SEXUAL MORALITY:
A CATHOLIC PERSPECTIVE

SEXUAL MORALITY:
A CATHOLIC PERSPECTIVE

by
Philip S. Keane, S.S.

PAULIST PRESS
New York/Ramsey/Toronto

NIHIL OBSTAT
Peter F. Chirico, S.S., S.T.D.
Censor Librorum

IMPRIMATUR
✠Raymond G. Hunthausen
Archbishop of Seattle

June 1, 1977

Library of Congress
Catalog Card Number: 77-83536

ISBN: 0-8091-2070-4

Published by Paulist Press
Editorial Office: 1865 Broadway, New York, N.Y. 10023
Business Office: 545 Island Road, Ramsey, N.J. 07446

Printed and bound in the
United States of America

Contents

Contents

To

Sally Anne McCarty
(1931–1974)

R.I.P.

Preface

A Roman Catholic moralist must necessarily feel a bit of apprehension in presenting another book on human sexuality. For so long, morality has been too closely identified with sexual morality whereas, in actual fact, there are many moral issues that are ultimately more important than sexuality. These more ultimate issues include especially the social issues, i.e., the question of achieving a more equitable distribution of the material and spiritual benefits available to humankind on this planet.

Sexuality is nevertheless a very meaningful aspect of human development. Catholics and others still have questions about how they might most responsibly live out their sexuality. Furthermore, human sexuality is a subject on which Catholic moral perspectives are in need of continuing reformulation so as to take account of new scientific information and changing socioeconomic conditions. Granted all of the other vital moral issues, human sexuality is still significant enough to deserve sober theological and pastoral reflection.

This book is written specifically from a Roman Catholic viewpoint. The author realizes that various religious groups have noteworthy contributions to make toward our understanding of sexuality, and at times these contributions are referred to. The explicit focus is on Roman Catholicism because its traditions of magisterium and natural law pose for it some particular questions concerning sexuality that do not exist in other traditions.

The author's basic position is that the Roman Catholic tradition does have a very worthwhile viewpoint on human sexuality. At the same time, the Roman Catholic tradition on human sexuality is impoverished because of certain historical distortions. Thus, the approach of the book will be neither to abandon our traditions on sexuality nor simply to repeat past formulations uncritically. Instead, the Roman Catholic tradition on sexuality will be seen as a living tradition, ever open to better expression. It seems critically necessary that the Church move toward this better expression in the area of sexuality. Otherwise, inadequate approaches to sexuality will keep on surfacing, while the Church's credibility, not only on sexuality but on all matters, continues to suffer.

Many of the issues touched on herein could be treated in much more detail. The format of this book is to survey moral perspectives on human sexuality, rather than to analyze thoroughly individual sexual questions. The footnote references may lead the interested reader to more complete information on specific topics. A few of the footnotes will also add more detailed philosophical specifications to the major lines of reasoning used in the book. It is hoped that this book, by means of its survey format, will achieve its primary purpose which is to demonstrate a consistent methodology for approaching all issues in sexual ethics.

The author wishes to thank all those who have contributed in any way to the writing of this book. In addition to the author's professors and students (both in seminaries and special programs) and the Society of St. Sulpice, the following persons deserve special mention: Archbishop Raymond G. Hunthausen, Frs. Paul P. Purta, Kevin A. Lynch, Peter F. Chirico, William H. Crisman, Lawrence T. Reilly, and Charles E. Curran, Sr. Ann Neale, Mrs. Marilyn Ochiltree, Mrs. Dorothy Ellis, Mr. Donald Kemple, Mr. Benjamin Ferarra, and Mr. Urban Intondi.

Friendsville, Pennsylvania
January 1, 1977

I
A Theological-Anthropological Overview of Human Sexuality

One of the difficulties under which Catholic moral theology labors concerning human sexuality is that all too often our moral theology talks about particular problems in human sexuality without formulating an overall perspective from which to view these problems. In the past century, there have been many significant developments in Roman Catholic thought. These developments have touched fields such as philosophy, biblical studies, Christian social ethics, the theology of the Church, and ecumenism, to name but a few of the areas. Surely all of these developments in Catholic thought should be applied to human sexuality so as to articulate an outlook on human sexuality that is integrated in itself and coherent with the Church's current philosophical and theological positions. To put the matter more simply, we have a crying need for a theological overview of human sexuality. In later chapters, this book will deal with some specific questions in Roman Catholic sexual ethics. But our approach to these questions is bound to run into problems unless we start with an overall theological position on human sexuality. Our project in this chapter is, therefore, to present a theology of human sexuality.

Basic Statement of a Theology of Human Sexuality

Two main elements must be set down as essential to a theology of human sexuality. First, human sexuality is a profound good, a great good given by God to human persons as part of creation. This notion that sexuality is a basic good. gift of God does not mean that we are naïve

3

about the fact that sexuality can be misused. In a sinful world, all of God's gifts can be misused, with God's greater gifts to us such as sexuality being subject to greater misuse. We cannot, however, let human sexuality's potential for misuse obscure the fundamental theological anthropological fact that human sexuality is God's good gift. "In the beginning, he created them; male and female he created them" (Gen. 1, 27).

The second essential theological element in sexuality is that the gift of sexuality is a gift that touches human persons on all levels of their existence. It is not a gift that touches us on just one or a few levels of our existence; rather, it is a gift that spans the whole gamut of human experience, thus becoming a basic or ontological determinant of human existence and personality. Sexuality touches us on the physical level, profoundly affecting our biological and physiological processes. It touches us on the personal or spiritual level, influencing our psychological and emotional life, our spiritual-religious-aesthetic nature, and our intersubjective relationships with both God and other people. Human sexuality also touches us on a larger social level, referring not only to our personal relationships but to our interaction with the structures and needs of society as a whole. To put all this in another way, human sexuality is a fundamental modality of the manner in which we relate to ourselves, to all other people, and to God. We always exist and function as sexed persons; at no time is our sexuality not a part of us. The gift of human sexuality is thus a wholistic or comprehensive gift; limiting its comprehensiveness will necessarily lead to an inadequate theological understanding of human sexuality.[1]

Some Clarifying Contrasts

To make our central position on sexuality stand out more clearly, it might help to contrast our position with some inadequate theories of human sexuality. In such a process we shall see how our briefly outlined theological anthropology of sexuality transcends such inadequate theories. Since we have described human sexuality as a good and then pointed to the physical, personal, and social aspects of this good, our clarifications will deal with four types of inadequate theories of sexuality: theories that see sexuality as an evil or that overstress the physical, personal, or social levels of sexuality.

Theories That Fail To Appreciate the Basic Goodness of Human Sexuality

The above insistence that we must begin by seeing the basic God-given goodness of human sexuality constitutes a decisive rejection of all systems or theologies that see human sexuality as fundamentally evil. The position that sexuality is an evil is basically anti-Christian. The Judaeo-Christian tradition is committed in its most primary roots to the fact that one God made the whole world and made it to be good.[2] Human sexuality is in no way an exception to this belief that God made the whole world and made it good. In addition, Christianity is committed to the reality of the Incarnation, i.e., to the notion that Christ took on the fullness of humanity. Again, there is no exception clause asserting that sexuality was left out of the Incarnation. Clearly the central roots of the Judaeo-Christian tradition are an assertion of the goodness, not the evil, of sexuality.

In candor, it must be admitted that the Christian tradition across the centuries has not always argued from its central teachings to the goodness of human sexuality as clearly as it might have. Probably the largest single reason for Christianity's failure to proclaim the goodness of sexuality clearly enough has been Christianity's ongoing association with various forms of the heresy of gnosticism. Gnosticism is a form of dualistic thought that arose at about the same time and in about the same part of the world as the Judaeo-Christian tradition.[3] In many respects, the two thought systems of Christianity and gnosticism have been fellow travelers ever since. The list of gnostic heresies that have affected Christianity across the centuries is too long to cite here; three prominent examples are Manicheanism, Albigensianism, and Jansenism.

For our purposes, the main problem with gnosticism is that it is a dualism holding that the world as it now exists is the result of a warlike conflict between two coequal principles (or Gods), a good principle that made the spiritual realities, including the human soul, and an evil principle that made the material realities, including the human body. Thus for gnosticism, the body and realities associated with it such as sexuality are basically evil. At times, gnosticism has been so opposed to the material order that it has rejected on principle the bearing of children because children continue human involvement in materiality. Indeed, some of the Church's earliest statements against birth control were directed against anti-material, completely anti-children forms of gnosticism.[4]

Roman Catholicism has never espoused gnosticism. Nonetheless, at times the Church and even its greatest leaders have lived in a world so influenced by gnosticism that the Church has tended to perpetuate gnostic fears of sex among its people. A classic case in point is St. Augustine. For a time before his conversion, Augustine was a member of a gnostic sect, the Manichees. The best modern opinion holds that after his conversion, Augustine did develop (especially in the *City of God*) a transformationist philosophy that in principle overcame his Manichean gnosticism.[5] On particular issues, however, Augustine did not always articulate his transformationist synthesis (in which Christ is redeeming all of reality) in such a way as to avoid the overly fearful interpretations that were part of his Manichean past. This was particularly the case in regard to human sexuality so that for Augustine the sinful aspects of sexual intercourse were stressed even when this intercourse was between married couples.[6] Augustine's thought (and thus his tendency to see sexuality as evil) was to dominate the Christian scene for nearly one thousand years.

The next great genius of the Roman Catholic tradition, Thomas Aquinas, was not directly influenced by gnostic currents of thought and thus was more positive in his views of human sexuality than was Augustine. The Greek philosophy from which Thomas drew did sometimes push the body/soul distinction a bit hard, thus reinforcing fears of the body and of sexuality. Note for instance that the Greek tradition and much Catholic theological speculation describe human destiny in terms of immortality of the soul, whereas the ancient Christian notion found in our primitive creeds speaks of the resurrection of the body, a notion much more favorable to the material order and to sexuality.[7] The Thomistic approach also slipped on occasion into other prejudicial descriptions of sexuality, e.g., the characterization in some moral manuals of the human genitals as our "dishonest" parts.[8]

Probably the most negative outlook on human sexuality produced by Roman Catholicism in recent centuries was French Jansenism. Jansenism was recognized as heretical, but its negative spirit vis-à-vis the world and sexuality perdured long after Jansenism itself had formally died. Jansenism is particularly important relative to the sexual negativities and fears of Roman Catholicism in America. Many of the religious communities that played key roles in the growth and development of American Catholicism had French, Jansenist-influenced backgrounds, and thus often unconsciously fostered notions of sex as evil among American Catholics.[9]

While the examples just cited have been drawn from Roman Catholic sources, it must also be acknowledged that Protestantism conveyed negative and ultimately anti-Christian notions of sexuality. In the American context we might recall especially the narrow-minded puritanical viewpoint on sexuality. Hawthorne's Hester Prynne with her red "A" may have been a fictional character but she reflects a consciousness about sexuality that was very real. The fear-ridden advice of nineteenth-century medical textbooks concerning sexual matters was not fictional.[10] It may well be that, in the long run, Puritanism was the single most important force in the development of overly negative views on sexuality here in America. In any case, it is clear that the overlay of gnosticism and the resultant suggestion that sexuality is basically evil have been problems for all of Christianity, not simply for Roman Catholics.

Some of the quaint customs connected with overly fearful views of sexuality serve to point out the pervasiveness of Christian fears of sexuality in the recent past. Parents in puritan New England were advised to put bells under the beds of their teenage sons so that the parents could detect and stop masturbation by their sons. Early in this century an electronic device was marketed to replace the bell. Some Roman Catholic seminaries furnished the students' rooms with paddles with which the students could tuck their shirts in. Girls were warned not to wear patent leather shoes because of the mirror effect these shoes might have. A lengthy list of similar examples could be compiled. It is probably good for us to laugh at these examples today, but in our laughter we must not forget the mentality that spawned them.

Without any exaggeration, it can be said that the lives of millions of people have been hurt by the failure of Christianity to reject more clearly the dualistic anti-Christian views of sexuality that have so repeatedly arisen in the Christian community. Some of these instances of persons being hurt are quite clear. Cases of sexual dysfunction such as frigidity and male impotence can have a variety of physical and psychological causes unrelated to religion, but religious hang-ups about sexuality are involved in many occurrences of sexual dysfunction. Beyond this obvious area of sexual dysfunction is the greater number of cases of persons who cannot relate to others as warmly and openly and confidently as they might, were they not beset with religiously inspired excessive fears of their sexuality.

In view of all this hurt and misunderstanding, it should be evident that one of the most basic tasks concerning sexuality for Christian communities today is to reject all gnosticism and proclaim the basic goodness of human sexuality, without of course ignoring the fact that there are significant moral concerns as to the proper use of the gift of sexuality. The brief historical review just given brings into sharp focus the reasons why we began our theological anthropology of sexuality by insisting that sexuality is God's good gift to us.

Theories Stressing the Physical Aspects of Human Sexuality

It comes as no surprise that sexuality has good physical aspects that must be incorporated into any theory of human sexuality. But our second key point on human sexuality called our attention to human sexuality's comprehensive goodness, i.e., to the fact that a sound theory of human sexuality must relate sexuality to every level of human existence. Thus the physical aspects of human sexuality, for all their goodness and importance, cannot be so stressed that we forget our sexuality's personal and social dimensions. Throughout history an excessive physicalism has often hindered the development of sound approaches to human sexuality. The gnostic dualism described above saw sexuality as exclusively physical and for this reason described sexuality as essentially evil. More refined systems of Christian thought rather quickly broke away (in theory if not always in practice) from gnosticism's notion that human sexuality is fundamentally evil. But the other aspect of gnosticism—that sexuality is exclusively or one-sidedly physical—has been even harder to overcome. There is still too much of a tendency for people to interpret their sexuality as a one-sidedly physical phenomenon and to act accordingly. The overly physical approaches to human sexuality fall into two main categories, procreationism and sex for physical fun.

Procreationism is the approach to human sexuality that holds that the only moral purpose of human sexual expression is the physical reproduction of children. To the extent that St. Augustine did break with the "sexuality is evil" notion, he tended to place himself in the "sexuality is for procreation" school. Much of Roman Catholic (and other Christian) theology across the centuries has also put itself in the procreationist school. Traditional theology did speak of marriage as a remedy for concupiscence and some important past Catholic documents such as the *Cate-*

chism of the Council of Trent spoke of the mutual help the spouses give each other in marital union.[11] But for many persons operating out of the popular Catholic mind, it was not until the mutual help of the spouses was called a secondary end of marriage by the *Code of Canon Law* in 1917[12] and by Pius XI in *Casti Connubii* in 1930[13] that a larger than procreationist approach to marriage began to develop.

Procreation is a good, a monumental good both for individuals and society. No theory of human sexuality can completely dismiss the role of procreation as some would tend to do today.[14] However, we cannot go the other direction either and limit the meaning of sexuality to procreation. One of the most central themes in our Scriptures from which to understand sexuality is the theme of covenant love. This theme is the background for Jesus' words about a married couple becoming one flesh (Matt. 19,6) and for Paul's description of marriage in Ephesians 5. Biblical scholarship tells us that the covenant theme includes a number of values (love, fidelity, etc.).[15] If we interpret the human sexual union in the light of covenant, we are clearly unable to speak of sexuality in terms of procreation alone. In the past many elements in the Church have been too procreationistic in their approach to sexuality. To be wholistic and biblical, we must transcend procreationist viewpoints on human sexuality.

The second major form of exaggeration of the physical aspect of human sexuality is found in those systems that place a one-sided stress on the physical or sensual pleasure associated with our sexuality. The physical pleasure associated with sexuality is a good, it is part of God's plan for humanity. The Christian tradition has at times failed to place sufficient value upon the physical pleasure inherent in sexuality. But at the same time, physical pleasure cannot be made the only or the major focus of an approach to sexuality. Overemphasis on physical pleasure in sexuality has been a problem throughout human history, and it is becoming an especially pressing problem in our own times. The proliferation of how-to-do-it sex manuals, often with ill-informed advice, shows the growth of a one-sided pleasure ethic of sexuality.[16] The frenzied search of some couples for mutual orgasm (Eugene Kennedy's "The Great Orgasm Hunt")[17] is another example. Probably the greatest instance of this sex-for-pleasure-only approach in our times can be found in the world of *Playboy* magazine and its publisher, Hugh M. Hefner. A perusal of *Playboy*, with its monthly circulation in the millions, graphically illustrates the overemphasis on sex for pleasure.[18] The magazine typically contains some good fiction, interesting interviews with famous persons, articles on subjects such as automobiles, stereo tape decks, fine wines, and several pieces prominently featuring pictures of women in the nude. The message that tends to come across is that the nudes are on about the same level as the cars, stereo sets, etc. The larger human dimensions of sexuality are lost sight of. Other examples of the shallow sensualist approach to sexuality might also be given,[19] but the point is obvious. While the physical pleasures of sexuality are a great good, these pleasures cannot be so stressed that we miss the larger or wholistic vision of sexuality.

Overly Romantic Theories of Human Sexuality

As we move away from physicalism in our approach to human sexuality, we become more and more aware of the personal elements in sexuality, more aware that our sexuality profoundly enters into our emotional and affective lives, and into our basic understanding of self and other people, always in relationship to God. Especially in this context we realize how human sexuality greatly deepens and enriches our interpersonal relationships. This enrichment is, above all, notable in the relationship of man and woman in marriage which in many ways is the paradigm for all human relationships. However, the sexual enrichment of human personality and relationships is by no means limited to marital relationships alone. Once we see that human sexuality is much more than physical or genital acts, our sexuality becomes a factor in, and contributes to, all human relationships. In the deepest sense of the word, there is never a human relationship that is not somehow sexual.

Because of some of the limitations of past Christian approaches (Protestant as well as Catholic) to human sexuality, people need to hear about the personal growth dimensions of human sexuality. But these dimensions can be taken out of the context of the inherent physical (procreative) and societal aspects of sexuality, leaving us with a narrow and overly romantic view of human sexuality.[20] Personal romanticism has arisen as a problem vis-à-vis sexuality repeatedly in history. In the medieval period the troubadours sought to separate love from marriage to the detriment of both. In our own times, personal commitment is sometimes so stressed as the ethical factor legitimating sexual intercourse that the need of society for stable marriages and families and the inherently procreative facets of human sexuality are written off as unimportant. These points are raised not to make a definitive moral judgment on particular cases of premarital sexual intercourse and contraception (of which more in a later chapter), but simply to reject any conception of human sexuality that so equates our sexuality with its personal and romantic aspects that all other considerations are unreasonably set aside.

Societal Theories of Sexuality

Without accepting Freud's idea that all of society's creative abilities come from sublimated forms of sexual energy,[21] the fact remains that society at large (often referred to as the common good) is closely related to the total dynamics of human sexuality and thus has legitimate concerns about how human sexuality is expressed. In particular, society needs stable families, and there is evidence that the increasing breakdown of family life in our era is creating a variety of emotional and psychological problems that redound to the detriment of society as a whole.[22] Thus a comprehensive theory of human sexuality cannot forget the societal aspects of sexuality.

It is also true that society's concerns for human sexuality cannot so predominate that sexuality's physical and personal dimensions are slighted. The medieval phenomenon of arranged marriages so as to provide heirs for kingdoms, etc., is one historic instance of society's slighting the personal side of sexuality.[23] Some contemporary proposals for compulsory sterilization and the genetic screening out of undesirable human beings would likewise be societal institutionalizations of sexuality that prejudice sexuality's personal dimensions.[24] We mentioned earlier that human sexuality has a religious dimension, a dimension in which human sexuality opens us up to the holy and wonderful mystery of God. This religious mystery dimension is perhaps the greatest reason why human sexuality must be seen wholistically, why there has to be a limit on how far society can control our sexuality, no matter how good society's intentions may be.[25]

Moral Perspectives in a Christian Sexual Anthropology

Hopefully our review of the strengths and the weaknesses of the partial positions on human sexuality has made clearer our fundamental Christian anthropology of sexuality: that we view sexuality as a comprehensive good touching all levels of human existence. But what does this say about a moral theology of sexuality? How do we assess moral responsibility in the area of human sexuality? To begin, our moral theology of sexuality should be catholic in the original or small "c" sense of the word. Our moral theology must be rigorously open to all aspects of human sexuality, refusing to forget anything that is important. This task will not be easy. No one ever has or ever will completely integrate all the aspects of human sexuality, thus making the search for the perfectly integrated sexual human being a waste of time. We are all pilgrims, on-the-way people, when it comes to being totally moral in the area of sexuality. Precisely for this reason—our pilgrim status—sexuality is a legitimate and ongoing moral concern. Asceticism and self-restraint in the area of sexuality will continue to be a need for us as human pilgrims who do not have our lives completely together.[26] The Catholic

Church has then been essentially correct in her moral care and concern for the area of sexuality. At times the Church's perspectives on sexuality may have been too negative and too physical, but she has surely been correct in seeing sexuality as a complex area of human life calling out for moral sensitivity.

To express the Christian and Catholic moral concern inherent in sexuality, the key question might be put as follows: how do I use my God-given gift of sexuality so as to relate most responsibly to myself (my *whole* self), to other people (both individually and societally), and to the holy mystery of God? The scriptural revival, looking at the mainstream theology of both Testaments, has suggested that the category of responsible relationship transcends the category of rule or law in assessing moral matters. Basic Christian dogmas such as the Incarnation (relating Christ to every facet of humanity) and the Trinity (asserting that personal relationships exist even within our utterly one God) also assert the importance of the category of responsible relationship. Our basic moral question about sexuality accepts this notion of responsibility in relationship and makes it the operative concept in a system of Christian sexual morality.[27] Again and again as we move on to specific sexual issues this question of how the person relates most responsibly as a sexual being to God, self, and others will be the background question underlying our deliberations. Not everyone will answer this question about responsible use of the gift of sexuality in the same way (e.g., celibates will answer it differently from married persons), but it will always be the key question.

Interestingly when we put the moral question about sexuality in terms of responsible relationality, the answers we shall give to specific questions of sexual morality will be, in general, fairly similar to those given in the Christian tradition of the past. But the whole spirit behind the answers will be different, for we will be focusing on the essential goodness of sexuality and on its applications to all of human life. This should enable people to live happier and healthier sexual lives because the unnecessary fears of human warmth and openness will no longer be present.

Religious and Christian Considerations

Our descriptions of a sexual anthropology have alluded to the religious and Christian dimensions of sexual experience. The wholistic viewpoint on sexuality is religious, particularly because of its insistence that no one aspect of life (biology, personal relationships, societal needs, etc.) can embrace the whole meaning of sexuality. This means that sexuality contains within it profound elements of mystery, of openness to God.

From primitive times, humanity has recognized the connection between religious experience and sexual experience. We must be careful not to so state the religious dimension of sexuality that religious experience and human sexuality are identified. Religious experience always transcends any particular categories of human experience. Along this line, the notion that sexuality explains virtually everything about human life must also be avoided.[28] The comprehensive notion of human sexuality proposed herein sees sexuality as relating to all of human experience and, therefore, as a religious or theological phenomenon. But our notion does not see human sexuality as the only explanation of the totality of our human existence. To make sexuality the total explanation would be to deify it.

The comments made so far have indicated that the wholistic perspective on human sexuality is a Christian perspective in accord with the deepest meaning of our Scriptures and traditions. Scriptural texts assert the primacy of the man/woman relationship in human existence.[29] Scriptural texts also explain the sacredness of the marriage relationship (one flesh) in terms of God's loving covenant with His people.[30] These biblical ideas and others like them are more consistent with a wholistic and positive viewpoint on human sexuality than with any other viewpoint. It is true that some passages in both Testaments appear to be quite anti-sexual: "A continual dripping on a rainy day and a contentious woman are alike" (Prov. 27, 15). "It is better to marry than to be on fire" (1 Cor. 7, 9). Scripture scholars today usually point out that such passages need special interpretations relative to their contexts (this is the hermeneutic problem), and are thus not as anti-sexual as they might appear. Paul, for instance, wrote first Corinthians with the expectation that the world was about to end. This fact, rather than any ultimate opposition to sexuality, was the reason for his negative remarks on marriage in first Corinthians.

The question might be asked whether the Scriptures have any other definitive teachings on sexuality besides the man/woman relationship and the sacredness of the marriage covenant. It can be said that the Scriptures definitively reject all dehumanizing forms of sexuality[31] such as sexual cruelty, rape, or prostitution. It is quite difficult, however, to push the Scriptures too far on specific questions of sexual morality such as masturbation and homosexuality. The interpretation or hermeneutic problem mentioned above implies that specific scriptural statements on subjects such as these are likely to be encrusted in cultural contexts that we can never fully recover.[32] The Scriptures, therefore, give us adequate materials with which to endorse as Christian the wholistic vision of sexuality presented in this chapter; they also give us guidelines on sexual conduct, but they do not provide detailed answers to all the sexual dilemmas of twentieth-century humanity.

We have already adverted to the centrality of the Incarnation in Christian thought. Christians have at times slipped into views of human sexuality that were too partial to one or another aspect of human sexuality. If we are believers in the Incarnation, we believe *ipso facto* that all things human, save sin, have been radically ennobled by the coming of Christ.[33] Thus for the true Christian, in the most primary sense of the term, there is no choice other than to properly value all the aspects of human sexuality. Whatever errors individual Christians may have made in past understandings of sexuality (and who are we to judge the context of the past or assert that we are any less biased?) we can confidently assert that our belief in the Incarnation of Jesus Christ supports the goodness and comprehensive character of human sexuality.

Besides the Incarnation with its central implications for a Christian approach to sexuality, there are two other

fundamental elements in any Christian anthropology: our
sinfulness, and our call to be sharers in the resurrection of
Christ. These two elements are also deeply related to the
theology of sexuality we have outlined in this chapter. For
the Christian, the ultimate problem with the partial views
of sexuality rejected in this chapter is that these partial
views are shot through with human sinfulness and human
selfishness. The Christian must also remember that he or
she, as a person called to share in Christ's resurrection,
should always strive for the highest possible expressions of
love and sexuality. Often, as this book unfolds, we shall
discuss sexual behaviors that, all things considered in our
finite world, seem morally acceptable in certain cases. Our
acceptance of such behaviors should not, however, obscure
the Christian call to resurrection, the call for us to strive,
both individually and societally, toward a state of integration in which our freedom will enable us to transcend all
limited forms of sexual behavior.[34]

A Corollary on Sexual Education

From all that has been said, it follows that one of our
most crucial responsibilities concerning sexuality is to provide for proper sexual education so that people will not
again revert to fearful or overly physical interpretations of
sexuality. The Catholic Church has called for proper sexual education several times in recent years,[35] an important
fact to note in a society that has many strident critics of
sexual education. If sexuality is as deeply related to human
life and human personality as we have argued above, education for sexuality becomes a key to mature and well-
rounded human living.

It is usually stated that parents are the primary sexual
educators of their children. No matter what the parents do
in terms of formal or explicit sexual education, they will
be, for well or ill, the primary sexual educators of their
children, inasmuch as the values the parents communicate
in relating to each other and to their children will have
more impact on the sexual development of their children
than all the formal sexual education in the world.

Because sexual education does have so much to do with values as well as with information, it is most ideal for the parents to play a formal role in the sexual education of their children as well as playing the value-imparting role that is theirs inevitably. Parents need not be afraid to begin the sexual education of their children at a reasonably early age. Adults and adolescents often have to deal with high levels of emotion or even of trauma when dealing with sexual matters. As a result, parents sometimes fail to realize that prepubertal children are relatively free of heavy overlays of emotion in regard to their sexuality. Thus honest explanations of issues in sexuality (made clear enough for the child's age, etc.) are usually the very best thing for the child. The withholding of sexual education, on the other hand, begins to instill in the child sexual fears that could be avoided by appropriate openness on the part of parents.

It is a regrettable fact that far too many parents fail to provide an adequate sexual education for their children. In light of the one-sided views of sexuality we have discussed above, this is no real surprise. Due to this parental lack, it is fitting and proper for other responsible agencies in society such as the Church and the school (parochial or public) to play a role in the sexual education of young people.[36] This is not to say that every program of sexual education taken on by a school or other group is perfectly sound and immune from all criticism. Nor does this mean that just anyone is qualified to be a sexual educator. A good sexual educator needs both accurate information and, much more importantly, a good personal integration of the many levels of value inherent in human sexuality. The whole point of this chapter is that we need a positive and comprehensive Christian viewpoint on human sexuality. The development of such a viewpoint in our young depends more on mature people who have integrated their sexuality than on any other factor.

These remarks on the need for good sexual education should not be concluded without our realizing that sexual education is needed as much by college-age persons and adults as by children.[37] When sexual education is given to persons on these more mature levels the process can be more objective with a lesser stress on normative guidance. If all facets of human sexuality are presented as fairly and completely as possible, adults in the Christian faith should be able to come to responsible moral judgments in the area of sexual ethics. This does not mean that we should refrain from presenting to adults the Church's norms on sexual ethics. But adult Christians will more readily come to a mature sexual orientation if they are given a chance to see the whole picture of sexuality rather than simply being told what they should do. Children and teenagers should also be helped to see the whole picture of sexuality; their lesser maturity does, however, imply that at times they may be in more need of relying on norms whose significance they have not yet fully grasped.

II
The Role of Women
as a Major Key
in the Whole Picture
of Human Sexuality

The reflections just given on sexual education were presented as a corollary to the wholistic viewpoint on human sexuality. Another even more significant set of corollaries has to do with the role of women, the man/woman relationship, and the whole question of masculine and feminine sexuality. Once we say that a Christian approach to sexuality must attend to all facets of sexuality, it becomes obvious that no approach to human sexuality can be called Christian unless it deals with the many issues concerning women in human life. Indeed, it could even be argued that all of the limitations of Christianity's sexual outlook seen in the last chapter might have been avoided if Christianity in past generations had faced up to the various questions related to women. Hence it is essential for us to develop and draw some conclusions from a theology of women before we take up any specific questions of sexual morality.[1] Our considerations in this chapter will have four parts: past inadequacies in Christian approaches to women; some critical current problems faced by women; a basic theological anthropological statement on women and the man/woman relationship; and women's liberation and the sexual maturation of all people.

Past Inadequacies in Christian Approaches to Women

In the last chapter, we reviewed a number of positions on human sexuality that were inadequate because of their negativity toward sexuality or because they placed too much stress on only one facet of human sexuality. Virtually every one of these inadequate approaches to sexuality translated itself early in Christian history into a poor view of women. Probably the most inadequate of all the philosophies of sexuality was the position that saw sexuality as essentially evil. It was part and parcel of this position to define women as evil, as the source of human sin. The gnosticism that gave rise to the idea that sexuality is evil was a dualism in which realities such as spirit, rationality, and logic were seen as good while matter and emotion were seen as evil. Masculinity and femininity were part of gnosticism's dualist model so that masculinity was seen as on the good side of the dualism while femininity was on the evil side. The classic stereotype of women as more carnal, more emotional, and less logical than men was inherent in this dualism.[2] If sexuality was evil, so were women. Our English word virtue, which connotes goodness, comes from the same root as our word virile which connotes maleness.

Christian Scriptures and patristic authors developed themes that continued this notion of women as evil. Some exegetes hold that Paul's famous dictum that women should keep their heads covered in church (1 Cor. 11,5-6) is based on Genesis 6,1-4 and implies that since women had once seduced the angels they should keep their heads covered in church lest they seduce men.[3] Tertullian calls woman the devil's gateway.[4] Jerome has passages in which he seems doubtful about women's washing themselves because this might increase their seductive potential.[5] Augustine states that nothing so debases man as the fondling of a woman.[6] It is not quite fair to look at only these passages in Scripture and the Fathers, since both Scriptures and the Fathers contain a larger context in which women are viewed more positively (e.g., Gal. 3,28: "In Christ there is neither Jew nor Greek, nor slave nor free, nor male nor female"). It is also true that Scriptures and the Fathers did not invent the stereotype of women as evil. Nonetheless, we cannot exonerate the Church of all blame for actions that perpetuated the notion of women as evil.[7]

We also considered in the last chapter the problems of procreation and sensualism, two approaches to sexuality that fail because they overemphasize the physical side of sex. Procreationism prejudiced the role of women by tending to see them as machines to bear children, rather than as full persons. Physical sensualism prejudiced women by seeing them as objects for the sexual delight of males. The double standard (males can have sex outside marriage, but females cannot), often called the oldest morality in the world, was one major fostering of the notion of women as children-producing machines and objects of sexual pleasure for males. The double standard barred intercourse outside marriage for females, so that a husband could be guaranteed that all the children his wife bore were surely his; the double standard did not exclude intercourse outside marriage for males because males had the right to the physical pleasure available from (unmarried) women's bodies. The reason why males could not have sex with other married women was not for the sake of the married women themselves, but to protect the rights of these women's husbands.[8] Divorce laws and other ancient and medieval forms of legislation often imply that women are their husbands' property and thus convey the notion of women as childbearing or pleasure-producing objects rather than as fully human persons.

The Church, of course, never officially approved of double-standard morality, and this is to her credit. But prominent Christian leaders of past centuries did sometimes help promote the idea that women were physical beings less than fully human. As late as the sixth century after Christ, a Catholic Bishop in a Synod expressed doubts as to whether women were human beings.[9] Thomas Aquinas did hold that women had souls but he followed Aristotle's idea that female souls were defective forms of male souls (the "misbegotten male" theory).[10] Up until the time of Albert the Great and Aquinas, the popular notion was that the human soul was infused by God forty days after conception in the case of males but only after eighty days in the case of females.[11] Cultural qualifications might be offered in defense of the medieval figures who had this less-than-fully-human view of women, but the Church cannot absolve itself of all responsibility on this matter.

The overly romantic conception of sexuality that began especially with the troubadours ("courtly love") also led to an inadequate view of women, to a view in which women were treated with great reverence (rising when they entered a room, kissing their hands, throwing capes over mud puddles before women crossed them, etc.) but at the same time carefully kept out of many important spheres of life. Important modern churchmen such as Cardinal Gibbons of Baltimore have supported the romanticist notion of women. Gibbons, in stating his unalterable opposition to women's suffrage, asserted that woman is queen, but her kingdom is the domestic kingdom.[12]

This overly romantic view of women is often called pedestalism because it puts women on a pedestal where they are praised while being excluded from much of life.[13] In our century, pedestalism is probably a greater social issue than the older notions of women as evil or women as physical objects (though all these inadequate notions interpenetrate). As an example of the problems that pedestalism causes us today, one author has suggested that the United States might have escaped the tragedy of Watergate were not women and the values they represent excluded from so many areas of public life.[14] Pedestalism is hard to combat because it seems to say good things about women and because many women are quite happy to be placed on pedestals so that they do not have to take their full responsibility for human life and the human future.[15]

The present author holds the opinion that many aspects of Roman Catholic Marian devotion in recent centuries have served to reinforce a pedestalistic view of women. This does not mean that the Church should give up devotion to Mary, but rather that such devotion needs to be revitalized and depedestalized. The great step of the Second Vatican Council in treating Mary within the *Constitution on the Church* instead of in a separate document will be an important help in this revitalization of true devotion

to Mary.[16] In its deepest roots, Marian devotion is, in spite
of some of its unfortunate forms, a theological statement
on the importance of the feminine in human life and
human destiny.

The last major inadequate view of human sexuality
discussed in chapter one had to do with society so stressing
and structuring its interests in sexuality (i.e., stable marriages and families for the common good) that the rights
of individual persons are prejudiced. Surely society has
prejudiced women in this respect. Inequitable laws concerning marriage and divorce, the lack of women's suffrage until recent times, and past exclusions of women
from higher education and from most professional fields
such as medicine, engineering, architecture, etc., are some
of the prime examples of how society's narrow conception
of the meaning of sexuality has worked against women.[17]
The concerns mentioned here obviously spill over into the
current problems of women that we are about to discuss.
But from our brief survey of history the point is clear: a
major difficulty with our past notions of sexuality has been
their view of women. Catholicism (and all of Christianity)
will not achieve a fully adequate understanding of human
sexuality until it achieves a more satisfactory theology of
women.

Current Difficulties of Women

To show that the remarks just made about the problems of women are not simply interesting historical pieces
of trivia, all one needs to do is to look to the world around
us and see that it still has an inadequate understanding of
women and their sexuality. Our language, which consistently uses male words to refer to both women and men,
subtly reinforces this notion that women are inferior to
men. The words we use may seem like a very minor matter, but we are much more conditioned by our words than
we generally realize. Thus our describing of both women
and men by the word "men" and our use of "he" to mean
both he and she tend to perpetuate the inequality of the
sexes. The constant use of such linguistic patterns should
therefore be avoided.

Women are still treated in our society as sexual objects for the pleasure of males. One great example of this is the pornography industry both in its hard- and soft-core forms. This industry has grown larger and larger in our times. Various approaches might be taken in objecting to pornography, but perhaps the worst single thing about pornography is that it continues to portray women as sexual playthings for the pleasure of men. There is a sort of reverse pornography on the market today, treating men as sex objects, but this phenomenon is probably better considered as an errant form of women's liberation rather than as an outright attack on the fuller humanity of males in the way that most pornography is an attack on the true humanity of women. In many respects, the softer forms of pornography (*Playboy* magazine and its imitators) are a more problematic attack on women than hard-core pornography. The softer material is so slickly packaged that its dehumanizing view of women (and of sexuality) is more subtle and, therefore, more likely to take people in.

There is some question as to whether strict censorship is always the best way to deal with the pornography problem. In certain cases, censorship is probably necessary, for instance, where the pornography industry is ruining a neighborhood that is committed to notable human values. In other cases, censorship may not be the answer since it may lead to the repression of legitimate material on human sexuality and legitimate types of nude photography (which do exist). As this implies, the communication of positive values about sexuality and about women may often be a better antidote to pornography than rigid censorship.[18]

Another example of our society's treating women as sexual objects is the advertising industry. For so many products (many having little to do with physical sexuality), an attractive woman's body is the focal point of the sales pitch. The frequent use of women in ads also ties in with the view of women as beings on pedestals. In contemporary ads, women are very often depicted as empty-headed consumers. The picture conveyed by these ads is that women who are not intelligent enough to be part of the economic power center of society exist as buyers of society's products, in addition to their role as sexual objects.

Further instances of women's being treated as sexual objects could easily be cited. The abuses reported by some women employees of the United States Congress are probably only the tip of the iceberg on the matter of the sexual dehumanization many women in the job market must endure. The widespread occurrences of rape and prostitution (which explicate the double-standard morality) are dehumanizations of women that are taken almost for granted by some.[19] Without a doubt, a top priority of the women's movement and of a wholistic approach to sexuality must be to stamp out all practices that carry the message that women are sexual objects.

Women today also have difficulty attaining their full humanity in the socioeconomic sphere. This subject is too large and complex for a complete treatment here, but the problems faced by women in obtaining credit, in being paid equally when they do the same work as men, and in breaking into the higher echelons of their professions are clear indications of women's socioeconomic problems. Those women who do go to the top in their professions often do so by buying into the male mentality that prejudices so many of their sisters. Progress is being made on women's socioeconomic concerns, but there is still a long way to go.

The various Christian Churches are at the present time in a period of a declining prestige and credibility in society as a whole. One of the most important things the churches might do in this trying period is to recognize clearly and encourage the many gifts that women might bring to the revitalization of the churches. In the past, there has been too much of a tendency to conceive of women as receivers of the Church's ministry rather than as part of that ministry. There are numerous aspects of the Church's ministry that are already being enriched by women, and numerous other aspects of ministry to which women could contribute, were they given the opportunity. In failing to acknowledge this, the churches are failing to acknowledge the full humanity of women. Roman Catholicism should be especially concerned about this question of ministry for women in the Church. For centuries Roman Catholicism, through its institutionalization of religious life, has admitted that other roles for women, besides marriage and family life, are possible in the Church. While women's religious communities of the past were not structured so as to recognize adequately the full humanity of women, they can be an important base for the development of new understandings of the role of women in the Church.

This chapter on women and sexuality cannot go into all the questions or arguments concerning the ordination of women in the Catholic Church. The present author does favor the ordination of women based especially on the notion that women and men are equal sharers in a co-humanity. Three major factors supporting women's ordination are as follows: first, the hermeneutic problem (i.e., the problem of contextualizing specific scriptural passages) and the historically conscious character of human life appear to exclude anti-ordination arguments asserting that women cannot ever be ordained because Jesus and the Church of the past did not ordain them. Secondly, the differences in the sexes (to be treated below) do not seem to be such as to prove that only one sex should be ordained. And third, the life of the Church would be markedly enhanced were the Church to ordain women. Much more than these three points would, of course, be necessary for a full treatment of the ordination question.[20]

Interestingly, there are some considerations suggesting that the ordination question is not the deepest or ultimately most important question on the subject of women's full humanity being recognized by the Church. In those churches that do ordain women, the ordained women are sometimes limited to ministries such as youth education and care for the aged, i.e., to ministries that continue to perpetuate the traditional feminine stereotype.[21] Thus, regardless of whether a given church has faced, is facing, or has not yet faced the ordination question, the matter of church structures opening themselves up to the full humanity of women is and will continue to be a central issue facing Christian women.

Against this background of ongoing problems of dehumanizing sexual objectification, socioeconomic prejudice, and lack of adequate roles in the churches, it is entirely proper that there is a women's liberation movement today, both in society as a whole and in the churches. Surely the basic thrust of this movement and of much of its literature is to be encouraged. There are some aspects of the women's liberation movement that are not as mature and wholistic in their view of sexuality as they ought to be, and these elements of the movement deserve criticism. The notion that the fetus is simply a tissue of the woman's body[22] and the idea that Christianity is completely useless in developing a satisfactory view of women[23] are two such unacceptable aspects of women's liberation literature.

Scholars of liberation movements sometimes suggest that all liberation movements must pass through three phases: a childlike phase in which those seeking liberation simply ape everything in the prevailing culture, an adolescent phase in which those seeking liberation reject everything in the prevailing culture, and finally an adult phase in which the liberation seekers learn to discriminate and accept the good and reject the bad in the prevailing culture.[24] If some of the earlier women's liberation material was in the childlike phase with its glorification of contemporary marriage and of sexual encounter in marriage,[25] it can also be said that some (not all) of the present-day women's literature, which stridently supports abortion and unisex theories, is in the adolescent phase of the liberation process. This adolescent phase may be necessary to the ultimate success of women's liberation, but this fact does not render it immune to constructive criticism.

A Theological Anthropology of Women and the Man/Woman Relationship

The deepest question underlying all these past and present inadequate views of women is the question of the ultimate goal or purpose of women's liberation. What really should we be aiming for in liberating women and coming to a more acceptable view of the whole mystery of human sexuality? What, in other words, is the theology of sexual equality? Perhaps the best preliminary response to such queries is full partnership in a common humanity. Women are human persons fully coequal to men. All practices that restrict women from sharing in the human goods as fully as men do are, therefore, unjust practices that must be transcended if humanity is to truly come of age.

But these fundamental principles on the meaning of women's liberation only raise another line of questions. Does women's full equality with men mean that women are exactly the same as men? Does women's full equality with men mean that human justice must always stipulate exactly the same provisions for women as for men? Our tradition on human justice has usually recognized that human persons are different from one another and that, therefore, true justice requires us to give each person his or her *due* rather than to treat each person exactly alike.[26] Obviously, there are dangers of favoritism in such a form of justice, but justice as giving each his or her due does respect the sacred uniqueness or individuality of each person.

As far as women and men are concerned, for all our common humanity, there are incontrovertible differences in the biological order. Probably the most notable example is the fact that only women may bear children. The differences in women and men created by childbearing are larger than the simple physical act of giving birth, since among higher animals and even among women who do not breast feed their children, infants have a stronger nurture-seeking orientation toward their mothers than toward their fathers.[27] This, of course, does not mean that mothers are exclusively responsible for changing, soothing, and feeding infants or children while fathers are off the hook on these matters. But the function of women as child bearers and nurturers does call on society in its norms of justice to provide what is due to women who bear children (adequate job leaves to working women who have children, etc.). Here the justice of treating women exactly the same as men would not be justice.

An even tougher question concerning the differences between the sexes is whether the obvious biological differ-

ences between women and men lead to any differences between them as persons. At first glance and with all our
current stress on sexual equality, it might seem best to reject all differences between the sexes except on the
biological-physiological-genetic level. However, if we look
to the history of human thought, we can see that it has
been much better for human beings to conceive of themselves as body-persons, as persons made up of an inextri-
cable union of body and soul, rather than as basically disin-
carnate spirits who happen to have bodies. Whenever
human thought has too radically separated our bodies
from our souls, poor theories of humanity have resulted.
Indeed, the largest problems of women across the centuries have come from an anthropology that overly divided
the human body from the soul. The notions of women as
evil, as child bearers, and as sexual pleasure objects all
came from such a divisive or even schizophrenic anthropology. Thus it seems that we must conceive of ourselves as body-persons in whom the tight linkage between
our bodies and our spirits does have implications for the
kind of persons we are. This, of course, does not mean
that bodily differences are totally determinative of who we
are as human persons (i.e., Freud's "anatomy is destiny"
theory must be rejected), but it does mean that theories of
human personhood cannot hold that the biological differences between the sexes have no impact on human personality.

To get more specific on how our physical differences
affect women and men as persons, I do not think we can
argue that either women or men are by their sexuality
clearly unsuited for any vocation (including the priesthood)
or profession, except in those cases where physical qualities
are a very predominant factor.[28] The vocations and professions chosen by either sex can evolve from age to age in
human history. I also do not think that there are any essential roles or stereotypes (husband as breadwinner and
wife as homemaker) that are inherent in the differences
between the sexes. These roles, too, can evolve with history. Rather it would seem that the difference between

women and men is best understood as a difference that
has its beginnings on the level of human relationships.
Women have a different sort of relational consciousness in
their relationships with men than in their relationships
with other women, and men have a different relational
consciousness vis-à-vis women than vis-à-vis other men.
This difference in relational consciousness is a fundamental anthropological factor of human coexistence and it is
experienced in all human relationships, not simply in those
relationships where physical or genital sexual expression is
or may well be present.[29]

At base, the difference in relational consciousness is a
call to all women and men to love other persons, in this
case, persons of the other sex, who are not exactly the
same as they themselves are. This challenge to love other
people in their differences from us is probably the most
fundamental challenge in all of human living. Loving
members of the other sex as full persons without fearing
their differences is the primary element in human
psychosexual development and maturation. All of human
life and Christian life is a life of loving in their full humanity different people, people who are different by race, age,
educational level, socioeconomic status, religious belief, etc.
In this light, the woman/man relationship can be seen as a
school for all of life. The relational difference factor of
sexuality is present to us earlier and more consistently in
life than the other difference factors just mentioned. If we
can learn to handle the relational difference factor in our
sexuality, we may well acquire a consciousness that will
help end all sorts of human oppression. This is why some
of its advocates assert that women's liberation is the most
fundamental form of human liberation.[30]

There are theories dealing with women's liberation
that take a unisex approach, that seek to deny all differences between the sexes except the strictly biological differences. The reflections just given suggest rather strongly
that for the sake of a true liberation and humanization of
all people, unisex theories must be rejected as a form of
closure to the richness and variety of human experience.

Women should be proud to be women, and men should be proud to be men. Hence we cannot say that it is completely inappropriate for societies to develop practices that help people become conscious of sexual differences and the challenges to growth that these differences imply. Not all societies will be the same in the practices they develop along these lines, and every society's practices to raise awareness of sexual differences need to be open to ongoing criticism and revision, so that these practices never place unjust limits on the access of any person to full humanity.

**Women's Liberation and the
Sexual Maturation of all People**

It was mentioned above that women's liberation has implications for the liberation of blacks, poor people, and other minorities. It should also be noted that women's liberation means almost by definition the liberation of men. The unsatisfactory stereotypes into which society and the churches have fit women have resulted in equally unsatisfactory stereotypes for men. Men are just as much hemmed in by the sexual roles they are expected to play as are women. In the last chapter, we spoke of sexuality as touching all levels of human existence. This means that sexuality is a wonderful mystery the human person never fully comprehends. Moreover, since sexuality is a wonderful mystery, there should be a healthy spectrum of styles with which both men and women integrate their sexuality. None of us will ever integrate sexuality in the exact same fashion as anyone else, granted, of course, that there are some moral limits on styles of sexual integration. The stereotyping of one sex serves to keep both sexes from a deeper appropriation of the mystery and variety inherent in sexuality.

The hemming-in that men experience vis-à-vis sexual roles is clear in regard to external behaviors. Men may very well like to cook, or sew, or clean house, and these activities should not be seen as inappropriate to maleness. The even deeper question about the sexual liberation of men is a question from the psychic level. It is fairly well agreed today that all persons of both sexes have within their psyches both masculine and feminine elements.[31] These elements are sometimes referred to as the *animus* and *anima*. The result of this theory about our psyches is that each of us must love and respect the elements of sexual differentiation not only in the world around us but in our very selves. Women must accept and appreciate their abilities to be assertive, highly logical, etc. Men must accept the sensitive and tender sides of their personalities.

In a sense, coming to terms with the *animus-anima* tension is harder for men than for women, because men have to learn not to be afraid of personal qualities that were traditionally feminine and, therefore, a sign of weakness or evil. The inability of many men to be tender and compassionate with their male peers has adversely influenced many areas of life, including modern governmental, economic, and military policies. Were there more of a feminine presence in today's economic system (both in women and in men unafraid of their *animae*), the enormous imbalances in the distribution of this world's goods might not be so great.[32] Churchmen, too, have been affected by their fear of certain elements of their own personalities. The style with which Church authority has sometimes been exercised and the great fears that homosexuality arouses in some priests and ministers seem at least partly due to churchmen who are afraid of the feminine elements in their own personalities. None of these criticisms mean that male world and Church leaders should downgrade their maleness. The point rather is that the healthy differences in sexuality that we experience in interpersonal relationships are differences that should be internalized to some degree in each of us.

On a more fundamentally theological level, there is today a growing awareness among theologians that the masculine/feminine dynamic which we have seen in the differences between the sexes and in the personalities of individuals is a dynamic that is somehow a part of the mystery of God. The notion of masculinity/femininity in God has roots in the Old Testament, especially in the notion of divine wisdom as feminine. Medieval theology also appealed to the masculinity/femininity dynamic in God, inspiring a few modern Russian theologians to understand the Holy Spirit as feminine.[33] In our own times, some authors are pointing to an element of femininity in Jesus insofar as his humanity was receptive (and therefore feminine) of the Word of God.[34] A detailed critique of this whole notion of masculinity/femininity in God is not possible here.[35] It might, however, help us to recall that the foundation of this book is that human sexuality is a good that touches us at all levels and is, therefore, profoundly related to the whole mystery of human existence. With this in mind, it seems entirely consistent that masculinity and femininity be somehow a part of our God who is the root or source of the mystery of human existence.

This chapter began with the thesis that our overview of human sexuality would never be complete unless we took up the question of the role of women and in that question the deeper questions of the man/woman relationship and masculinity/femininity. We have seen how our answers to and personal integrations of these questions have an immense influence on the quality of consciousness with which we relate to other people, to ourselves, and to God. If people can learn to integrate the kinds of sexual consciousness this chapter has proposed, perhaps the perennial demons of sexuality as essentially evil or exclusively physical can be exorcised to the benefit not only of women, but of all of us.

III
Some Pertinent Themes in Fundamental Moral Theology

One more topic remains to be considered before we turn to contemporary Roman Catholic perspectives on specific sexual questions. At the beginning of this book, we alluded to developments in the Roman Catholic outlook on philosophy, biblical studies, ecclesiology, etc. These developments have impacted much more than our overview of human sexuality. Moral theology as a whole has been greatly influenced by these developments. As we take up specific questions of sexual morality in subsequent chapters, reference will be made quite frequently to certain key themes of current Roman Catholic moral theology. Our purpose in this chapter is to describe some of the fundamental themes of today's moral theology that will come up most often later in the book. By no stretch of the imagination will we be presenting a complete summary of the foundations of moral theology. Only those themes most pertinent to our purposes will be discussed. These themes will be six in number: the meaning of sin, moral growth and development, a renewed understanding of the natural law, moral absolutes and moral evil, conscience and the Church's magisterium, and discernment of spirits.

The Meaning of Sin

Many traditional moral textbooks defined sin as the breaking of God's eternal law.[1] Moral theologians today do not dispute the fact that we humans need laws or rules, nor do they dispute the fact that when sin takes place, laws are very often broken. What moral theologians do question today is whether lawbreaking should be understood as the most central or formal element in the definition of sin. A very significant percentage of moral theologians would assert that it is inadequate to hold that the essence of sin is breaking God's law.[2] Law tends to measure what is on the surface of the human person whereas sin would seem to come from a deeper level in the person. In rejecting law-breaking as the central element in the concept of sin, moralists find significant support in Scripture, particularly in St. Paul.[3]

In place of the lawbreaking approach to sin, moral theologians assert that in the Scriptures and in the Christian tradition the most central moral teaching is that all of us are called into a loving personal relationship with God. We took note of this theme earlier when we asserted that the central moral question concerning sexuality is the question of responsible relationship to God, others, and self. Once we commit ourselves to the centrality of the responsible relationship theme, it clearly becomes best to define the essence of sin as the breaking or rupturing of our loving personal relationship with God. Sin is estrangement from God. When we estrange ourselves from God, we in the process become estranged from neighbor and self as well. God must be kept in the center of our definition, however. If we reduce sin simply to estrangement from other people and from ourselves, we will too easily forget the seriousness of sin and understand it only as some sort of social or psychological maladjustment.[4]

The biggest question inherent in the notion of sin as estrangement from God is the question of how this estrangement takes place. How do we break our loving personal relationship with God? In the past, the trend in moral theology was to say that we estranged ourselves from God through single, isolated, external actions in such a way that one external action in and of itself was apt to alienate a person from God for all eternity. Many readers of these pages may be old enough to remember the sermons about the evil of "one mortal sin" that were a standard part of the repertoire of so many old-time retreat masters.[5] In those sermons, one mortal sin and one external action were usually synonymous terms.

A key foundational contribution to contemporary moral theology has been the development by scholars such as Karl Rahner and Bernard Lonergan of a religious anthropology, i.e., an in-depth study of the human person in relationship with God.[6] One big insight of religious anthropology is that the human person is extremely complex, a being boundlessly open to mystery, as Rahner would say.[7] This means that there are many levels or strata or layers in the human person from which the acts of the person might spring. This also means that the human person never completely expresses or actualizes the mystery of who he or she is in any one action. To use an example from agriculture, modern religious anthropology envisions the human person as being something like an artichoke. In the artichoke, there are all sorts of leaves with varying degrees of toughness and tenderness. These leaves, coming from the many diverse layers of the artichoke may or may not tell us that much about the heart of the artichoke which is by far the most important part. Individual human actions, like artichoke leaves, come from various levels in the human person (emotions, moods, drives, needs, etc.). These acts may or may not give us a clear picture of the human person's heart.

Basing ourselves on this religious anthropology, we can say that our past tendency to identify sin with wrong external actions was an incorrect tendency. If the human person is as complex as we now understand him or her to be, what we must do in assessing the presence or absence of sin is to look to the whole person so as to grasp what the person is like on the core level of his or her being. To see the whole person, to see the core or heart of a person, we should take into account the entire pattern of the person's actions. We should look to a series of actions emerging from the person rather than to any one act alone. Our assessment of where a person is before God (in sin or in grace) will be far more likely to be accurate if we look to the overall life-style of the person, and see sin or grace as emerging from this life-style instead of from individual external actions alone. Even when we do look at a person's overall pattern of life, we can never be absolutely certain of the person's state before God,[8] since only God can ultimately tell what a person's state is (which explains the Scripture passage: "Judge not, that you not be judged" Luke 6,37). But our chances of making a correct assessment of any person's state before God will be much better if we look to the person's pattern of life.

A number of theological authors have described the current view of sin by calling sin the breaking of our fundamental option for God.[9] The term "fundamental option" means the stable orientation or life direction that exists at the core level of the human person. One's fundamental option can be either toward God or away from God. When we sin, we separate ourselves from God at the core level and thus break our fundamental option for God. The term fundamental option implies the nuances of religious anthropology mentioned above, i.e., that the human person is a complex person in such wise that we cannot simplistically argue the character of a person's fundamental option based on individual external acts taken out of context.

Upon reflection, it emerges that the fundamental option theory of sin is not all that different from the best of traditional Roman Catholic moral theology. Our tradition argued that there were three things necessary for mortal sin: serious matter, sufficient reflection, and full consent of the will. Since sufficient reflection and full consent are terms that do refer to the deepest qualities of the human person, our tradition recognized that something significantly more than external action was necessary for sin. The problem was that in recent centuries the categories of sufficient reflection and full consent came to be treated very superficially so that at least in the popular Catholic mind, seriously wrong external actions and mortal sin became virtually identified.[10] Thus the fundamental option theory can be seen as calling us toward a notion of sin that is not less traditional but ultimately more traditional. This is not to say that fundamental option and the sufficient reflection/full consent theory are identical. The latter would be more ready to see itself verified in individual actions than would the former with its deeper appreciation of the complexities of religious anthropology.

There are a few cautions that ought to be made about the fundamental option approach to sin. One caution is that the frequent references to the human person in fundamental option theory should always be understood to mean person-in-society. In other words, the fundamental option theory should not be used to reinforce overly individualistic notions of sin that forget about the sinfulness inherent in larger social matters.[11] Roman Catholicism's past tendency to equate sin and individual external acts often led to a forgetfulness of the social dimensions of sin. Fundamental option theory must be used in such a way that it will not continue the same problem.

Another caution is that the fundamental option concept of sin should not be taken as meaning that we can dismiss all concern with the sinfulness of our individual external acts. In the final analysis, the series of actions moral theologians look for today as a sign of sin is a series made up of particular actions. Just as we cannot say for certain (as we facilely did in the past) that the individual action does reflect a person who is turned away from God at the core, so we cannot say for certain either that the individual action does not reflect alienation from God at the deepest level. There remains the possibility that a person, in a rare set of circumstances, might so fully actualize himself or herself in a single act that he or she becomes completely alienated from God. Even in such a rare case, it would seem that the estranging action must have had a long history inside the person; it is not something whose total reality happens all at once. Hence, not even this kind of action can be fully analyzed or evaluated by our finite human minds.

As all this implies, the individual external act of a person has about it an inherent ambiguity that always raises the question of whether the person is in sin or in grace. Roman Catholics of the past tended to be very sure that some of their acts were good and others were bad. The newer approach, in questioning whether the badness of our bad acts always implies personal sinfulness, also serves to make us a little less confident that our good acts are as unequivocally good as we sometimes think. With these perspectives in mind, we can say that while the contemporary theology of sin does not stress individual acts taken out of the context of the person as we did in the past, it does not write off the moral significance of external actions either.[12] Some popularized versions of the contemporary theology of sin have done this theology a disservice by overly minimalizing external acts.

On both of these two matters of caution (the social nature of sin and the continuing importance of individual acts in an understanding of sin), Roman Catholics might be helped by dialogue with Protestant notions of sin,[13] though as a proponent of the natural law tradition (of which more later) I would certainly not be calling for the negativity about humanity that has existed in some segments of the Protestant past.[14]

On the whole, the fundamental option concept of sin has been widely accepted in Roman Catholic thinking and it has been used with some favor by the magisterium.[15] There are all sorts of applications for the fundamental option theory in moral and spiritual theology. Ultimate estrangement from God due to failure to respect the command to worship is probably better assessed from an overall style of life than from an individual action (e.g., of a priest not saying his office, of someone missing Mass on a single Sunday). Ultimate readiness for a vocational sacrament (marriage or holy orders) is best judged on the basis of a person's pattern of life rather than from more superficial criteria. In the area of sexuality, it seems quite unlikely that in certain types of sexual behavior a person totally estranges himself or herself from God in a single act. This and other implications of fundamental option for sexuality will be developed in subsequent chapters.

Moral Growth and Moral Development

A noteworthy occurrence in Roman Catholic thought and in Christian thought as a whole in recent decades has been the far greater significance attached to history and historical processes. Past theologies organized their view of life around fixed and static principles. Today's theologians, while not denying the presence of stable or continuing elements in human life and in the realm of faith, are much more aware of the many ways in which history and historical development condition our understanding of life and of faith. Bernard Lonergan has described philosophy and theology's new interest in history as the transition from a classicist world view to historical mindedness.[16]

Many aspects of theological thought have been influenced by present-day historical mindedness. The whole thrust of modern biblical exegesis which was clearly accepted by Vatican II[17] is based on using historical techniques (studies of archaeology, culture, language, etc.) so as to get at the context and thus the more exact meaning of various biblical passages. The effort of the Church to renew her celebration of liturgy has drawn much of its impetus from historical studies of eucharist, penance, etc.[18] The concern with social problems that has marked almost all Christian denominations in the twentieth century has its roots in the insight that the Gospel needs ever to be thought out afresh in changing historical circumstances. Example after example of this type could be cited.

In moral questions, it can certainly be anticipated that in the light of historical developments the Church as a whole might change some aspects of its position on one or another moral issue. This has happened in the past, for instance, on the subject of usury.[19] Since not all historical development is necessarily positive (there can be regress as well as progress) the Church has reason to be cautious in changing aspects of her moral teachings due to historical development. Nonetheless, there surely can be cases where changed human understandings are positive steps forward and where the Church should be open to changing her approach to particular moral questions. This is true in various moral areas including sexuality.

When talking about moral change and development we must note that it is not only the Christian people as a whole that has a history. Each individual within the Church has his or her own personal history that qualifies the individual's response to moral matters. At some points in our lives we relate in one fashion to various issues of morality whereas at other points in our lives we relate to the same moral issues quite differently because our personal histories are in an ongoing process of growth and development. Some of this personal historical development is unique to each person because of his or her particular circumstances. A pastor who has had a very positive experience with a group of Sisters in his parish will probably be much more aware of (and, therefore, responsible for) women's liberation as an ethical issue than a pastor who has not had such an experience. Neither of these priests would be any more or less responsible as a person but each would be quite different in his moral attitude to the women's issue.

Other aspects of each person's individual historical development are not quite so unique, at least for those who live in a common society. All of us grow through childhood, adolescence, young and mature adulthood, and old age. It is only to be expected that most persons' awareness of various moral topics will develop with the movement through these various phases of life. A teenager's sense of property might tell him that he should not steal from local merchants, but it will very likely not tell him too much about his responsibility for distribution of goods on an international level. Thirty-year-olds, on the other hand, would be fairly likely to be morally sensitive toward some questions of international (or at least of local or national) economics. Some scholars have sought to study in detail those developing stages of moral consciousness that we all might hope to move through in life, granting, of course, that not everyone will achieve the same level of adult moral development. Lawrence Kohlberg is perhaps the best-known author in this field.[20]

Catholic moral theology in the past tended to be somewhat unaware of this reality of personal moral development, with the result that our moral norms were phrased in such a way as to expect the exact same behavior from every person, regardless of his or her stage of moral development. This was especially true of sexual morality.

Allowance was made for the subjective non-culpability of persons in particular circumstances, but there was very little awareness that stages of moral development, particularly stages shared by whole groups such as adolescents, should be part of moral norms in the first place so that the moral norms themselves would clearly allow for different expectations of behavior for persons at different levels of growth.[21]

Three consequences of this notion of personal moral development seem to stand out for use in our moral theology (on sexuality or on any other subject). First, our moral norms should be formulated as just described, i.e., with a consciousness of common human development patterns. Second, those applying the moral norms should always be aware of the unique factors of a given person's history. These factors could never be part of moral norms (as could the common development factors), but we cannot leave aside aspects of a person's unique growth circumstances that have rendered him or her unable to see an issue the way a wiser and more morally mature person might see it. Third, in dealing with these moral growth questions, we must never lose sight of our best moral ideals. These ideals must always be before us as a challenge to keep on growing. The danger of moral development theories, if they are overstressed, is that we might become so tolerant of various stages of growth that we lose sight of the ideals we are moving toward. When this happens, moral growth, which is the very basis of moral development theories, stops and we are in trouble. The delicate art in moral development is, therefore, to accept people's particular growth stages and at the same time to keep on challenging them. Our reflections on particular sexual topics will try to reflect this delicate art.

The Transcendence of Physicalism: A Renewed Understanding of Natural Law

Probably the single most significant element in the traditional Roman Catholic understanding of morality is natural law. Natural law, of course, predates Christianity, but it was used by Aquinas in his great synthesis of Christianity and Aristotelian philosophy.[22] Roman Catholicism has just reason to be proud of the natural law tradition. The Catholic belief in the basic goodness of human persons and human communities is rooted in the natural law tradition. The fundamental Catholic trust in the sciences and their data comes from the natural law tradition. Our notion that human sexuality, marriage, and the family are central human goods finds sources in the natural law tradition. The Catholic approach to government and politics (relatively optimistic compared to segments of Protestant theology) is strongly supported by our natural law theory. The themes Americans celebrated during their bicentennial (that all are equal and have unalienable rights) are natural law themes. Hence, there is no reason for Roman Catholics to consider abandoning the natural law tradition as such. In recent decades, some Protestant thinkers have begun to recognize the values of the natural law tradition and to call for a qualified acceptance of it.[23]

Our affirmation of the natural law tradition does not mean that we should simply accept all facets of past Catholic natural law theory without any criticism or ongoing evaluation. If a tradition like natural law is to remain strong and vital, it must constantly be restudied and renewed. It is not our purpose to review all the important aspects of the ongoing study of natural law.[24] There is, however, one element in the present-day renewal of natural law that is especially pertinent to various questions in sexual ethics and that, therefore, calls for our reflection.

Among the historical theorists of natural law, one well-known author was the Roman lawyer Ulpian who died in 228 A.D. Ulpian described natural law as that which is common to all the animals and to humans before any intervention of reason.[25] This conception of natural law tends to lead to a determination of morality that judges what humans should do by seeing what animals do. This conception also leads to a great deal of concern with the physical structure of acts as the source of morality since natural law is seen primarily on the physical level, previous to any reflection on morality by human reason. This physicalist conception of natural law is obviously rather one-sided since human nature is more than physical. Human nature includes reason as well.

Thomas Aquinas cited a variety of ancient authors on the natural law and he did not completely espouse any of them. Ulpian was among the authors Thomas cited with the result that there have been fairly clear Ulpianist or physicalist leanings in Thomas,[26] the Thomists, and in much of the Roman Catholic tradition on moral matters. The Roman Catholic bias toward the physical aspects of moral questions has shown up in two prominent ways. First, the *content* of Roman Catholic moral theology has been quite physical. Our morality has spent a great deal of time talking about moral questions with clearly physical overtones (especially medical and sexual questions), while other moral questions such as economic justice tended to be ignored. The magisterium began to move into economic questions with *Rerum Novarum* in 1891, but many Catholics, due to their physicalist approach to morality, have still not become particularly concerned about moral questions with a less prominent physical orientation. The fact that our language often uses the term "morals" (e.g., "morals charges") as a synonym for sexual offenses may be at least partly reflective of an overly physical understanding of the content of moral theology.

The second effect of physicalism in past Catholic moral theology has been the *method* or reasoning pattern of Catholic morality. Quite often in reasoning to the rightness or wrongness of an action, Catholic morality has relied excessively on the physical structure of the action. The applications of the double-effect principle offer a number of examples of physicalism in moral reasoning. It was all right, for instance, to terminate a tubal pregnancy by removing the fallopian tube. Removing the contents of the tube ("shelling it out") was immoral, however, even though the latter process would leave the woman more able to bear children at a later time.[27] Many traditional Roman Catholic arguments in sexual matters also relied very heavily on physical criteria. For instance, the goal of maintaining the physical structure of each individual act of sexual intercourse was the major factor in past arguments against birth control.

The trend in natural law theorizing among Catholic theologians today is to go beyond physicalism and to try to achieve a larger view of human nature and human persons.[28] There are many human qualities besides the physical qualities, and all of these qualities should enter into our calculation of what it means to be human and what moral demands our humanness makes on us. Sexual morality is certainly among the areas where this larger view of the natural law should be involved.

The more broadly human view of natural law being proposed today does not mean that we can dismiss the physical structure of human acts as part of our moral estimate of such acts. Indeed, there may be times when the physical structure of an act is virtually all that is needed to determine the objective immorality of an act. The human body is an integral part of the human being, a fact that was very strong in Hebrew consciousness as Paul Ramsey reminds us.[29] The move away from physicalism also cannot be employed to justify the use of a morally evil means to achieve a good end, e.g., to argue that once we de-emphasize the physical structure of acts, it will make no difference whether we let a terminally ill person die by discontinuing extraordinary life-sustaining means or directly kill the dying person by means of an injection. Even in the past, our theology accepted the use of physically evil means (amputation of a limb) for a good end (saving a life). But neither tradition nor newer Catholic theological patterns of thought would justify the use of a morally evil means to accomplish a good end.

What Is Moral Evil?

These last remarks bring us to a question in fundamental moral theology that is more important for moral theology in general and for specific issues in sexual ethics than any other fundamental question we shall treat in this book. How do we determine if an action is morally evil and, therefore, not to be done? We said a moment ago that Catholic moral theology can accept the positing of physical evils to achieve good ends, but must reject the positing of moral evils for any purpose. But how do we know when the evil to be done is a moral evil as opposed to some other kind of evil? In answering, we shall have to bypass many helpful considerations and nuances,[30] but we shall try to get at the main lines of thought that prevail on this question among today's most respected Roman Catholic moral theologians.

Two propositions can be offered to summarize what the mainstream of Roman Catholic theologians are saying on this question of moral evil. First, there are many actions in life that for one reason or another significantly fail to reach the full potential of human goodness and possibility. Second, such actions can be judged to be seriously morally evil only when they are evaluated in their total concrete context and only when this context shows that there is not a sufficient proportionate reason for permitting or even causing the actions to occur. Each of these propositions will be given some explanation.

On the first proposition it can be said that no human act ever actualizes the fullness of human possibility. All human acts contain within themselves elements of non-good. Even listening to a Beethoven concerto temporarily deprives the listener of other human goods such as rest, food, exercise, etc. These minor lacks of good we simply take for granted.[31] In other human actions, the lack of good is much more significant. The journeys into space by astronauts and cosmonauts have much higher elements of non-good (risks of death, injury, health loss, etc.) than does the listening to the Beethoven concerto.

Moral theologians are divided on how to describe this evil that attaches itself to all human acts. Peter Knauer follows the traditional language and calls such evil physical evil.[32] The elements of non-good attached to an action may, however, be elements belonging to orders other than the physical order, a fact that has led some of today's

moralists to suggest other terms. Louis Janssens has proposed the term ontic evil,[33] implying that the evil is somehow part of the being of the act. Josef Fuchs has used the
term premoral evil,[34] so as to suggest that in speaking of
this kind of evil, we are not yet on the level where judgments about morality are made. Bruno Schüller and
Richard McCormick, to make a simple distinction between
this kind of evil and moral evil, have favored the term
nonmoral evil.[35] Without taking a stand on the merits of
these terms, we will, for purposes of simplicity, use the
term ontic evil in this book.[36]

The second proposition is the heart of the matter and
it holds that to determine whether an action containing
significant ontic evil is a seriously morally evil action, we
must look not to the action alone, but to the action in its
total context. In other words, intrinsic moral evil, objectively grave moral evil, and evil *ex toto genere suo* are all
concepts that are found only when the action is considered
in its total concrete reality. Past theologies have tended to
see these concepts in the action apart from its context, i.e.,
to see them in what we used to call the object of the act.
Today's moral theologians would tend to say that the
moral truth (objectivity in the most genuine sense) of an
action stems partly from the end and circumstances of an
action in such a way that the question about the morality
of an action is never determined from the act alone, i.e.,
from the object of the act. Thomas Aquinas did assert that
morality came from the object, end, and circumstances of
an action.[37] The current position of moral theology is that
it is more consistent philosophically (and more faithful to
Thomas) to see the object, end, and circumstances as part
of a continuum so that, at least metaphysically, moral evil
never comes from any one of these three factors separated
from the other two. This understanding of the nature of
moral evil has been developed by various authors, perhaps
most thoroughly and articulately by Josef Fuchs.[38]

How do we look at the concrete totality of an action
and decide whether the action is morally good or morally
evil? When the action is done to achieve a bad end, the

existence of moral evil is rather obvious. But what about the case in which the person doing the action has a good purpose, but due to some circumstances can achieve the good purpose only by performing an action that either contains significant degrees of ontic evil in itself or leads to other results that contain significant degrees of ontic evil? In these cases, the category of proportionate reason, based on the total concreteness of the action, is the best way to assess whether the ontic evil is also a moral evil.[39] In the total story of the action, are there factors that make the level of ontic evil present in the action reasonably acceptable? If so, the act might be considered not to be a moral evil. If such factors are not present, the action would be a moral evil.

In my phrasings, I have hinted that ontic evil might be related to an action in two ways, either as part of the action or as a result of the action. The traditional moral theology of the double effect regularly allowed the positing for proportionate reasons of an action that resulted in ontic evil, but it was inconsistent about those cases in which the ontic evil (for a good end) was part of, rather than the result of, the action. Thus traditional moral theology allowed the ontic evils of killing (in a just war), untruth (to an unreasonably inquisitive person), and taking someone's property (when in danger of death), in proportionate circumstances, but it did not allow the ontic evil in certain types of sexual actions (e.g., masturbation for the purposes of sperm testing) no matter what the circumstances were. Perhaps the problem in the past was that our theology could not admit the existence of ontic but not moral evil in sexual matters due to the physicalism mentioned earlier. In this light, the contemporary approach to moral evil might be said to be summoning our theology and Church teaching to a greater philosophical consistency on moral evil than it has exhibited in the past.

These comments are not meant to question that there is a significant difference between doing an ontic evil for a good end and letting the ontic evil happen as a result of some other act aimed at a good end. In the case where the ontic evil is directly done rather than being indirectly permitted, there would have to be a greater proportionate reason present for the act to be called moral, and there would be a greater likelihood of the ontic evil in the act becoming moral evil. In other words, differences in the physical structure of acts may often be the ground of moral differences in the acts as well.[40] We noted earlier that for most in the Catholic tradition, killing a dying person instead of letting him or her die would be a case in which the physical differences in the way these acts relate to their ends are also moral differences.[41]

The position that the moral evil or lack thereof in an action comes from the proportionality found in the total concreteness of the action does not mean that an act is proportionate and free of moral evil simply because the individual doing the act thinks there is a proportionate reason for the act. Subjectivity does not make for proportionality unless the proportionality is there in the first place. There may, of course, be individuals who innocently fail to see the moral evil in their acts and who are thus subjectively not responsible for the evil in their acts. But there is objectivity in morality and these subjectively not-responsible persons need to be challenged to see the immoral character of their actions.

What happens to absolute moral principles if we accept the current theological understanding of moral evil? Three things can be said. First, absolute moral obligation exists most truly in the total concreteness of our individual acts. In total concreteness, God does at times call us— absolutely—to do this and not that. We cannot generalize from this unequivocal moral absoluteness of God's call to all other cases involving the same act because the total concreteness of these cases may differ. But—in total concreteness—God does impose moral obligation absolutely and objectively.[42] Contemporary Catholic moralists are thus not the "anything goes" types they are sometimes accused of being.

Second, there are some actions in which the ontic evil is so predominant that it is virtually impossible for us humans to conceive of concrete cases where there might be anything related to the concreteness of the act that would justify it morally. Concerning such actions, we can formulate virtually exceptionless or virtually absolute moral norms that we understand as applying to all concrete cases in which the acts occur.[43] There are and there should be quite a number of virtually exceptionless moral norms. Cruelty to children, indiscriminate bombing of noncombatants, and genocide are examples of actions that we might call virtually exceptionless moral evils. In the area of sexuality, rape and incest are examples of virtually exceptionless moral evils. The force of the word "virtually" in this context is that, while we know there is not an absolute metaphysical ground for universalizing the moral evil of the actions just cited, for all practical purposes the prohibitions of these actions are universal.

Third, it is possible to develop descriptions of moral acts that are universally and absolutely proscribed, realizing that we must always check to see whether the moral act we have described is or is not present in a given concrete case. We can say in other words that murder, lying, and stealing are always wrong. But since murder is unjust killing, lying unjust withholding of truth, and stealing the unjust taking of property, we must always examine specific acts of killing, truth withholding, and property taking to see if these specific acts contain the injustice that makes them murder, lying, and stealing. Universal moral norms of this type are sometimes called formal norms. They are very important because they do help us to see what our moral values are; formal norms do not, however, call into question our main point: that we must look at cases in their total concreteness to see whether ontic evil in an act is at the same time moral evil.

The thinking about moral evil and moral absolutes just outlined needs a good deal of searching and creative application in the area of sexual ethics. Many of our future chapters will refer to this thinking, especially to the distinction between ontic and moral evil.

Conscience and the Magisterium

We argued earlier that there is objectivity in moral

matters and that individuals can make mistaken moral judgments. This means that all individual persons have to examine their moral judgments in the light of the broader sources of moral wisdom available to them. In moral matters there is thus an ongoing dialogue between the individual who makes decisions and the sources that guide the individual to his or her decisions. For Roman Catholics, there is in particular an ongoing dialogue between the person's conscience and the moral teaching or moral magisterium of the Church. Because this dialogue between conscience and the magisterium will be a factor in so many decisions in the sexual area, some comments will be made on the two dialogue partners (conscience and the magisterium) to see how they relate to one another.

Roman Catholic morality has held for centuries that it is the individual human conscience that ultimately makes decisions about moral matters.[44] The Thomistic tradition taught that a person with a certain conscience must follow it.[45] In modern times, Cardinal Newman was perhaps the greatest theologian of conscience: "If I am obliged to bring religion into after dinner toasts ... I shall drink ... to the Pope if you please ... still, to conscience first, and to the Pope afterward."[46] One of the great achievements of Vatican II was the *Declaration on Religious Liberty*, a declaration that is based strongly on the priority of conscience.

Some care is needed in discussing these traditional and modern statements about conscience. All of these statements presuppose that a person's conscience—to put it redundantly—must be conscientious. In other words, the presupposition is that conscience in making its choices will guard against the possibility of error by obtaining as much pertinent information as possible from the sources that guide or help its choices. While our primary reference in this section is to conscience using the magisterium, there are actually a number of sources that can help guide one's conscience. These sources include Scripture, tradition, the teaching of theologians, scientific information, community standards, etc. To do its job, conscience must pay attention to all of these sources including the magisterium. Some popular notions of conscience in the past few years have created the mistaken impression that conscience is completely autonomous, that it can "do its own thing" without regard for the magisterium or other sources of wisdom. These one-sided notions of conscience must be corrected.

At the same time, the theology of conscience cannot go to the other (and in the past more common) extreme which says that conscience is simply a computer-like ratification of what the Church teaches. The normal presupposition is that conscience will support the magisterium, but if we say that there is never the possibility that conscience may in good faith depart from a specific moral teaching of the Church, we have destroyed the priority of conscience that is inherent in the Catholic tradition both past and present.

Proceeding from this understanding of conscience, we can say that there are very good reasons why the Catholic Church offers official teaching on moral matters. We proposed above a partial listing of the sources of moral wisdom (the Scriptures, the teaching of theologians, scientific information, etc.). These sources of wisdom are so many and so complex that it is extremely difficult for the individual person to know about all of them, to understand them, and to put them together to make a good decision. Hence, the individual person can be markedly helped by the Church's effort, based on her life of faith, her experience, and her worldwide resources, to put together various perspectives and take a moral stand on one or another topic. In general, the Church's moral magisterium has rendered very good service to God's people and deserves praise for its efforts. This is especially true of the Church's social teachings in the past century.[47]

The complexity of sources the individual faces in making moral choices must also be faced by the Church. If we accept the notion that the ultimate morality of an action comes from the action in its total concreteness, the Church can never fully catch up with this total concreteness in such a way as to make infallible or fully absolute decisions on all the aspects of concrete or specific moral cases. The Church

herself seems to be aware of this fact. The theologies of
the magisterium found in the manuals always distinguished
between the Church's infallible magisterium and her authentic non-infallible magisterium.[48] In the area of morals,
while many would argue that the Church can teach moral
principles infallibly, there is a fairly widespread consensus
that the Church has not taught and cannot teach infallibly
on specific moral cases.[49] This does not mean that the
Church's teachings on specific moral cases are unimportant, nor does it imply that there ought to be widespread
disagreement between the teaching Church and the faithful on all sorts of moral cases. Rather, the general pre-
sumption would be that the Church's specific moral teachings are correct, particularly in those areas that are covered by what we have called virtually exceptionless moral
norms.

At the same time, however, if we accept the limitations
the Church's magisterium has to face in regard to specific
moral cases, it does not seem that we can exclude all possible disagreements between the magisterium and members
of the faithful on concrete moral questions. Nor can we assume that when such disagreements arise the magisterium
will always be right and the person or persons questioning
it wrong. We spoke earlier of a dialogue between the
magisterium and the individual conscience. On clearly
non-infallible moral matters, this dialogue will continue as
long as the Church and her people are pilgrims in this
world.

It is to be hoped that this ongoing dialogue will be
carried out with a spirit of mutual respect and trust on
both sides. The individual conscience should listen carefully to the magisterium, respecting the value of the tradition it represents and seeking to understand and accept its
positions on specific moral issues. At the same time, when
there are weighty reasons, the individual should be free,
both in theory and practice, to take stands that go beyond
or even disagree with certain aspects of the magisterium's
approach to specific moral questions. On its part, the
magisterium should be unafraid to present its position with

forcefulness and clarity. But the magisterium should also listen carefully to the people and to the experts in fields that relate to its decisions. Both the individual conscience and the magisterium will be enhanced by such a trusting dialogue and listening.[50] On occasion in the following chapters alternate approaches to the magisterium's teachings on specific sexual questions will be presented, but always in the context of responsible dialogue oriented toward mutual respect.

Discernment of Spirits

The net result of all the matters considered in this chapter is that both the believing person and the Church share in a continuing project of applying valid moral norms to ever-new historical realities. To see how a moral norm applies in concrete cases, we have to assess the proportionality or proportionate reason that exists in the totality of the concrete case. But how is this done? How is this proportionality found? In a Christian perspective, we get at this proportionality by looking for God, by seeing how God is working and what he is asking for in the totality of the case.

Across the centuries of the Christian tradition, the theme that has best expressed this notion of listening for God in all cases is the theme of discernment of spirits. The discernment theme is deeply rooted in the Scriptures and it has been employed by many of the great saints and scholars of the Christian era.[51] The basic idea behind discernment is that, while God does speak in norms and principles, he never fully expresses himself in norms and principles.[52] Thus, to find God's call, we must look into the hearts and souls of persons and communities as well as to norms. We must decide which movements or impulses in human hearts and souls come from God and which movements or impulses come from other sources. The gift of distinguishing which movements in the life of a person or group come from God and which do not is the gift of discernment: "Beloved, do not trust every spirit, but put the spirits to the test to see if they belong to God" (1 Jn. 4,1).

In this passage from John, the word "spirits" refers precisely to the impulses that a person or community must test (discern) to see if they belong to God.

In the deepest sense, all of moral theology is an exercise in discernment of spirits, an exercise in looking for God wherever he chooses to manifest himself. When the magisterium makes authentic non-infallible pronouncements, what it is ultimately doing is making an effort to discern spirits. When the theologian or the ordinary believer takes a stand on a moral issue, he or she is trying to discern spirits. The whole moral process is synthesized or unified by the reality of discernment. While discernment may not be explicitly mentioned in this book as often as the other fundamental moral categories we have reviewed, it will be implicitly present in everything that is said.

The crucial background necessary for discernment of spirits is the background of prayerful union with the Lord. Only with such prayerfulness can the narrow biases of individuals and communities be overcome, and particular discernments will be more or less successful in proportion to the degree of openness to the Lord from which they spring. This does not mean that discernment can be made into a shortcut around the hard work of analysis that must enter into moral choices. But in a theological perspective, a God-oriented attitude is the most basic requirement for decision making. Moral theology today is rightly seeking a greater and greater union with spiritual theology so that our daily choices and our relationship with God work hand in hand instead of separately.[53] In the past, for too many Catholics there was a gap between moral choices and prayer. A focal point of discernment is to overcome this gap.

Each of the themes reviewed in this chapter could easily have been the subject of a full-length chapter or even of a book. But at least in brief we have taken cognizance of some fundamental moral notions that will be pivotal in subsequent chapters.

IV
Autosexual Activities and Morality

Much of the content of this and the next two chapters will deal with moral questions related to certain physical sexual acts (masturbation, premarital sexual intercourse, etc.). The material on these physical sexual acts will be broken into three categories: sexual actions involving one person alone (autosexual acts), sexual actions involving two persons of the same sex (homosexual acts), and sexual actions involving two persons of opposite sexes (heterosexual acts). In our first chapter, the point was made that human sexuality involves much more than the physical level of the human person. Thus it would be more precise to speak of the physical actions to be discussed in these chapters as genital or erotic actions rather than sexual actions. This would make the point that there are many other ways besides physical sexual acts in which the life of one person or the relationship between two people is sexual. For the sake of simplicity, we will use the more conventional terms: autosexuality, homosexuality, and heterosexuality. But the distinction between sexual action (larger sense) and genital or erotic action is certainly valid and should be borne in mind.

Sexual Thoughts and Fantasies

There are three major actions involving the physical sexual arousal of one person alone: nocturnal emissions, sexual thoughts and fantasies, and masturbation. Since there are no major moral questions involved in nocturnal emissions or in the content of dreams,[1] we turn immediately to the area of sexual thoughts and fantasies.

The Roman Catholic tradition has held that except for those sexually arousing thoughts oriented toward intercourse with a person's own marriage partner, all thoughts that arouse sexual pleasure and are deliberately consented to are mortally sinful. Such thoughts are often referred to as "bad thoughts" and worry about them has been a significant source of anxiety for many Catholics, especially teenagers. The term "bad thoughts" belongs in the same family as the term "morals charge"; there are many areas of morality and of "bad thinking" (plotting a murder, etc.), but "bad thoughts" tends to refer immediately to sexuality. The Roman Catholic position on sexual thoughts and fantasies is based on the venereal pleasure principle, which holds that all directly intended genital sexual arousal outside of marriage is an objectively grave moral evil, and, therefore, mortally sinful when it is fully and deliberately consented to.[2] The venereal pleasure principle applies both to complete instances of sexual arousal (those terminating in orgasm) and to the incomplete sexual arousals (no orgasm) that are much more likely to be the case in our present context of sexual thoughts and fantasies. Later on, the veneral pleasure principle will be evaluated at more length.

Several comments are in order so as to set the Catholic position on sexual thoughts and fantasies into a better context. First of all, sexual thoughts and fantasies happen with a good deal of frequency in most people's lives. Accurate statistics on the rate of occurrence of sexual fantasies would be virtually impossible to obtain, but it seems safe to say that the person who never has such fantasies would be a rarity and perhaps a cause for more concern than most people who do have sexual fantasies. It can also be said that most sexual fantasies occur so casually and so spontaneously that the person having them is not that deeply involved in his or her fantasies, i.e., these fantasies do not come from a level that would involve a person's fundamental option or deepest state before God. The data available from the behavioral sciences is another addition to our knowledge about sexual fantasies. These sciences tell us that sexual fantasies serve as a means by which people deal with minor sexual tensions that might otherwise build up and be released in more explicit and less acceptable fashions.[3] This means that at least in general sexual fantasies are more likely to eliminate problematic sexual behaviors than to cause them.

Without getting into a detailed moral analysis, it can thus be said that in most cases sexual thoughts and fantasies do not deeply involve the average person; they are not very significant as an area of moral concern. If the term ontic evil which we will use for other issues in sexual ethics were to be applied to sexual fantasies, it would apply only in a very minor way to the majority of such fantasies. There can, of course, be cases in which an individual seeks to fill himself or herself with sexual fantasies in a degree that is all out of proportion to the human meaning of life. In such cases, the use of considerable pornographic material might well be involved. With respect to these kinds of cases, the Church's traditional teaching on fantasies as an area of sexual immorality should still stand.

Masturbation: Updated Information

Technically, we are speaking in this section of self-stimulation to orgasm. The term masturbation (from *manus*, hand, and *stuprare*, to defile)[4] is not a completely accurate term to describe self-stimulation to orgasm since there are other ways besides the use of hands with which a person can stimulate himself or herself to orgasm; also another person can stimulate or masturbate someone to orgasm, a practice that is sometimes called masturbation (mutual masturbation), but that is not self-stimulation. We will use the common term masturbation in the text, but it is meant in the specific sense of self-stimulation to orgasm. The traditional Roman Catholic teaching on masturbation is much the same as that on sexual thoughts and fantasies: due to the venereal pleasure principle, all cases of masturbation are objectively grave moral evils; every act of masturbation done with sufficient reflection and full consent is mortally sinful.[5]

In our times, updated information on masturbation

has come from a variety of sources, with this information often setting aside past misconceptions about masturbation. It is essential for us to review this updated information before taking a moral position on masturbation. The updated information may be divided into the following categories:

Biological Perspectives

For a large part of human history, it was thought that the woman contributed nothing active to the birth of the child. Rather the woman was like a "watered garden" in which the seed of the man was planted. The total human product that would become the child was thought to be contained in the male semen or seed. After the spermatazoa were described by Anton van Leeuwenhoek in 1677, some scientists published pictures of the *homounculi* or little men swimming about in the male seed. In retrospect, it is fairly easy to see how this misconception about reproduction began. The male genital equipment is external where its functioning can be fairly easily seen. The female genitals are mostly internal and, therefore, more difficult to understand. It was not until modern times, beginning with the still partially mistaken work of Gabriello Fallopio (16th century),[6] that the female reproductive system began to be more accurately understood, and a reasonably complete understanding of human reproduction has existed only for the past one hundred years or so.[7] Prejudices against women probably both contributed to and resulted from this mistaken biology that defined woman as merely a carrier of rather than a contributor to new human life.

As far as masturbation is concerned, once the total human product is seen as being in the male seed, the preserving of the seed becomes a high priority and it is quite difficult to distinguish masturbation from contraception or abortion, since in all of these acts the total human product is being killed or wasted. Classic arguments against masturbation often relied heavily on the loss of the seed in explaining the evil of masturbation. Some moral theologians in earlier times even argued that women lost seed when they masturbated, stating that the secretions of the Bartholin glands (near the entrance of the vagina, and, therefore, visible before the advent of modern biology) contained seed.[8] Such arguments were probably constructed out of a perceived need to have seed loss so as to explain the evil of female masturbation. Today, when we know that the average male ejaculation contains 150-160 million sperm,[9] and that even in intercourse few ejaculations of sperm will be made when the woman is fertile, the traditional concern about loss of seed in masturbation seems to be poorly placed. Clearly, therefore, the traditional condemnation of masturbation was based on an erroneous biology. This alone does not invalidate the traditional position on masturbation, but it is a factor prompting reevaluation of the tradition.

Masturbation and Myths

In the past, masturbation was surrounded by an almost unbelievable number of myths. It was said to cause acne, odors of the skin, dilated pupils and dark rings around the eyes, nosebleeds, asthma, heart murmurs, and insanity, to give only a partial listing.[10] Medical research today rejects all such myths related to masturbation. Underlying all these myths is a notion still fairly widespread today, that masturbation and other forms of sexual arousal and orgasm are injurious to health, particularly when practiced to an excessive degree. Medical opinion today rejects this notion.[11] The human organism is now understood to be balanced in such a way that a person does not seek excessive orgasmic experience, granting of course that the amount of orgasmic experience varies greatly from individual to individual. Thus, excepting in cases where a person is in poor health to begin with, the notion of excessive masturbation or excessive sexual indulgence is not correct. Past myths surrounding masturbation can no longer be used as an argument for masturbation's immorality.

Statistics

Recent decades have seen the collection of statistics,

which for the first time give us at least something of a reading on the percentage of human persons who have at least some incidence of masturbatory activity in their lives. The statistical surveys done on masturbation have shown it to be a phenomenon that happens in a great many human lives, i.e., in about ninety percent of men's lives and in about sixty percent of women's lives.[12] Care is needed in reading these statistics; a person who has only masturbated once in a lifetime is counted among the ninety percent or sixty percent. Thus the statistics do not reflect the frequency of masturbation in human life. They do not tell us how many persons have frequent and ongoing occurrences of masturbation over long periods. Some of the statistics on masturbation do show that nearly all males who masturbate will do so for the first time by the time they are twenty, whereas for females masturbation will happen for the first time about as often after twenty as before with a number of first experiences of masturbation coming in women's thirties or forties or later. This fact is part of an overall picture showing that while males are most sexually active in their twenties, women are more sexually active in their thirties and forties than in their twenties.[13]

Sound moral theology cannot be based solely on statistics. The fact that all sorts of people do something does not automatically make it right. But at the same time, sound moral theology should not dismiss statistics out of hand. Especially when something such as masturbation happens in the lives of nine of ten men and six of ten women, there ought to be some honest questioning by moralists. Our tradition believes in a loving and merciful God. It is a bit hard to conceive of such a God as judging something that happens almost as a matter of course in so many human lives to be always a major moral offense.

Psychological Input

Modern psychological theory has sought to offer an evaluation of masturbation.[14] While the results of psychological efforts on this subject are by no means uniform, two major insights from modern psychology can be proposed here: first, a great deal of masturbation, especially among adolescents, can be interpreted as part of a normal human growth pattern. In other words, masturbatory activity is a phase to be grown through as the person moves toward a mature sexual life that is directed toward other people and that most probably will include marriage. From this psychological perspective, masturbation is not a topic of complete unconcern since fixation or arrest at this level of sexual growth must be avoided. At the same time, from this perspective, masturbation is not a major moral dilemma. It is simply something for a person to work through. The Vatican, in its recent *Declaration on Sexual Ethics*, appeared to be open to this kind of psychology of masturbation,[15] though it may not have applied it in the same fashion as the psychologists themselves.

The second insight stemming from modern psychology vis-à-vis masturbation is that there are times when masturbation may be symptomatic of deeper questions concerning an individual's overall personal growth and adjustment. Care must be used in employing this insight. Some counselors and pastoral ministers, perhaps because of their own ambivalence on masturbation, seem determined to probe for a deeper personal problem every time they are confronted with a case of masturbation, whereas in actual fact many cases of masturbation are, psychologically speaking, simply the normal growth and adjustment cases described above. The second psychological insight is true, however. Masturbation can be connected with more serious problems of human adjustment. This is one reason why a sense of unease about masturbation should not be completely dismissed in efforts to re-evaluate it.

History of Theology

We mentioned earlier that the focal point of Roman Catholicism's traditional position on masturbation is the venereal pleasure principle with its assertion that all directly sought genital pleasure outside of marriage is an objectively grave moral evil. Historical examination shows that the magisterium has consistently asserted the immorality of masturbation, premarital sexual intercourse, and other actions arousing venereal pleasure outside of marriage.[16] At the same time, however, it should be noted that the magisterium has been careful and nuanced in its condemnations of such venereal pleasure-causing actions. Often in such condemnations, the words "at least scandalous and dangerous in practice"[17] or similar phrases were used to reject arguments for the liceity of non-marital, venereal pleasure-causing actions. In the technical language of theology, words such as "at least scandalous" do not constitute an absolutely unchangeable stand on the part of the magisterium.

The fact that the magisterium has now and again made these carefully worded condemnations brings to the fore another important point: namely, that from time to time across the centuries, certain Roman Catholic theologians have questioned one or another aspect of the Church's teaching on venereal pleasure. Perhaps the most eminent of past moralists to question the total applicability of the Church's teaching on venereal pleasure was the Jesuit Thomas Sanchez (1550-1610), who raised his questions in the context of petting and other forms of incomplete sexual arousal.[18] Two years after Sanchez's death, the Jesuit General Claudius Aquaviva forbade all Jesuit teaching contrary to the Church's teaching on venereal pleasure (Sanchez's works on the point were posthumously rewritten), but it was later made clear that Aquaviva's action was disciplinary and not intended to permanently solve the questions concerning venereal pleasure.[19] All in all, the character of the Church's condemnatory statements in this area, and the occasional recurrence of counter positions by theologians, show that the Roman Catholic teaching on the immorality of all non-marital sexual arousal is consistent, but not as fixed and closed to development as it might seem at a casual glance.[20]

We have already seen that, due to the hermeneutic problem, Scripture is not fully decisive on all cases of concrete sexual acts such as masturbation. Moreover, the opinion of St. Thomas on this matter needs to be subjected to a distinction that Thomas himself makes. The distinction here referred to is Thomas's distinction between the primary and secondary principles of the natural law,[21] a distinction that holds that the natural law is absolutely changeless in its first and most basic principles, but that in the conclusions from these principles the natural law is valid in the majority of cases (*ut in pluribus*) but not always. Using this distinction, it becomes difficult to see how all the applications of Thomas's basic and still-sound theory on marriage as the best context for sexual expression[22] could be construed as being other than secondary (and, therefore, changeable) elements in the natural law.

Religious Anthropology

The essential character of contemporary religious anthropology was described earlier when we noted that a human being is a complex person, some of whose actions do not very well reflect his or her deepest life orientation. In the light of this anthropology, it seems quite reasonable to argue that many acts of masturbation stem from emotional and physical pressures that build up inside the person in such a way that these acts of masturbation are simply not that deeply reflective of who the person is before God. Such an insight from religious anthropology is another factor that needs to be included in today's assessment of masturbation.

Masturbation: Shifting Moral Perspectives

In light of all this updated information on masturbation, there seems to be a fairly widespread consensus in Roman Catholicism today that we should approach masturbation somewhat differently than we have in the past.[23] Within this consensus there are two main schools of thought on how to apply the aforementioned data on masturbation in theology and pastoral practice. The first school of thought would use the insights we have outlined to argue that in a very significant number of cases (more than we realized in the past), masturbation occurs in such a way that sufficient reflection and full consent do not ac-

company it. With this in mind, the individual who mastur-
bates is to be treated with pastoral care and understanding.
Quick judgments as to his or her guilt are to be avoided.[24]
Some pastors in the Church are learning to use this approach to masturbation quite sensitively, e.g., by explaining
to adolescents who masturbate the human growth and
challenges related to masturbation, and by welcoming such
masturbators to the Eucharist without always expecting a
previous confession of masturbatory activity. The recent
Vatican document on sexual ethics seems to be open to
such an approach to masturbation.[25] This approach does
maintain the principle that masturbation is an objectively
grave moral evil but it is certainly more pastoral in using
this principle than was much of the traditional Roman
Catholic practice on masturbation.

This first contemporary Catholic approach to rethinking the morality of masturbation is a step forward. It still
seems to have some limitations, however. It continues to
see all cases of masturbation as serious deordinations of
the moral order, regardless of their circumstances, and it
bases itself on the premise that often there is a significant
defect in the ability of many people to form or act upon a
correct moral judgment about masturbation. Neither the
serious objective immorality of all cases of masturbation
nor the idea that the moral sense of many masturbators is
greatly impaired seems to cohere completely with the
aforementioned data on masturbation or with the major
insights of today's moral theology as outlined in the last
chapter. Thus some Catholic authors have proposed or at
least hinted at a second approach to masturbation.[26] The
present author favors such a second approach and would
try to spell it out as follows:

Viewed from the whole perspective of human life and
human goodness, masturbation should always be understood as an ontic evil, that is as a practice that clearly does
not actualize all the potential open to humanity through
sexual expression. Masturbation contains ontic evil because
it closes both the personal union aspect and the procreative
aspect of physical sexual expression. Hence, the Church

and other agencies concerned with promoting human values can never be completely indifferent toward masturbation. The trend toward interpreting masturbation as a fully normal and fully human form of sexual activity, a trend implied even in some Roman Catholic writing, must be called into question.[27] There is, in other words, a fundamental element of truth in the Church's traditional concern about masturbation.

At the same time, and based on the best contemporary literature on moral norms and moral evil, it cannot be said that the ontic evil present in masturbation becomes an objectively grave moral evil in every case. Metaphysically speaking, no ontic evil is *ipso facto* a moral evil in all cases. In areas other than human sexuality, Catholicism has consistently recognized that ontic evils are not always moral evils. With this in mind, it seems particularly opportune to hold that with all the concrete factors related to masturbation (e.g., its statistical frequency, its relation to human growth and development, its usually minor anthropological status vis-à-vis our relationship to God, and its enshrouding in myths and medical misconceptions), there are many cases in which acts of masturbation in their total concreteness are not objectively gravely morally wrong.

Related to our earlier remarks about moral growth and moral development, it seems best to understand the gravity of the ontic evil involved in masturbation on some sort of a sliding scale. Infantile and prepubertal masturbation should be seen as a very minor ontic evil on such a scale. Adolescent masturbation should be seen as a somewhat morally significant (but still not all that weighty) ontic evil. Adolescents should be mature enough to be aware that they ought to transcend masturbation and grow toward a higher expression of their sexuality; on the other hand, adolescents are adolescents and the fact that they have not yet moved to higher sexual maturity should not be given undue moral significance. Pastorally, adolescents should be welcomed to the sacraments as in the first contemporary approach to masturbation.

In adulthood, the ontic evil involved in masturbation

should in general be seen to be quite morally significant, though by no means comparable to the evil involved in sexual activities such as rape and incest. By and large, adults should have arrived at a mature post-masturbatory stage of sexual expression and it does seem possible that adult masturbatory activity, especially when frequent, might be part of a life-style that is notably disordered in its total concreteness and, therefore, seriously morally wrong. One thinks of adults who use life-size dolls in their masturbatory activity, etc. Some of these cases evoke the insights of psychologists about the connection of some masturbation with deeper personal disorders and it may also be that in certain of these cases we should use the traditional notion of an objectively grave moral evil for which there is diminished or no subjective culpability.[28]

These remarks about the greater significance of the ontic evil of masturbation in adults are not intended to exclude the fact that fairly often adult masturbation remains only an ontic evil rather than a moral evil when it is looked at in concrete cases. The person who chooses to remain single for some important reason (care of a sick parent, a worthwhile professional career, etc.) may have acquired a habit of masturbation in adolescence that he or she cannot perfectly overcome in an adulthood in which the more common step toward heterosexual marriage is not taken. In these cases, the masturbation might well be interpreted as a sign calling for humility and indicating that the individual lacks complete personal maturity. But such masturbation would not be an objectively grave moral evil.

In marriage, there would also seem to be possible cases where the ontic evil of masturbation is not a serious moral evil in the concrete. Examples might include (but not be limited to) instances when a married couple is facing lengthy periods of separation or an illness of one of the spouses. It seems that the key question to be asked about masturbation when it occurs in marriage is how much the masturbation interferes with the total married love and sexual communion of the couple. A high ongoing rate of masturbation would seem to have a significant adverse effect on any marriage and, therefore, to be a moral as well as an ontic evil. Isolated instances of marital masturbation, such as those in the circumstances described above, may not have such a major adverse influence upon the marriage. Another circumstance wherein adult masturbation (either of a single or married person) might be concretely reckoned an ontic but not a moral evil is the case in which someone (in all probability a woman) first discovers masturbation (and orgasm) at a mature age such as twenty-five to forty-five. The adjustments to be made by the person in such cases might suggest that moral and pastoral approaches appropriate to adolescents should be used for a time.

Of all the cases involving adult masturbation, the case that most clearly argues that we should not always think of masturbation as an objectively grave moral evil is the case of masturbation for the purposes of sperm testing. Masturbation for sperm testing is manifestly an isolated instance and is done precisely to enhance the person's marriage and its procreative possibilities. Bernard Häring endorsed this sort of masturbation some years ago (1963)[29] and it is quite regrettable that his opinion has not won wider acceptance. Masturbation for the purposes of sperm testing may be an act of self-stimulation or it may be mutual (involving one's spouse) and thus not technically the concern of this chapter. In either case, such masturbation gives support to the reinterpretation of the morality of masturbation that has been suggested here.

The sliding scale of ontic evil in masturbation and the many different types of cases of masturbation on each part of the sliding scale require that a great deal of moral discernment be exercised by those whose pastoral ministries bring them into contact with actual cases of masturbation. Pastorally speaking, quick judgments that the ontic evil in masturbation leads to serious moral evil are to be avoided. It would also be wise if those pastoring in this area could help equip the individual masturbator to make his or her own discernments on this matter and to stay with such discernments once they are made.

By way of summary, the second contemporary approach to masturbation supported by some Roman Catholic authors might be called the "ontic but not necessarily moral evil" approach to masturbation. The "ontic but not necessarily moral evil" approach does not agree with the present magisterial formulations on masturbation. But the present author would argue that dialogue on such matters is appropriate and as a proponent of the second contemporary approach to masturbation, he would assert that, properly understood, the second approach is in accord with the deepest instincts and traditions of the teaching Church on masturbation, and that the second approach articulates these deepest instincts and traditions in a more philosophically and theologically sound fashion by using the concept of ontic evil.

The "ontic but not necessarily moral evil" approach to masturbation cannot be fully reconciled with the Church's traditional formula that all venereal pleasure outside marriage is an objectively grave moral evil. In subsequent chapters, we shall see other issues that raise doubts about this formula. Toward the end of the book, we shall offer a reformulation of the traditional teaching on venereal pleasure. Hopefully, the notion of ontic evil will help us maintain what is true in the Church's tradition, while avoiding some of the problems of the past.

V
Moral Considerations
on Homosexuality

Our procedure in this chapter will be as follows: first we shall attempt to describe the complicated phenomenon of homosexuality and to set aside some myths surrounding it. Second, we shall review some background factors that will help us form our moral evaluation of homosexuality. These factors will include the frequency of homosexuality, the psychological adjustments of homosexuals, the causes of homosexuality, possible changes in the homosexual orientation, and the Scriptures' evaluation of homosexuality. Finally, and most significantly, we shall attempt to develop social, ecclesial, and moral approaches to homosexuality and homosexual acts.

What is Homosexuality?

The term homosexuality is based on the Greek word *homos*, meaning the same, and the Latin word *sexus*, meaning sex. Thus homosexuality means literally the same sex or the same sexuality. Some authors have used the literal definition to describe as homosexual all friendships or relationships involving persons of the same sex regardless of whether any physical, genital or erotic attractions are involved.[1] This broadest definition of homosexuality is legitimate and it does us the service of pointing out our need for healthy friendships with members of our own sex. This broad definition is not, however, what most people or most dictionaries have in mind when they think of homosexuality. The more common meaning of homosexuality is that homosexuality is an erotic or genital or sexual attraction toward persons of one's own sex.

71

To get at what is involved in the common and accepted definition of homosexuality, the proponents of the broader definition of homosexuality (any relationship to members of one's own sex) have suggested the term homogenital to describe those relationships to members of one's own sex that specifically do involve erotic or physical sexual attraction. Since the word genital is based on the word generation and, therefore, implies an openness to procreation, the term homogenital does not seem entirely satisfactory in describing erotic attractions for members of one's own sex. Whatever positive things can be said about the creativity of intrasexual relationships that do involve erotic attraction, these relationships are not open to the generation or procreation of children. The term homoerotic relationships has also been suggested in this context and it seems to more accurately describe what the users of the term homogenital are trying to convey.[2]

In any case, the present author's conviction is that both the use of the term homosexual to refer to any relationship between persons of the same sex and the use of terms such as homogenital or homoerotic are rather likely to create confusion even though their uses have some validity. Thus we shall use the more frequent definition in which homosexuality refers to an erotic or physically arousing sexual attraction to a person of one's own sex, an attraction that may possibly lead to orgasm. In this context homosexuality includes erotic relationships both between males and between females. There is another term, Lesbianism, that is sometimes used to describe female homosexuality, but as a general rule, we will employ the generic term homosexuality.

This preliminary arrival at a definition of the word homosexuality actually opens us up to a whole range of variety in human sexual adjustment rather than describing a clear and distinct pattern of homosexual orientation that is the same in all cases in which homosexuality occurs. In the final analysis all persons may well be open to some occurrence of homosexual attractions in their lives. For some persons, the conscious awareness of homosexual attraction virtually never happens. For others, the conscious awareness of heterosexual attraction virtually never happens. Between those two positions of virtually no conscious homosexuality and virtually no conscious heterosexuality there falls a great variety of human combinations of heterosexual and homosexual attractions. Thus homosexuality is anything but a monolithic notion. It describes sexual attractions for one's own sex running all the way from the most temporary and minor inclinations in teenagers and young adults to permanent, exclusive, and deeply rooted patterns of homosexual preference in mature adults. Environmental factors will often influence the degree of conscious homosexual orientation a person experiences, e.g., a person placed in a predominantly one-sexed situation (school, military service, etc.) may experience homosexual attractions that he or she would not experience in other circumstances.[3]

Two conclusions can be drawn immediately from the great variation referred to by the notion of homosexuality. First, in light of the multiplicity of adjustments to which we can apply the word homosexuality, it is better to avoid the facile labelling of specific persons as homosexuals. This book has argued that sexuality is inherent in all aspects of human life, but it has tried to avoid a pansexualism in which all human motivation and activity is explained on the basis of sexuality. Thus it seems inaccurate to define any person by his or her sexuality. We do not usually label persons heterosexuals as if this were a complete and exhaustive description of them and this approach of non-labelling should apply also to persons with greater or lesser homosexual orientations. At times, in what follows, we will use the term homosexual, but always remembering the cautions just mentioned.

Second, and even more importantly, the variety of degrees of manifestation of homosexuality means that there is a critically significant (though not fully adequate) distinction between slight and occasionally acted out tendencies toward homosexuality and orientations toward homosexuality that are deep, permanent, and usually acted out fairly regularly.[4] Often these more deep and permanent homosexual orientations are described as true homosexuality and they sometimes involve a clear aversion toward members of the opposite sex.

The distinction between occasional tendencies toward homosexuality and true homosexuality is important because occasional homosexual tendencies, especially those occurring in teenagers and young adults, will very often be grown out of as a person matures. If a parent or priest or counselor reacts too strongly to occasional homosexual tendencies and acts, the person experiencing these tendencies and acts may suffer needless guilt and may even feel pushed toward ongoing patterns of homosexual activity that he or she would not otherwise choose. The point is that occasional homosexual tendencies and acts are a normal and usually transcended phenomenon that should not be treated as if they were the same as true homosexuality. The major concern of this chapter will be with true homosexuality and true homosexuals. When we speak of homosexuality in subsequent sections of the chapter we shall be referring to true homosexuality unless we explicitly enlarge the context to include other homosexual manifestations.

Rejection of Myths

To expand our description of homosexuality a bit further, we must put aside the myths that surround true homosexuality. Classic stereotypes have been developed for both male and female homosexuality. In these stereotypes, the male homosexual is understood to be effeminate in appearance, dress, occupation, etc. Often he is thought to be an interior decorator, an artist, an actor, or something similar. The female homosexual is stereotyped as a very masculine-appearing woman, again marked by certain preferences in dress, jobs, and so on.[5]

These classic stereotypes of male and female homosexuals are unfair to persons with both homosexual and heterosexual orientations. There are some male homosexuals who appear effeminate, but there are a great many more who do not. There are also some males who appear effeminate who are very thoroughly heterosexual in their orientation. Similarly while there are some female homosexuals who appear to be masculine, many do not; many masculine-appearing women are thoroughly heterosexual in their orientation.

Another stereotype concerning homosexuality is that it typically involves one-night stands and other promiscuous behaviors that we would consider immoral whether they occurred in homosexual or heterosexual contexts. It is true that some homosexual activity involves one-night stands, etc., but a great deal of homosexuality does not involve such contexts and in general there is quite a variety of contexts in which homosexual activity occurs ranging from supportive personal relationship contexts to the crass and exploitive use of other homosexuals.[6] Society is more hostile to male homosexuality than to female homosexuality, meaning that it is easier for women homosexuals to form lasting homosexual relationships. But such lasting homosexual relationships do occur in both sexes and the one-night-stand stereotype for all homosexual activity must be avoided.

An issue related to the myths and stereotypes connected with homosexuality is that today's changing patterns of dress and occupation are said by some to be an indication of growing homosexuality in our times. Women are more active in athletics and wear traditionally male attire such as slacks much more often. More men are into things like knitting and more men wear bright-colored and delicately tailored clothing that we would traditionally have called feminine. These developments can be said to be part of a pattern of changing cultural valuation as to what constitutes maleness and femaleness. These developments are not, however, in themselves an indication of homosexuality and they need not be interpreted as such.

Statistics and Psychological Adjustment

As a background for our moral reflections on homosexuality it will help us to know something both about the frequency of and the psychological adjustment factors involved in true homosexuality. Regrettably our information on both of these categories is limited and somewhat uncertain. As far as statistics are concerned, the problem in getting accurate information is that some homosexuals may fear to indicate themselves as such while others may aggressively seek inclusion in statistical surveys so as to make society more aware of the phenomenon of true or exclusive homosexuality. Dr. Kinsey and his associates found from three to sixteen percent of the male population to be exclusively homosexual;[7] other surveys done in Europe place the incidence of true male homosexuality at only two to four percent.[8] The same surveys found true female homosexuality to occur about one third as often as true male homosexuality.[9] These statistical surveys, for all their limitations, do seem to show that homosexuality in the true sense does occur reasonably frequently in human life. In a typical group of one hundred people, there will be a few homosexuals. Homosexuality as a life-style is not, therefore, something that hardly ever happens.

The information relating to the psychological adjustment of homosexuals is even more difficult to sort out than the statistics. The American Psychiatric Association has lifted its description of homosexuality as an illness, but many psychiatrists and other professionals disagree and the association itself may have been under some political pressures when it changed its description of homosexuality.[10]

Two points do seem clear concerning the psychological adjustment of homosexuals. First, there are many homosexuals who do not have significant psychological or psychiatric problems. Second, there are a large number of homosexuals who do have such problems. What is unclear is this: have those homosexuals who have achieved a well-adjusted psychological life accomplished this because they are extraordinary persons who have transcended psychological difficulties that are intrinsic to homosexuality? Or are these individuals well adjusted because homosexuality is not a major psychological problem in the first place?

Similarly are psychologically maladjusted homosexuals maladjusted because of their homosexuality or for other reasons (pressures from society, unrelated behavioral problems)? One set of answers to these questions would imply that homosexuality is a basic psychological problem though some have transcended it. Another set of answers would imply that homosexuality is not a basic psychological problem and that those homosexuals who do have psychological difficulties have them for reasons extrinsic to homosexuality itself. At the present time, partly due to the lack of thorough statistical analyses of homosexuality, there is no clear answer to these questions. Caution is, therefore, called for in the use of psychological evidence by both the opponents and the proponents of homosexuality. The psychological and psychiatric data are not a decisive argument in discussions of homosexuality.

Causes and Changes of the Homosexual Orientation

As far as the cause or the etiology of homosexuality is concerned, the most honest thing that can be said is that no one really knows why some people become true homosexuals. For a large part of human history, it has been thought that homosexuality has a biological basis, though there is no certainty as to what this basis is. In our own century, especially due to the impetus of Freud, there has been a tendency to offer psychological or environmental explanations for the fact that some people are homosexuals. These psychological or environmental explanations often center on the person's family background as the cause of homosexuality. Neither the biological nor the psychological explanations for the origin of homosexuality are completely satisfactory. Both biological and psychological research into the origins of homosexuality are continuing at the present time and perhaps in the future there will be a definitive explanation as to why some people become homosexuals. But as of now, no such explanation exists.[11]

On the subject of changing a person's homosexual orientation into a heterosexual orientation, the possibilities

vary with the varying degrees of homosexual orientation
mentioned earlier.[12] There are many persons with
homosexual tendencies, even fairly strong homosexual
tendencies, who can be helped through psychological
counseling, etc., to become heterosexual persons. But at
the same time, there is very clearly a group of homosexuals for whom no change in their orientation is possible with
all the good will in the world. This group of homosexuals
who cannot change their sexual preference are probably to
be identified with those whom we previously called true
homosexuals. Both the American Catholic bishops and,
even more clearly, the Vatican document on sexual ethics
seem to acknowledge the position that there are some
homosexuals who are irreversibly such.[13]

If we put together the affirmations of the last two
paragraphs, that we do not know the ultimate cause of
homosexuality and that true homosexuals cannot change
their sexual orientation, the conclusion to be drawn is that
true homosexuals are no more responsible for being
homosexuals than heterosexual persons are for being heterosexuals. This is a critically important fact that must be
kept in mind as we seek to develop social and moral evaluations of homosexuality and homosexual acts. True
homosexuals are not to be blamed for being homosexual.
Somehow in God's providence certain people are
homosexuals. This basic perspective must enter into the
way we face homosexuality.

One key consequence of the fact that homosexuals are
not responsible for their state is that words like "pervert"
or "unnatural" are best avoided as characterizations of
homosexuals. Homosexuals certainly do not experience
their sexual orientation (which they did not choose) as a
perversion. Nor do they see themselves as unnatural.
There may be a limited and qualified sense in which
homosexuality is not in accord with human nature but
homosexuals are not unnatural in the sense the word used
to connote when it was applied to them.

Homosexuality and the Scriptures
We have already taken the stand that, due to the her-

meneutic problem, the Scriptures do not fully explain the morality of all specific cases of sexual behavior whether in regard to homosexuality or in regard to other issues in sexual morality. Because the Scriptures are so often brought into the picture in arguments concerning homosexuality, we shall move beyond this general stance concerning the Scriptures and sexual morality and go into a bit of detail on the subject of the Scriptures and homosexuality. Two comments in particular can be made about scriptural passages dealing with homosexuality. First of all, some of the most celebrated passages in the Scripture that have been traditionally construed as condemnations of homosexuality may possibly be referring to other matters if we read these passages in the light of some contemporary exegesis. This could be the case in the famous story of the destruction of Sodom and Gomorrah in Genesis 19. Though many exegetes do not accept his opinion, D. S. Bailey has noted that the evil of the Sodomites may be related to the hospitality traditions of the ancient Near East rather than being an exclusive or primary reference to homosexual acts.[14] If it is true that not all the biblical passages traditionally associated with homosexuality are really references to it, then the evil of homosexuality may not be as pressing a concern in the Scriptures as we have tended to think it is.

Secondly, we should note that those biblical passages that definitely refer to and point out the evil of homosexual acts are passages that were written in relation to particular problems and situations. Romans 1, 26-28, which is one of the clearest statements against homosexual acts in the Bible, is written in the context of the idolatry of pagan culture and its evaluation of homosexual acts is to be understood in light of this context.[15] The same sort of thing can be said about other passages where homosexual acts are certainly mentioned.

There is an important methodological question to be asked when we admit that the Bible's statements against homosexual acts were spoken in specific contexts. Does this fact mean that the Scriptures' negative judgment about homosexual acts applies only to those cases of homosexual acts the Scriptures precisely take up, in such a way that the

Scriptures express no general negative valuation of homosexual acts per se? Or should the Scriptures' negative judgments about homosexual acts be understood on the level of a general principle about homosexual acts, granting of course that since Scripture expresses its negative statements about homosexual acts in specific cases, there may be other specific cases not discussed in the Scriptures that would lead to careful qualifications and nuances of the Scriptures' general negative stance toward homosexual acts? In his recent book *The Church and the Homosexual*, Father John McNeill appears to answer the first of these two questions affirmatively, thus holding that the Scripture has no negative judgment on homosexual acts except in the specific cases that it treats.[16] The present author disagrees with Father McNeill on this point and holds that the Scriptures do take a general or universal-level stand to the effect that homosexual activity always involves evil, even though we may have to very sensitively define just what this evil means in particular cases.

The major reason for the author's disagreement with Father McNeill on this matter is that the Scriptures' statements about homosexual acts cannot be read in isolation from the great priority the Scriptures give to the man/woman relationship and to marriage. This priority indicates that the Scriptures' concern about homosexual acts is a basic concern rather than something only relevant to a few isolated types of homosexual activity. Father McNeill seeks to argue that the New Testament, with its statements about celibacy, is not as interested in the priority of the man/woman relationship and marriage as is the Old Testament.[17] Father McNeill implies by this that it is harder to argue that the New Testament has any basic attitude on heterosexual or homosexual activity. It does seem, however, that there are some powerful New Testament statements on marriage and the man/woman relationship, e.g., Matthew 19:4-7 ("What God has joined together, let no man put asunder"), and Ephesians 5:25-34 ("Husbands love your wives just as Christ loved the Church"). Also the New Testament teaching on celibacy can hardly be construed as condoning orgasmic activities in any context other than marriage. Hence the suggestion that the Scripture is concerned only with certain cases of homosexual activity, but not with homosexual acts in general, seems difficult to support.

To sum up, this book's position is that in the Scriptures there is a basic attitude toward sexuality in the light of which homosexual acts are seen as an evil.[18] Since Scripture does not deal with all the cases in which homosexual acts occur, caution is called for in applying the Scripture's notion that homosexual acts are evil. Moreover, that fact that some biblical passages traditionally related to homosexual acts may have other meanings suggests that homosexual acts may not be as great a preoccupation in the Bible is as we have tended to think.

A review of traditional Roman Catholic moral teaching on homosexual acts would lead to much the same sort of conclusion just drawn about homosexual acts in the Scripture. There is a constant sense in our tradition of the presence of some type of evil in homosexual acts.[19] However, because the debates on objectively grave moral evil in all sexually arousing acts outside of marriage have never been definitively or infallibly resolved, it does not seem that Roman Catholicism has completely settled all moral questions that might come up concerning specific types of cases of homosexual activity.

Social and Ecclesial Attitudes on Homosexuality

When we speak of our basic social attitude toward homosexuality, the major factor behind our attitude should be the previously described position that homosexuals are no more responsible for their sexual orientation than heterosexuals. In this light our goal should be to give homosexuals a true welcome into society, a true sense of belonging. Homosexuals are as much a part of the human race as any other persons. They have a variety of talents and skills that can be used for the service of humanity, and there should be an opportunity for them to develop these

skills and talents. While some of the rhetoric and some of
the specific positions taken by homosexual liberation
groups may be ill advised, the general effort of homosexual liberation groups to secure a more human acceptance
for homosexuals is an effort that is going in the right direction.

There are many examples (housing, education, etc.) of
areas in which homosexual persons should be given a more
fully human acceptance into society. The two examples we
shall comment on are the areas of economic stability and
reasonable legal treatment. Economically speaking,
homosexuals have a right to use their skills to support
themselves. In the past, there has been too much of a
tendency to refuse homosexuals jobs on the basis of their
homosexuality. Admittedly there may be some special situations in which a person might be refused a job for
reasons related to homosexuality. If a certain job will
create all sorts of harassment and pressure for a homosexual, the job might legitimately be refused to the homosexual, granting, of course, that the problem causing this particular job refusal is a problem caused by the narrowmin-
dedness of society rather than by the homosexual seeking
the job. If a given homosexual has a record of not controlling his or her sexual attraction toward young people, this
homosexual might be refused a job (teaching, etc.) involving lots of contact with young people. (Note that a heterosexual person would be subject to job refusal for the same
reasons.) Other cases of legitimate job refusals to
homosexuals might also be developed, but the principle
should be clear: except in special circumstances, homosexuals should not be refused jobs for reasons related to their
homosexuality.

On the subject of homosexuality and the law, the goal
should be for homosexuals to be treated with sensitivity
and by the same standards as other persons.[20] At the present time oral-genital sexual contacts and oral intercourse
are against the law in most states in the United States.[21]
The laws prohibiting these actions apply whether the acts
are done in heterosexual or homosexual contexts, but the

laws are much more strictly enforced against homosexual persons than against heterosexual persons. Many experts would favor the elimination of such laws in those cases involving consenting adults.[22] Granting that some homosexual persons are irreversibly so, it simply does not seem that that much harm would be done to the public good by legalizing private homosexual behavior among consenting adults. There should, of course, be laws against some types of homosexual behavior (seduction of children and young people) but there should also be such laws against similar behaviors on the part of heterosexual persons.

As far as the Church is concerned, its response to homosexuals should be to help them understand themselves as part of the people of God. Regardless of where one stands on the morality of specific homosexual acts, homosexual persons should have the ministry of the Church available to them. Workable solutions within which homosexuals can receive the sacraments should be sought after. The aim of an organization like *Dignity*, which seeks to establish a place for homosexuals in the Church, is to be honored as a good aim even if there occasionally may be questions about some of the approaches with which *Dignity* pursues its objectives.[23] The Church, more than almost any other element in life, offers people a sense of social belonging. With all the bias and unjust treatment homosexuals have received in the past, they especially need to belong. Thus they especially need to be welcomed by the Church.

The preceding remarks on the attitude of both society and Church toward homosexuality have—correctly, I believe—called for a positive attitude toward homosexuality. This does not mean, however, that all societal and ecclesial difficulties about homosexuality are to be eliminated. In the next section, we shall take up the question of the morality of homosexual acts, a matter not discussed in our social and ecclesial remarks about homosexuality. Once we have evaluated the morality of homosexual acts, we shall be able to see the sense in which homosexuality remains a source of difficulty for society and for the Church.

The Morality of Homosexual Acts

To deal with the morality of homosexual acts that lead to erotic arousal or more especially to orgasm, it will help us to make a fourfold division of the cases in which homosexual acts occur. First, there is the case in which homosexual acts are taking place in the life of a person who is not irreversibly homosexual but who instead has the prospect of developing and strengthening a heterosexual orientation. In this case, the person's goal or objective must clearly be to develop toward heterosexuality. We shall not offer a detailed moral analysis of individual homosexual acts on the part of such persons. If the person is clearly intending and trying to grow toward heterosexuality, his or her individual homosexual acts are probably not that important, probably not a sign that the person is alienated from God. On the other hand, if the person who is free to develop as a heterosexual is not seeking to do so, but is deliberately seeking homosexual acts, these acts are objectively immoral. This is especially true of homosexual acts involved in any exploitive use of other persons.

The second case is the case of the true or irreversible homosexual who is expressing his or her homosexuality in a manifestly irresponsible fashion. This irresponsibility might include a variety of behaviors (the seduction of youth, homosexual prostitution, etc.). The homosexual acts that occur in such behaviors are objectively immoral.[24] Similar actions on the part of heterosexual persons would likewise be objectively immoral.

Our third case is the situation of a true homosexual who feels genuinely free to live a life of perfect chastity, i.e., to engage in no prominently erotic or orgasm-producing behavior. The homosexual who can make a genuine option for perfect chastity ought morally to take this option. Active homosexuality involves so many pressures, partly external (societal prejudice), partly internal (psychological adjustment), that the person who can avoid explicit homosexual acts is better off doing so. Roman Catholicism has always held up perfect chastity as the goal for all unmarried persons including true homosexuals. While we might today seek other options, we should not overlook the fact that for some homosexuals, perfect chastity might be a very good choice.[25]

By far the most complex of our cases is the fourth one. This is the case of the true homosexual who is committed to avoiding the manifest sexual abuses found in case two and who at the same time does not experience himself or herself as being free to choose perfect chastity. This homosexual wishes to live a responsible homosexual life-style involving as far as possible a stable relationship with another homosexual, a relationship in which the sexual acts contribute to the growth and development of both parties. The experience of homosexuals is that this sort of homosexual relationship strengthens the homosexual couple's sense of self-worth and enables them to contribute more effectively to the good of society.

In Roman Catholicism today, there are a fairly good number of persons (theologians, pastors, etc.) who sense that we should take a more enlightened and positive approach to this fourth case in which homosexual acts occur. The current proposals made to deal with this fourth case vary quite a bit from author to author. For purposes of simplicity, we can distinguish three different current approaches to the fourth case, i.e., to the case in which homosexual acts are performed in a responsible context by persons who have no real choice not to perform homosexual acts.

One approach to this case uses the objectively grave/subjectively not culpable methodology. In other words, even in this case all homosexual acts remain an objectively grave moral evil. However, because of all the factors surrounding the case, the persons performing the homosexual acts are not morally guilty for their homosexual acts. Thus the persons remain members of the Church in good standing and are free to receive the sacraments. This methodology concerning responsible homosexual acts can, if used carefully, be of help to people and it is in accord with the formulations used in the recent Vatican document on sexual ethics which states that the homosexuals now under consideration are to be treated with understanding and with prudence in judging their culpability.[26]

Our chapter on masturbation dealt with the objectively grave/subjectively not culpable method as it applies to masturbation. There we took the position that while this method has values, it also has its limitations, especially in its refusal to admit that the circumstances bearing on an act can change not only the person's moral relationship to the act but also the substantive moral character of the act itself. Much the same critique ought to be made of the use of the objectively grave/subjectively not culpable method as it applies to those homosexuals who are seeking to live as responsibly as they can. Thus we need to look to further models with which to relate to this particular type of homosexuality.

A second approach to this kind of explicit homosexual activity argues that when homosexual acts occur in a responsibility-seeking context, these acts are evil in no way whatsoever. Catholic authors who tend to go in this direction include Gregory Baum and John McNeill.[27] While the exact positions of such authors differ slightly, there seems to be a common note among them that responsibility-seeking homosexual activity is a fully coequal alternative to heterosexual activity. The position of the *Dignity* organization on homosexual acts is not uniform throughout *Dignity*, but it can be said that many elements in *Dignity* tend to lean toward the notion that there is no evil whatsoever in certain homosexual acts.[28]

It is true that certain homosexual acts can contribute to the growth and creativity of the persons involved. It is also true that Catholic homosexuals need a better treatment than they have gotten in the past. However, it simply does not seem philosophically or theologically sound to drop all notion of evil or lack of being from our description of homosexual acts that occur in good contexts. For one thing, homosexual acts will never be open to the specific value of the procreation of children, a value without which humanity (even homosexual humanity) cannot exist and accomplish its great goals in this world. The one-sided procreationism of the past may have been mistaken, but we cannot go the other route and say that procreation is not a key element in the meaning of sexuality. Perhaps even more significantly, homosexual acts and the relationships that surround them will also never be open to the deepest levels of the relational consciousness differential we earlier described as the key to understanding the value of the man/woman relationship. We have also seen that it is possible that homosexuality and homosexual acts may always demand major psychological adjustments (which some admittedly do make) and we have held that the Scriptures' sense of problem vis-à-vis homosexual acts relates to homosexual acts in general, not simply to specific cases.

Based on all these considerations, the position taken herein (and I believe in the best of the Christian tradition) is that there is a priority or normativity to heterosexual acts and relationships that cannot be dismissed in any theology of homosexuality. This priority will be crucial in our upcoming chapter on heterosexuality and marriage. In light of this priority, positions that resolve the case of the responsibility-seeking homosexual by equating or tending to equate homosexual acts and heterosexual acts as simply alternate preferences do not seem to be adequate.

How then do we explain the case of the homosexual who acts as responsibly as he or she can? The third approach to this case holds that homosexual acts always involve a significant degree of ontic evil because of their lack of openness to procreation and to the man/woman relationship as it functions in marriage. At the same time, the third approach holds that there are cases in which the ontic evil in homosexual acts does not become an objective moral evil because in the circumstances germane to these cases it is truly proportionate for the homosexual acts to be posited. When the homosexual who is not free to be otherwise or to be perfectly chaste is achieving responsible relationships and personal growth in his or her homosexual acts, these acts are ontically evil in what they lack, but not morally evil in the actual concrete totality in which they exist. In the present author's perspective, this "ontic but not necessarily moral evil" approach to certain homosexual acts is the soundest approach.[29] With this approach, as with the two previous approaches to the homosexual who does the best he or she can, there should be the clear pastoral possibility for such a homosexual to receive the Eucharist regularly.

The question might be asked whether the circumstances that make the ontic evil of homosexual acts proportionately acceptable can exist only in homosexual relationships that have the same degree of stability as heterosexual marriages. In general, this question can be answered affirmatively. We should note, however, that societal prejudice makes it harder for homosexuals to achieve permanent relationships, a fact that calls for some caution as to the degree of stability in relationships we can expect from homosexuals who are truly trying to do the best they can. Later on we shall deal with the question of stability in heterosexual marriage and see that there may possibly be a need for some slight nuancing of our approach to permanent marriage. While the stable homosexual relationship is not the same as marriage, the qualifications some suggest in applying the norm of marital indissolubility may be seen to apply by analogy to homosexual relationships.

Some further precision is called for on exactly what it means and does not mean to say that even the best homosexual acts always contain a significant aspect of ontic evil. This position does not mean that, unlike homosexual acts, heterosexual acts in marriage are completely free of ontic evil. We live in a finite and sinful world and the expressions of sexual love in marriage are all too often marked by selfishness, exploitiveness, etc. The reasons for the presence of ontic evil in heterosexual marital acts are not identical with the reasons why ontic evil is present in homosexual acts and in fact there are more reasons for the presence of ontic evil in homosexual acts than in heterosexual acts. But both heterosexual marital and homosexual acts are marked by ontic evil. This kind of evil does not belong exclusively to homosexual acts.

The notion that homosexual acts always contain ontic evil also does not mean that homosexuals are any less moral in God's eyes or any less worthy of dignity as human persons. Ontic evil is not the same as moral evil. We all struggle against various forms of ontic evil in our lives. Our worth as persons comes from our success in finding moral ways to deal with the ontic evils we face. The homosexual who does find a morally acceptable way to deal with his or her situation is not inferior as a person, even though there are limitations involved in some of his or her particular activities.

What the ontic evil always present in even the best homosexual acts does mean is that, on the universal level, the Church and society must never lose their sense of the fact that no homosexual acts open up to humanity the full possibilities inherent in the human sexual experience. For the human race as a whole, heterosexual marital sex acts will always have a priority in such a way that the human race can never be fully comfortable about homosexual acts, even in the cases in which homosexual acts are judged as moral due to their special circumstances. The Church and society at large need to have a humility when dealing with sexual matters. They do not have all the answers to sexual questions and they need to be willing to keep on studying these questions. But in their humility, the Church and society at large must also have the courage to stand for those values in human sexual activity that, as far as we can tell, will best foster the growth and development of the human community. It is in this spirit of making the greater potential value of heterosexual acts stand out that we have described all homosexual acts as ontically evil.

One way in which Church and society ought to witness this sense of ontic evil in homosexual acts is by refusing to permit homosexual marriages. Some theological authors who are very favorable toward homosexuals have indicated their opposition to homosexual marriage, a position consistent with the fact that homosexual acts do not make available to humanity all the possibilities found in heterosexual acts.[30] The Church and society should be open to finding other ways of supporting stable homosexual unions, but these unions should not be equated with marriage. The Church and society also have a legitimate right to bar the adoption of children by homosexual couples. We do not know exactly why homosexuality happens, but there is a very significant possibility that childhood experiences are related to the origin and development of homosexuality. The instinct of Christianity and of society across the centuries has been that the heterosexual family is the best atmosphere for the rearing of children. This instinct deserves to be maintained[31]

The author closes this section on the morality of homosexuality realizing that he has probably gone too far in his views on homosexuality to please many persons working out of the traditional morality while at the same time he has not gone far enough to satisfy those who believe that homosexual acts are fully on a par with heterosexual acts. What the author has tried to do is to follow as objectively as possible the Christian tradition, contemporary understandings of moral principles, and contemporary insights on homosexuality and homosexual acts. If the author's position does mediate between two counter positions on homosexual acts, its mediation may in the long run prove to be a strength and a way of bringing all people together into consensus on the difficult question of homosexuality.

A Note on Bisexuality and Transsexuality

This chapter has treated homosexuality and homosexual acts. It might be appropriate to comment very briefly on two other phenomena that, while related to homosexuality, are quite different. The phenomenon of bisexuality refers to the situation of persons who experience themselves as sexually attracted to persons of both sexes. Recalling what was said earlier about the great variability of the homosexual tendency in human persons, it should be no surprise that some persons have both heterosexual and homosexual tendencies. What is not so clear—and bisexuality has not been studied nearly so much as homosexuality[32]—is whether bisexual attractions are only a temporary sexual adjustment phenomenon that can be dealt with through counseling or sometimes an irreversible state that some persons will have to face for a lifetime. If bisexuality is a temporary phenomenon, the bisexual person is obligated to seek to work toward heterosexuality, following much the same moral judgment process outlined above for homosexuals who are free to overcome their homosexuality. If and when bisexuality is a permanent fact, the bisexual person who is not capable of perfect chastity should be counseled to control one of his or her sexual orientations, so as to create the possibility of a stable personal relationship involving sexuality. Other things being equal,[33] the bisexual person should seek to control his or her homosexual orientation. Marriage for bisexuals would seem inadvisable until clear control over the bisexual's homosexual drive has been established. Again, we should emphasize that the phenomenon of bisexuality is relatively little understood. For that reason, the moral guidelines suggested here are very tentative.

The phenomenon of transsexualism refers to people who sincerely wish to be, or even believe that they are, members of the opposite sex. Thus they differ from homosexuals who clearly identify themselves as members of their own sex, even though they have sexual desires for members of their own sex. The major moral question related to transsexuals (who are rare in comparison to homosexuals) has to do with sex-changing surgery. This question will be dealt with later in a chapter on some specialized questions of sexual ethics.

VI
Heterosexual Expression, Marriage and Morality

Though this chapter will be our longest, it will be impossible to take up all aspects of heterosexual activity and marriage. Rather our purpose will be to treat a few key questions about heterosexual activity and marriage. We will begin with a basic statement about heterosexual genital activity and marriage, and then move on to treat premarital and extramarital sexual activities, sexual communion in marriage, means of controlling birth, and finally divorce and remarriage.

The Fundamental Catholic Christian Values on Heterosexual Acts and Marriage

The Beginning Point: Genital Sexual Acts
and Marriage Go Together

As this book has unfolded, many of the wonderful and deeply significant aspects of human sexuality have been touched upon. We have seen how profoundly human sexuality affects our capacity for physical intimacy, for meaningful personal relationships, for the creation of new life (both physical and spiritual), for insertion into society as a whole and for relationship to the mystery of God. Across the centuries Christianity has deepened and is still deepening its appreciation of all these aspects of human sexuality. While no one insight or value can ever completely integrate all the aspects of our sexuality, the Roman Catholic tradition has constantly offered one key insight, that, perhaps more than any other insight, has served to unify and give coherence to the many values pertinent to human sexuality.

This key insight is that genital sexual activity so deeply

involves all the potentials of the human person that it is best expressed and protected in a stable and enduring union between a man and a woman. To put it in other terms, the meaning of genital sexual activity is such that it calls for the personal union we know as marriage. Only in the context of marital fidelity can genital sexual acts have the possibility of accomplishing all the goodness for which such acts are apt. This is not to say that all types of marriage concretely structured in modern societies sufficiently reflect and give to people the opportunities that genital sexual union calls for. Nor is it to say that all marriages are automatically accomplishing more than other unions involving explicitly sexual activity, e.g., premarital unions or homosexual unions. But the point is that Roman Catholicism (and I think all of Christianity) has a clear value system in which genital sexual activity is linked with marriage.[1]

The insight of our faith on this point is not something that has come down upon humanity strictly from on high with no foundation in human life and experience. Rather there has been the experience of countless persons throughout the ages on the value of uniting genital sexual activity and marriage. Granted the many issues and difficulties of our own times (premarital sex and the divorce rate), the personally experienced intuition that genital sexual acts and marriage ought to be united remains quite prominent today. It is true that in our era many persons have more of a need to try a variety of adjustments out (in all areas of life) so as to decide for themselves what really seems to be most meaningful. Such experimentation has gone on in the area of genital sexual activity. Very interestingly, the experiments in the area of genital sexual activity have tended to lead many of the experimenters to discover on an inductive or experiential basis that monogamous marriage works better for most human beings. The work of Carl Rogers and other authors summarizes some of the inductively made discoveries of the value of monogamous marriage.[2]

Deeper Christian Insights into Marriage

What we have so far described about the union between genital sexual activity and marriage might be said to have a primarily natural basis. We have talked about the conjugal love of spouses for each other and indicated that the character of the conjugal love union between spouses argues for the union of sexual acts and permanent marriage. If we reflect more deeply on the Christian tradition, we can find an even deeper basis for our insight about heterosexual activity and marriage. This deeper basis is that the conjugal love of a married couple mysteriously and wonderfully symbolizes and makes real in this world the covenantal love God has for all of us. Earlier it was stated that Yahweh's covenant of love for his people is the most ultimate basis from which to understand the mystery of human sexuality. Our present position on marriage (and on sexual acts in marriage) as a sign of God's love explicates this connection between human sexuality and God's covenant love.

Additional metaphors and images besides covenant can also be used to make the point about sexuality and marriage as a mirror of God and his love for us. St. Paul uses Christ's love for the Church as the theological point to which marriage ought to be compared. "Husbands love your wives as Christ loved the Church" (Eph. 5,25). Those theologians who hold that the Trinity is a profound teaching on the existence of dynamic and intimate personal relationships in God would see marriage as a beautiful symbol of the trinitarian life of God. Other theologians would make the highly significant point that the married couple give love as growing members of the communion of saints. Their love is not only for themselves but for all people.[3] In the final analysis, married love proclaims that the whole people of God is called to newness of life in the resurrection. Hence, the married couple's covenantal love is a proclamation of hope for the whole communion of saints.

In Roman Catholicism, and in other Christian communities as well, all these insights about marriage (its witness to God's covenantal love, to the inner life of the Trinity, to Christ's love for the Church, and to our resurrection destiny in the communion of saints) have led to our key faith consciousness on marriage, namely that marriage is a sacrament. It took the Church a number of centuries to recognize clearly the sacramentality of marriage, but this recognition is essential in our faith perspective concerning marriage. The fact that marriage existed as a very meaningful human good before the time of Christ probably explains why it took so long for the explicitly religious aspects of marriage to be distinguished in such a way that we could perceive the sacramentality of marriage.[4]

Because the context of this book is human sexuality, it is especially important for us to note that everything about a marriage, including its explicitly sexual aspects, is part of the sacrament. Sometimes there is too much of a tendency to think of the sacrament of matrimony as only the ceremony that begins the marriage, not the whole marriage. Past fear of human sexuality may have been part of the reason why the marriage ceremony, rather than the whole marriage, popped into mind when we spoke about the sacrament of marriage. But all of the married couple's giving to one another and to their children is part of the sacrament of marriage.[5] Sexual intercourse, as a major sign of the total union of spouses, is surely to be conceived of as a significant element in the sacramental life of married couples. In this context, sexual intercourse can be understood as a liturgical or worshipful action.

The Purposes or Ends of Marriage

As we have reflected on the natural and religious aspects (which are never fully separable in the concrete) of heterosexual acts and marriage, mention has been made of both the union between the spouses and their openness to having children. The question might be asked as to how these elements or ends of marriage (mutual love, children) and indeed other aspects of a marriage are best integrated into a synthesis. Past Catholic teaching used to express its synthesis of the ends of marriage by the statement that the procreation of children is the primary end of marriage. This teaching was not, however, used by the Second Vatican Council,[6] so it seems that we are free to search for other formulations in our effort to integrate all the values pertinent to sexual activity and marriage.

Our purpose in these pages has been to be wholistic, human, and Christian in our approach to sexuality. With this in mind it seems best to take the union between the spouses as the most integrating factor in our description of the meaning and purposes of sexuality and marriage. It is this conjugal union of the couples that makes possible all the values at stake in marriage. The man/woman relationship which is so meaningful in life as a whole is most deeply realized by the personal union of spouses in marriage. The capacity for physical intimacy, which is a universal human need, is most fully able to be realized through the union of spouses in marriage. Creative life-giving service and witness to others comes as a result of the personal union of the spouses in marriage. This life-giving creativity includes but goes far beyond the procreation of children. In other words, all the values at stake in sexuality and marriage (physical, personal, social, and spiritual values) seem to have roots in the total union of the couple and in their experience of loving each other in their differences. When a couple marries, their clear commitment is to each other; this commitment (which witnesses God's love and gift of resurrection) will continue even if there are no children or even after the children have moved away. This commitment or two-in-oneness of the married couple is what society and individuals concretely and really have in mind when they think of conjugal or married love. For Christians, this commitment sacramentalizes God's love for the human family.[7]

Properly understood, this description of married love in no way minimalizes the place of children in marriage. Children are the supreme concrete manifestation of the physical, personal, and social union of the spouses. But marriage is still marriage even when there are no children, (e.g., in cases of sterility). And unless children spring from the kind of total personal and permanent union of spouses just described, the life situation of children will be sadly lacking. Thus it seems essential that we declare the union of the spouses in their otherness to be the focal point from which marriage is to be understood both humanly and Christianly. If we too quickly move to the children in defining marriage, values essential to the marriage and to the children may be lost sight of.

In a way this question about synthesizing the ends of marriage reflects a false problem, brought on by the popular Catholic impression (for which the Church must bear some responsibility) that children were far more important than anything else in marriage. For the couple who have a dynamically growing and wholistic view of their marriage, all the various "ends" of marriage (each other, their children, if any, and union with all of God's people) fit together integrally into a total pattern of life that emerges out of lived experience and does not require a lot of theorizing. Our reflections have made covenantal, conjugal love the focal point of marriage since it is from this love that the whole picture of marriage flows and toward this love (ultimately consummated in our resurrected life) that the whole picture of marriage moves.

Some Problems with the Current Catholic Proclamation of Marriage
   The past few pages have described the beauty and sacramentality of marriage, and the Christian insight that genital sexual activity belongs in marriage. Yet in today's world the incidence of premarital sex and divorce is very high. One may wonder why, if the Church's viewpoint is as sound as we have argued, there is not more appreciation of the approach to sexuality and marriage just outlined. There are a number of reasons why many persons in our society disagree with the Church's approach to sexuality and marriage. The selfishness and sinfulness of various persons and social structures certainly cannot be omitted from any list of reasons to be proposed on this point. From our vantage point, however, it might be well to develop at more length one particular reason why the Church's views on sexuality and marriage are less appreciated than they ought to be. The reason we shall develop is the failure of the Church (and here we mean all in the Church, not simply those in authority) to make her teaching on sexuality and marriage stand out as clearly as possible.
   Several factors enter into the Church's failure to make her fundamental position on sexual acts and marriage more clear to people at large. First, the Church has spent too much time making one-sided and unnuanced condemnations of sexual acts that fall short of her basic position on sexual acts and marriage. The result is that people have to spend so much time wrestling with the Church's approach to non-marital sexual acts that they do not appreciate the positive strength of

what the Church has to say about marriage and sexuality. If the Church more carefully nuanced its stands on other sexual questions, people would be more free to appreciate the positive side of the Church's teaching on the normativity of heterosexual acts in marriage. This book has attempted to develop more nuanced positions on masturbation and homosexuality and will later do so on premarital sex and divorce. The recent Vatican document on sexual ethics did attempt to be more pastoral on the matters it treated, though it could have gone further. Individual leaders such as Bishop Mugavero of Brooklyn have tried to develop sensitive positions on issues such as homosexuality.[8] The Canon Law Society of America and the Catholic Theological Society of America have done the same in the whole area of second marriages.[9] More steps need to be taken in this direction so that a harshness on particular problems does not continue to be an obstacle keeping people from seeing the basic strength of the Church's insight that genital sexual acts are best protected in stable marriages. Those who simply and unqualifiedly repeat traditional condemnations of various sexual matters may in fact be helping to undermine the Church's teaching on marriage.

Another way in which the Church can obscure the value of her position on sexuality and marriage is by being too physical in her explanation of marriage. Marriage is a personal union of the couple, a union that of its very nature calls out for fidelity and, therefore, for personal maturity. If the notion that marriage is basically for physical sex and for children is stressed without emphasis on the notions of union, human fidelity, and maturity, there are bound to be difficult marriages, many of which end in divorce. The Church, of course, knows that there is more to marriage than physical sex and children, but she does sometimes leave the popular impression that these are the main values at stake in marriage.[10] Since marriage calls for fidelity and commitment, the Church has a responsibility to sponsor careful education and preparation for marriage, especially in an era when human maturity seems on average to come at an older age than in the past.[11] We will talk later about the Church's stand on divorce, but it should be noted now that the real issue raised by divorce is the Church's need to attain to a deeper vision of marriage and prepare people for marriage on the basis of such a vision.

Needed: A Richer Theology of Marriage

These last comments indicate the greatest single task for the Church to undertake if her approach to sexuality and marriage is to win wider acceptance. This task is the building of a well-articulated theology of marriage, a theology that will give a more substantial grounding to the basic insight that genital sexual acts best take place in marriage. It was mentioned earlier that it took the Church centuries to understand that marriage is a sacrament in the first place. This fact, plus the various currents of misunderstanding that have surrounded human sexuality, make it no surprise that we do not have a very extensive theology of marriage. A great deal of material has been written on particular sexual questions and problems both in and outside of marriage. But there has been relatively little written on the theology of marriage itself.[12]

This lack must be overcome. We live in a world that has come of age, to use Bonhoeffer's phrase. In such a world we are much more conscious of the dignity and worth of human persons. We are also conscious of the great richness and variety in human relationships, a richness available to all persons including married couples.[13] Simple stereotyped descriptions of marriage that do not treat it as a relational reality and that tend to close the development of the marriage partners both toward each other and toward all persons will not work. Much of the theology we do have on marriage still comes from the era of arranged marriages, i.e., from the era when older relatives made marital decisions with a view to inheritances, etc., not with a view to whether the married couple themselves loved each other and wanted to foster each other's personal dignity and worth through their marriage.[14] In our age, which has transcended these past customs, there exists both the possibility and the necessity of enunciating a richer theology of marriage that will be more widely understood and accepted on the popular level.

Some of the bare rudiments of this in-depth theology of

marriage have been suggested herein. We have noted for instance that human sexuality opens up avenues to personal growth both in and outside of the marriage union itself. We have tried to suggest that the awesome and enriching character of human sexual intercourse calls for fidelity and commitment,[15] with these notions not being as old-fashioned as they sometimes sound. We have stressed the central importance (though not absolute necessity) of children to marriage, an importance that in itself demands marital stability for the sake of the best human development of the children. Finally, we have asserted that marriage as a human reality and as a sacrament bears witness to God and enriches the lives of all people by proclaiming our resurrection destiny. Hopefully others will pick up these rudiments and build a theology of marriage. The present author is convinced that the Church has the necessary roots for sound theology of marriage and that the explication of this theology will serve to increase significantly the acceptance of a Christian viewpoint on sexuality and marriage.

Many of the remarks made so far in this chapter have stressed the beauty and goodness of Christian marriage. It might be well to close this section on a note of realism so that the foregoing will not be written off as pie in the sky. Marriage is hard work. For all its value it will not cure people of all their problems as some seem to think when they enter it. Indeed, it would be very foolish to look upon marriage as a solution to problems. No marriage will ever fully actualize all the values described above. Every marriage will have its difficult times. But many marriages, for all their limitations, will be very good marriages that do go a long way toward realizing the values of marriage described above.

Premarital and Extramarital Sexual Activities

Premarital and Extramarital Intercourse: Definitions and Statistics
    One issue that must be treated in light of the above remarks on heterosexual activity and marriage is premarital and extramarital intercourse. In our present context premarital sexual intercourse refers to any intercourse before mar-

riage, whether with one's future marriage partner or someone else. Extramarital sexual intercourse refers to that extramarital intercourse taking place when there is an existing, functioning marriage. The case of someone who marries a second time after a first marriage has broken up (and who is thus guilty of adultery and extramarital sex in the traditional Catholic view) will be considered later.

Before getting into some specific types of cases of premarital and extramarital sexual intercourse, a few statistical reflections might help set a context. There is a very widespread opinion that the rates of premarital and extramarital intercourse have increased enormously in the last decade or so. Stories about college campuses, wife-swapping parties, etc., promote this opinion. The statistics we have available show that the rate of premarital sexual intercourse in the United States has increased gradually over our century instead of all at once in recent years. The really big change in participation in premarital sex in the United States in our century has involved women, inasmuch as the percentage of twentieth-century American males having premarital sexual intercourse has always been quite high (eighty to ninety percent in most surveys). Of American women born before 1900 only fourteen percent had premarital intercourse. About thirty-six percent of women born around 1925 had premarital intercourse. Of those women born in the World War II era, sixty-five percent have had premarital sexual intercourse, with the figure reaching eighty-one percent in the youngest age group surveyed.[16]

One interesting aspect of the fact that the number of women having premarital intercourse has come to almost equal the number of men doing so is that premarital sexual intercourse seems to have become more affectionate and personal than it was earlier in the century when the many men having premarital intercourse had to do so with fewer available women, often with prostitutes. In addition, while much premarital sex has been narrowly premarital (only with one's fiancé) throughout the twentieth century, even more premarital sexual intercourse is limited to fiancés only today than was the case earlier in our century.[17] This seems to imply that premarital intercourse is more connected with permanent commitment today than it was in past decades. Another important point is that the statistical research done so far has failed to show any clear correlation, positive or negative, between premarital intercourse and the success or failure of marriages. It should also be noted that premarital intercourse is less frequent among the very devout in all religious groups.[18]

These statistics are not presented to condone premarital sexual intercourse but simply to bring us abreast of the results of some admittedly limited surveys of premarital sexual intercourse. Possibly these surveys indicate a change for the better in the context in which premarital intercourse is occurring. The statistics also suggest that older generations in our society ought not to cry out against premarital intercourse as if it had never happened before the sixties and seventies.

As far as extramarital sexual intercourse is concerned it is harder to get a complete picture since statistics are much less available and reliable. In general however, extramarital intercourse happens a lot less often than premarital intercourse. Kinsey's report placed the extramarital intercourse rate at fifty percent for men and twenty-six percent for women, and noted that among devoutly religious people the rate was much less than this.[19] There appears to have been very little change on this issue since Kinsey's time except that the adultery rates for both sexes are equalizing.[20] Those Americans who have been involved in adultery have generally found the experience notably less satisfying than they find sexual intercourse in marriage.[21] The adultery that does happen in our country is only very rarely of the wife-swapping, group-sex, swinging-orgy variety that gets so much publicity. Only about two percent of American men and even fewer women have ever been involved in these so called "swinging" activities.[22] All in all, therefore, the statistics suggest that twentieth-century America's opposition to extramarital intercourse remains fairly high. If our society has shifted somewhat in its attitude toward premarital intercourse, it has not done so on any large scale in regard to extramarital intercourse.

Casual Premarital Intercourse and Adultery

With the background of Roman Catholicism's basic position on heterosexual acts and marriage, and with the statistical facts in mind, we can now consider the morality of premarital and extramarital intercourse. Our considerations will cover three types of non-marital intercourse, two of which will be fairly easy to handle since the Church's teaching and the statistical input tend to support one another. The first of our cases has to do with the casual use of sexual intercourse by the unmarried, i.e., with intercourse for physical fun or pleasure. This type of intercourse falls very far short of the Church's insight that intercourse is best expressed in the personal union known as marriage.[23] Since this form of intercourse is so lacking in personal commitment, it seems impossible to justify it. The data in our statistics suggest that society is still quite opposed to this sort of intercourse on an experiential or practical level. If anything, there is even less of this casual intercourse practiced today per capita than fifty years ago. Hence in the case of casual premarital intercourse, the best judgment seems to be that there are no circumstances in which the ontic evil contained in such intercourse does not become a moral evil. To put it in another way, the Church's traditional opposition to casual premarital intercourse is still quite coherent in our times.[24]

The statement that casual premarital intercourse always involves a moral as well as an ontic evil should not be taken as meaning that every couple who engages in casual premarital intercourse is guilty of mortal sin, i.e., guilty of breaking their fundamental option for God. Regrettably, there are sources in our society that strongly promote casual premarital intercourse, and thus pressure some of our young people (e.g., college students) into acts of premarital intercourse for which they are not fully personally responsible. At times this pressure is such that young unmarried women can feel "out of it" if they are not having intercourse. All this means that we must be pastorally sensitive in dealing with young people who are having casual premarital intercourse. Some of them may not be involved in the total turning away from God that is necessary for the breaking of their fundamental options. In no way, however, should our pastoral sensitivity lead us to give the impression that there is any moral justification for casual premarital intercourse.

Our second case of non-marital sexual intercourse is the case of adultery, i.e., the case of a married person having intercourse with someone other than his or her spouse. As indicated above, we are not including in this case those persons who are in second marriages that are invalid from the Church's viewpoint. Our focus is on those acts of extramarital intercourse that are engaged in by partners in concretely existing marriages. The trust, openness, and self-giving to one's spouse that marriage calls for seems clearly to exclude acts of intercourse outside the marriage, since such acts indicate a division of the deep, personal self-giving that belongs in marriage. The act of sexual intercourse inherently contains a meaning level involving personal fidelity and commitment. Human beings cannot deny this meaning level in sexual intercourse and act as if any meaning whatever can be attached to intercourse.[25] One of our key theses in this book is that body and soul are inseparable in the human person. This thesis means that sexual intercourse will never achieve its real human potential except in the context of the personal commitment we call marriage. The statistical fact that so many married persons who have tried extramarital intercourse have found it to be less satisfying than married intercourse seems to bear out this fundamental philosophical and Christian insight. Hence we must conclude that in normal life there are virtually no circumstances that would give moral justification to the ontic evil inherent in extramarital sexual intercourse.[26] As with casual premarital intercourse, this position does not imply that all adulterers are guilty of broken fundamental option and personal mortal sin. At the same time, in the case of extramarital intercourse we are ordinarily dealing with persons older than the young adults who might be led to engage in casual premarital intercourse. Thus the possibility of extramarital intercourse's involving someone's fundamental option seems more likely than in the case of casual premarital intercourse, especially when there are repeated instances of extramarital intercourse over an extended period of time.

The Dilemma of Committed Premarital Intercourse

The third and by far the most difficult case of sexual intercourse outside of marriage is the case of sexual intercourse by a man and a woman who are deeply personally committed to each other and whose intercourse takes place in this context of personal commitment. In this case the union of the partners has much of the personal and human reality of marriage. Often the partners in such intercourse intend to marry and will do so if and when their circumstances permit. These factors do make this sort of intercourse complex and challenging to evaluate. Our review of statistics has suggested that society at large is rather open to this particular type of intercourse, which, as we shall see, may never have existed in former societies in quite the way it exists today.

Several perspectives need to be developed to evaluate fully this case of premarital intercourse with personal commitment and affection. First, it must be said that even in this case the Church's basic norm that genital sexual activity is best protected and expressed in marriage remains clearly in place. Marriage has about it an inherent social dimension as well as a personal dimension. Thus a deep heterosexual love union between two persons needs to be publicly witnessed. Such a union by its very nature is apt to contribute to the growth and development of society. As long as the union remains on a purely private level it is not achieving its fullness, it is not clearly sacramentally witnessing to society the love of God for his people.[27] Part of the reason, but by no means the whole reason, why such a union is not witnessing to society is because it is not open (most probably through birth control) to the procreation of children. When all of these factors are put together, the conclusion to be drawn is that there is no case of premarital intercourse, even in the best of circumstances, that does not contain a morally significant level of ontic evil or lack of due fullness of being. This conviction about ontic evil will be an element in all our evaluations of premarital intercourse.

A second point to be made is that many of these cases of committed premarital sexual intercourse are not as good as they look at first glance. A lot of the rhetoric about love and commitment in these cases is simply rhetoric and it can cover a fair degree of selfishness and immaturity. Part of the problem here is that one partner can never be sure that the other partner's words of commitment—which are not public—are genuine. It all too often and all too traumatically happens that one deeply committed partner in such a union discovers that the other person's commitment, though spoken, was really not meant.[28] Admittedly this problem could also happen after marriage, but the social character of marriage does help make such a problem less likely.

Third, it must be acknowledged that, in our highly complicated and industrialized society, loving heterosexual unions of people are sometimes affected by some very difficult circumstances. For centuries, the Church has taught that people have a right to marry, a right that society cannot unreasonably infringe upon.[29] With this in mind, it can be argued that in our times there are perhaps some cases in which society does unreasonably impede people's right to marry. One example is the situation of a widow who falls in love and wishes to marry, but faces significant financial problems (loss of pension benefits, etc.) if she does so. In an older, simpler society, this widow and her first husband probably would have saved their own retirement income so that she would have had no financial problems relative to a second marriage. In our society, with its socialized retirement programs, she does have a problem. Another example would be the case of a young man and woman in their later twenties who are mature, deeply committed to each other, and fully intending to marry. Before they are free to do so, the young man is having to work through a whole series of socially structured delays: college, military service, graduate school, the achievement of financial independence, etc. These factors might not delay all couples from marriage, but they tend to do so for some of our best young people. If all the delay factors just mentioned operate in a given case, marriage might be postponed ten full years beyond the time when the couple is physically prepared for it, ten years beyond the time when people married in an older, more agrarian type of society. It is perhaps no surprise that society began to adopt a new attitude toward committed premarital intercourse at about the same time that our industrial society altered the usual age and financial conditions necessary for marriage (cf. our statistics showing that the change on this matter began early in our century). It may also be quite possible that the delay in achieving maturity that many notice in our young adults is related to the fact that many young adults cannot achieve financial independence until they near the age of thirty.[30]

Both of the examples just given make the same key point: our society has established a socioeconomic structure for marriage and family life that may unreasonably restrict some persons' fundamental freedom to marry. Because of this situation, the present author's position is that, in a limited number of cases, the circumstances surrounding the intercourse of a couple who are deeply committed to each other and who fully intend to marry may render their premarital intercourse an ontic evil but not a moral evil.[31] The possibility of such intercourse being an ontic but not a moral evil would seem to be present especially when the committed couple whose marriage rights are unreasonably prejudiced by society do not experience themselves as genuinely free to take the more ideal route of abstaining from that intercourse that cannot be publicly proclaimed as part of a marriage. In these cases the intercourse's lack of public proclamation is not due to any defect in the intention of the couple; it is due rather to certain problematic characteristics of modern society. The couple in such a situation needs to have the humility to recognize that their intercourse is still lacking an important dimension; morally speaking, however, their intercourse may not be wrong.

From a pastoral viewpoint, the most important thing to recognize about the cases we have just described is that they are rare. The great problem is that when we admit the existence of such rare cases, all sorts of people will conclude that their case is one of the rare cases.[32] Ways must be found to avoid this difficulty. Of the issues we treated earlier, masturbation is obviously a transitional phase of sexual development and homosexual acts based on a permanent homosexual orientation are relevant for only a small (but significant) portion of humanity. Thus there is little danger that our positions on certain cases of masturbation and homosexual activity will be applied permanently to the larger part of the human race.

But with premarital intercourse the danger of our carefully outlined cases being carelessly extended to large segments of humanity is quite real.

In terms of what we might do to cut down on the increased occurrence of such unwarranted premarital sex, the first priority is a theme we have already touched on: the deepening of our theology of marriage. With a richer vision of marriage, perhaps more people would freely respond to the ascetic challenge to abstain from intercourse until marriage. Besides this step we should clearly assert once again that the only cases where premarital intercourse seems morally justifiable are the cases where there is a real maturity and commitment including the intention to marry when and if the interfering social obstacles are removed. If in such cases the couple breaks up or fails to marry when the opportunity comes, they ought to be judged by moral standards similar to those that apply to formally married couples who break up.

We should also note that there may be cases of committed premarital intercourse in which, while the degree of commitment and social pressures do not offer a moral justification, the emotional attachment of the couple and the attitudes of our society are such as to bring about a situation in which the couple do not break their fundamental option for God through their intercourse. This, in other words, is the objectively grave but subjectively not culpable case. The case in which we would offer a moral justification for premarital intercourse (ontic evil but not moral evil) is very rare. The objectively grave but subjectively not culpable case seems likely to happen somewhat more often.[33]

Three issues ought to be raised as a follow-up to our whole approach to premarital intercourse. First, some might pose the question whether those few cases where premarital intercourse does seem morally justifiable could be handled through the traditional notion of a secret marriage (i.e., a marriage secretly witnessed by the priest) since in these cases the couple's intention toward each other is basically the same as if they were married. There is a somewhat unfortunate legalism underlying this question, a legalism assuming that the problem involved in premarital intercourse is completely solved when a priest blesses a genuine intention to marry that is frustrated by unreasonable external factors. Some would even suggest that fully committed premarital intercourse is not premarital intercourse at all, but only preceremonial intercourse. To those who would assert such a distinction or who would hold that a secret ceremony would take care of such a case,[34] it must be asserted that public proclamation (so that the couple can witness God's love) is an essential element in marriage. Thus even a secret marriage is an ontic evil; it is not a complete solution to the difficulty that committed but not publicly marriageable couples face.

Also, while the cases of justifiable premarital intercourse, even in our times, are few, our dealing with them on the basis of secret marriages would lead to significantly more secret marriages than in past nonindustrial societies. This in turn could lead to a variety of social and legal problems. Hence, a secret marriage might be used in cases of grave pastoral necessity (e.g., the case of an elderly couple having weighty problems of conscience about their love relationship), but it does not seem wise to expand the notion of secret marriages too greatly.

Another issue has to do with the use of birth control devices by those whose premarital intercourse may be morally justifiable or even by those whose premarital intercourse is not morally justifiable. It used to be said that the employment of birth control devices always added to the wrong of premarital intercourse. Our more complete treatment of birth control will come later in this chapter. For now we can briefly anticipate that treatment by saying that if a premarried couple is truly justified in having intercourse, their use of birth control devices does not seem morally wrong provided that they are open to having children when the right opportunity comes. As for those whose premarital intercourse does not seem morally justified, it might be suggested today that such a couple, by using birth control devices, is actually lessening the wrong in their intercourse since at least they are avoiding the procreation of new life for which they are unable to take responsibility.

Finally, nothing that has been said about some cases of

premarital sexual intercourse gives any credibility at all to the notion of trial marriage. Our basic notion is that marriage is permanent and the few exceptions we did make concerning premarital intercourse were made precisely because these exceptions involved the basic reality of a permanent marital commitment. Married love is difficult to achieve amid life's ups and downs. Trial marriage for a few years would almost guarantee that marriage would not work. Without permanent commitment, too many couples would take the easy way out when they ran into problems. The growth that is part of committed marriages would not take place. There is a big difference between being open to a few premarital dilemmas such as those described above and setting up a legal-social structure that literally invites marriage to fail. The Church, in its tradition on marriage, must remain steadfastly opposed to trial marriages.

Premarital Petting

Our past theology, with its position that all sexual arousal outside of marriage is an objectively grave moral evil, tended to place premarital sexual petting in more or less the same category of condemnation as premarital intercourse. Perhaps a bit more refinement is called for on this matter. For one thing, statistical surveys seem to suggest that petting has increased in our industrially and socially complicated century because persons whose marriage has been delayed beyond the age when they are physically ready to marry (college students, etc.) have turned to petting precisely as a means to avoid sexual intercourse.[35] In other words, some petting is an effort by physically mature young people to deal with their sexual tensions in a way that respects the fact that intercourse ought to be reserved for marriage. Another point is that not all petting is the same. Some of it is very mild, really intended more as a sign of affection than as a means to intense sexual arousal. Other petting is more intense, perhaps involving protracted lying together, deep and erotic kissing, fondling of the breasts or genitals, partial or total nudity, and possibly even orgasm. Some would say that a distinction should be made between deep petting that is not orgasm-producing and deep petting that leads to orgasm. Others might see this particular distinction as based on an overly physical understanding of human sexuality.[36] Regardless of the exact distinctions made, premarital petting is a complex enough issue that it deserves some comment in addition to what has already been said about premarital intercourse.

As far as mild petting activities (kisses, brief embraces, etc.) are concerned, it should be acknowledged that the signs of human affection involved in such mild petting are signs that are not exclusively oriented toward marriage or sexual intercourse. All persons in all states of life have a need for affection and support. Thus, in situations when close human affection is appropriate, mild gestures of embrace and kissing are certainly acceptable. Such mild gestures are acceptable not only for premarried couples, but also for married couples with persons other than their spouses, for celibates, and indeed for everyone. These gestures are part of the basic human need for intimacy; growing comfortable with them is an important human learning process. It is a bit difficult to draw an exact line between petting that is mild and not directly intended for sexual arousal (though it may indirectly cause some arousal) and petting that is not so mild and more clearly arousing. The level of response and stimulation from the activities we are discussing can vary greatly from individual to individual, meaning that different persons (possibly in consultation with a confessor or other counselor) will have to make their own best decisions on what is acceptable for them in this area. Some cases of acceptable human kissing and embracing outside the context of marriage (funerals, weddings of good friends, etc.) should be fairly obvious to all of us.

The position that there are clear instances in which mild forms of petting are acceptable in non-marital contexts does not mean that these mild forms of petting should be taken for granted. Such petting can easily incline people toward sexual involvement and, even apart from this fact, human embrace and the respect for the other that it bespeaks should never be treated lightly. There are persons who seem almost too ready to make use of the gift of embrace in practically any circumstances. People, their backgrounds, and their cultures do differ, but the importance of human embrace ("the theology of hugging") is such that we ought to be careful not to cheapen it.

On the subject of deeper and more protracted petting, the clear orientation of this petting toward sexual intercourse and marriage suggests that this kind of petting falls under our basic norm that genital sexual activity is best expressed in marriage. Thus heavy petting before marriage should always be understood as involving ontic evil, i.e., as not being a fully satisfactory form of human sexual expression. We noted earlier that there may be some cases in which the ontic evil of premarital intercourse does not become a moral evil. This same judgment should be applied to heavy premarital petting. In the same sort of circumstances in which premarital intercourse might not be a moral evil, premarital petting might also not be a moral evil.

Moreover, if we seek to compare the ontic evil involved in heavy premarital petting with the ontic evil involved in premarital intercourse, it seems reasonable to assert that the ontic evil in premarital petting, while quite important, is not as significant as the ontic evil involved in premarital intercourse. In the special circumstances of a societally hindered commitment to marry, the couple who limit themselves to heavy petting (possibly including orgasm) are trying, in their difficult situation, to respect the fact that intercourse is best expressed in marriage. It is this which suggests that the ontic evil involved in heavy premarital petting may be somewhat less significant than the ontic evil in premarital intercourse. If this line of argument is correct, the proportionate reasons necessary to give moral justification to heavy premarital petting may not be quite as weighty as the proportionate reasons necessary to justify premarital intercourse. A couple who find themselves in a borderline situation might keep this in mind.

We might also argue that, even in those cases (and there are many) where the ontic evil of heavy premarital petting cannot be given any objective moral justification, the fact that the ontic evil in heavy petting is less significant than the ontic evil in premarital intercourse implies that there may be more likelihood of heavy premarital petters not breaking their fundamental option for God than would be the case with those engaging in premarital intercourse. Of course, in both of these matters (heavy premarital petting and premarital intercourse), the breaking of a fundamental option is more prone to occur when there is a series of actions rather than one act or incident alone.

In applying these remarks about heavy premarital petting, we should note that the psychological implications of heavy petting (in many ways a practice new to the twentieth century) without intercourse are not fully understood. For instance, might the interruption of sexual arousal before it leads to intercourse cause psychological problems for the persons involved? This does not seem very likely in occasional instances of petting, since petting can be understood as part of a learning process that will eventually and integrally lead one to intercourse. But regular non-coital petting over a lengthy period of time might possibly be a cause of notable psychological frustrations. We really do not know the answer on this matter, and until we do caution is called for, especially in regard to petting over protracted periods of months and years. If it should emerge that certain types of premarital petting situations do lead to significant psychological problems, our above-stated tentative conclusion about the weight of the ontic evil of heavy premarital petting would have to be revised, at least for the pertinent cases.[37]

The Sexual Communion of the Married Couple

Basic Observations on This Communion

A variety of issues of sexual morality ought to be considered as we move from unmarried to married persons. The physical sexual communion of the married couple is by no means the whole of married life, but it is one issue on which it is important to form some moral values.[38] In treating this issue, it is not our purpose either to sensationalize or to trivialize the physical sexual relationship of the married couple, even though both of these dangers exist when sexual communion is discussed. Our first chapter made the point that human sexuality must be seen as wholistic, as touching us on all levels. More recently we made the point that sexual intercourse in marriage ought to be seen as sacramental and perhaps even as liturgical.[39] In our articulation of moral values pertinent to the physical sexual communion of the married couple, our major objective will be to see how the married couple's sexual relationship might best reflect the deeper human and religious values inherent in the sexual experience.

To begin, it is very important for married couples to see their explicitly sexual activity as integrally related to the whole fabric of their married life. They should not expect their intercourse or other sexual actions to achieve their full potential if they are not making efforts to relate honestly and openly and caringly to each other in all sorts of ways. Intercourse can at times be healing of tensions that exist in a marriage relationship, but it is unwise for a couple to assume that they can automatically turn on to sexual expression at the deepest level when they are being inconsiderate of one another and failing to make the human effort to love each other as total beings.

On a more explicit level, married couples ought to try to take sufficient time in preparing for sexual intercourse. Such preparation involves not only the context of the intercourse (most ideally in relaxed circumstances allowing the opportunity for deeply human interaction), but also taking enough time for foreplay, i.e., for sexual arousal through petting, kissing, caressing, etc. While both men and women are capable of sexual arousal that is more or less equally intense, many women do need more time to achieve intense sexual arousal than do their husbands. Since sexual intercourse should be a mutual experience, it is important that it not be rushed into before the woman is fully prepared for it. Even if both spouses do become aroused quite quickly, adequate foreplay is still to be desired so as to heighten the couple's sense of union and love for each other.

Another point in the area of preparation for sexual intercourse is the need for both members of the couple to practice good hygiene. Failures against hygiene (e.g., the presence of fecal matter) can be harmful to the couple's sexual sharing. Standard sexual education textbooks can be consulted for information on the best methods of sexual hygiene.[40]

Some comments can be made about the married couple's intercourse in and of itself. First, complete nudity is perfectly normal and acceptable for married couples having intercourse. Nudity for the couple is meaningful not only for the physical pleasure it brings, but because it is a sign of the complete personal giving to each other that is part of married love. Some persons still have fears of nudity even in marriage, but hopefully these fears can be set aside as nudity is seen as a sign of marital self-giving. Second, contrary to what was taught in some quarters in the past,[41] there is no one morally preferred position for sexual intercourse. Thus, since intercourse should involve play and spontaneity, it is entirely appropriate that a couple engage in a variety of intercourse positions on different occasions. At the same time, positions and other forms of physical sexual technique should not be overstressed as the one great answer to a better sex life. Some literature on the market today does overstress positions and related matters, leading to what Paul Ramsey calls the "calisthenic sexuality" approach to intercourse.[42] Our first chapter noted that one aspect of this sexual calisthenics approach can be a major preoccupation with each member of the couple's achieving orgasm at the exact same instant. Granted the value of mutual orgasm, the couple's rooting of orgasm in their human commitment to one another is a good deal more important than questions of physical technique and exact timing.

The frequency of sexual intercourse is an issue that must ultimately be determined by the married couple themselves. The general principle would be that since intercourse is an important part of the couple's life, it should happen reasonably frequently.[43] The rate of this frequency will vary with factors such as a couple's health, working circumstances, etc. These factors should not, however, be used as an excuse for reducing the frequency of intercourse too sharply. A matter related to the frequency of intercourse is that either spouse ought to be free to initiate sexual intercourse. In the past there was a tendency to say that only the husband should initiate intercourse, with the implication being that it was not ladylike to ask for intercourse. The traditional description of intercourse as a debt one rendered when asked was part of the context in which it was thought that married women should not initiate intercourse.[44] This notion of intercourse as a debt helped to make it sound something like a business deal instead of a deeply human experience. But intercourse is deeply human and all its aspects, including its initiation, ought to be shared in by both spouses. There may, of course, be times when either partner might have good reason to turn aside the other partner's request for intercourse. But in a good marriage such refusals ought not to be habitual.

The moments after the act of intercourse are a significant time for the married couple. These moments should be spent in physical and, more importantly, human closeness. Hence these moments are not a good time for one of the spouses (more likely the husband) simply to fall asleep. Nor are they a time for one of the spouses to rush immediately on to other business (such as the wife putting the cat out or getting up to leave a note for the milkman). At times falling asleep or other business must inevitably follow intercourse in our complicated world, but if such things happen consistently after intercourse, the impression is given that intercourse is basically a physical reality with not much human meaning on other levels.

Probably the single most vital aspect of the sexual communion of the married couple is that they need to engage regularly in good human communication about the sexual aspects of their life together. Everything we have said in this section has been aimed at helping couples to see their intercourse as a beautiful and human experience. Regular communication is a key to making married sexuality human. Often couples are threatened by their sexuality (due to values projected on them by our culture). This sense of sexuality as a threat makes them afraid to speak with each other about sex, afraid to share their deeper human sexual needs with each other. The wife may be afraid that her outlook on one or another aspect of sexuality will upset the husband and vice versa. The result is that too many couples fail to communicate in this area even though they talk about almost everything else under the sun.

Some pastors and marriage counselors advise couples

preparing to marry to set up a regularly scheduled time (e.g., once a week) to talk about their sexual lives during the early years of marriage. This may be a bit artificial, but the need for communication is real. It is not that unusual to find persons who are dissatisfied with one or another aspect of their sexual communion (e.g., the type of foreplay they use, the time of day at which to have intercourse) and who have not mentioned this dissatisfaction to their spouses even though they have experienced the dissatisfaction over a period of many years. Obviously matters such as the type of foreplay and the time of day for intercourse need to be settled through a mutual trusting and respecting that can happen only through honest communication. If there is a great need to make marital sexuality and intercourse a fully human experience of communion, there is *ipso facto* a need for good marital communication about sexuality. Perhaps as much as ninety percent of the difficulty married couples have about their sexual lives is at least partly a communication difficulty.

Some Special Questions

Three special issues can be mentioned relating to the sexual life of the married couple. The first of these issues has to do with oral sexual intercourse and, to a significantly lesser extent because of its lesser frequency, with anal intercourse. The traditional teaching of the Church has been that oral and anal sexual arousal might both be used as a prelude to normal sexual intercourse but that orgasm with the penis in the wife's mouth (fellatio), with the husband's tongue in the vagina (cunnilingual sex), or through anal intercourse is never morally acceptable.[45] The traditional teaching would, of course, have acknowledged that there might be cases in which the couple's subjective culpability in oral or anal intercourse might be lessened or taken away. A more contemporary moral theology might suggest that while oral and anal intercourse always involve ontic evil in their lack of openness to all the potentials of sexual intercourse, there might be cases in which the circumstances related to oral or anal intercourse are such that the ontic evil is not a moral evil. If both members of the couple are open to oral or anal intercourse and if this intercourse moves the couple toward greater love and greater openness to procreation, there might be a substantial argument that moral evil is not present.

A couple who must endure lengthy periods of separation (due to the husband's profession, etc.) might find that the use of oral intercourse at the times of their reunions serves to avoid aggressive and somewhat impersonal experiences of sexual intercourse with the result that while they are together the couple experience a greater love for one another, have more frequent sexual intercourse, and are ultimately more open to procreation. On the other hand, such a couple might find that without the use of oral intercourse, their sexual intercourse is very rushed and unsatisfactory with the result that it happens less often and that they become less personally close to one another. Other examples might also be suggested, but the point is that modern life does place people in rather complicated situations. Thus perhaps we should be more willing to consider the questions people raise on matters such as oral and anal intercourse.[46]

On the subject of oral and anal intercourse it might be helpful if more of the reflecting were done by married couples, since the aesthetic sense of celibates might be a bit idealistic on issues of this sort. Couples who do feel that they have genuinely good reasons for oral or anal intercourse do not experience this behavior as perverse whereas celibates might be quite ready to do so. Another consideration on oral and anal intercourse is that, regardless of where one stands on the morality of these behaviors, they should not be against the law for consenting adults as they presently are in so many places in the United States.[47]

Our second special issue concerning the married couple's sexual communion has to do with their early experiences of sexual intercourse. It is important to help couples preparing for marriage to set aside fears that might be associated with early experiences of intercourse. Normally the woman's hymen can be penetrated without any great difficulty. Bloody tales on this subject are out of order. There can, of course, be some cases in which the hymen will be difficult to penetrate, so that every woman planning on marriage ought to have a gynecological examination in which the doctor could offer any necessary medical attention.

From the man's viewpoint, the fear of early intercourse experiences may be related to the question of premature ejaculation. In his excitement will he be able to retain his semen long enough to have intercourse? It may well be that in some of his early intercourse experiences the seed is spilled before intercourse takes place. We have already noted that it is important for the man to learn to pace himself during intercourse so that both partners may fully participate in the experience. For some men this having to pace themselves will take a bit of time and they will not always be successful at first. Such men should be told that there is no moral problem with their premature ejaculation since it is not something they are intending but simply a part of the sexual adjustment process. There are cases in which premature ejaculation continues well into the marriage and becomes a more complex issue. Even in these cases premature ejaculation should not be looked upon as a moral problem. Fortunately, some rather effective therapeutic techniques have been developed to deal with more persistent cases of premature ejaculation. [48]

Another observation about the couple's early experiences of sexual intercourse has to do with what we might well call "the American Way of Getting Married," paralleling Jessica Mitford's *The American Way of Death*. [49] The American Way of Getting Married often includes a whole round of social events before the wedding (showers, bachelor parties, etc.), an elaborate ceremony and reception, and a lengthy drive to the place where the wedding night will be spent. These customs may bring the couple to their wedding night in a state of physical exhaustion, hardly the best context for sexual intercourse. The ideal way to face this situation might be by changing some elements in the American Way of Getting Married, perhaps making the big reception and celebration something that happens a few weeks after the wedding. We might also remind young couples that if they are exhausted there is no reason why they have to have intercourse the first evening, especially if their honeymoon is to be of an adequate duration. There is, of course, real doubt whether very many couples would want to wait beyond the first night.

A final note on early experiences of intercourse in marriage is that in our times many persons will have had intercourse before marriage either with their prospective spouses or with other persons. Pastors and other counselors helping people prepare for marriage ought to keep this in mind and not naïvely act as if no couple to whom they give instructions have ever had intercourse before. Especially when it is clear that a couple planning marriage has had intercourse, the counselor should work with this fact, and help the couple to see the deepening and broadening their personal commitment is taking on as they express it publicly. The counselor who does not treat past premarital intercourse in this way may fail in his efforts to reach certain couples who are preparing for marriage.

The third special issue related to the sexual communion of married couples has to do with the sex lives of aging couples. It is a well-known fact that for many persons, sexual interest and activity continues until very late in life. This fact is pertinent not only for older married couples, but also for those persons, even in nursing homes, who may be interested in marrying again. Unfortunately, there exists a fair amount of prejudice in our society against the sexual interests of older people. We need only think of phrases like "lecherous old man" (and other variations) to make this prejudice concrete. Some of the prejudice against sex among older people may stem from the feeling that sexual intercourse is somehow wrong when it is not open to procreation. But there is nothing wrong about any married couple's personally and humanly enjoying intercourse regardless of their age. We have already noted that the economic structures of our society sometimes hinder widows and widowers from marrying again. The policies of homes for the aged and similar facilities are also structured in some instances so as to hinder the sexual freedoms of married couples or couples desiring to marry. All such prejudicial structures should be done away with, and sexual relationships for older married couples who desire them and whose health warrants them may be looked upon as perfectly acceptable.

It does happen fairly often that older couples who are interested in sexual relations with each other will find that they cannot become aroused as quickly or by using the same means that suited them when they were younger. This is normal and is not a sexual dysfunction. Researchers into sexual functioning have discovered some methods that can help older couples achieve a sufficient degree of sexual arousal for intercourse. One technique often used in this context is the direct stimulation of the penis and the area around it. Older couples need not be at all embarrassed about their slower rate of sexual response or about learning special techniques to facilitate sexual arousal. Most older couples will not have intercourse as frequently as they once did. The techniques they learn to use during lovemaking can be a very beautiful part of their ongoing life together.[50]

Means of Controlling Birth

Clarification of the Issue

In facing the complex problem of married couples making decisions about the size of their families, it might help us to begin by seeking to clarify what the disputed moral issue is in the area of birth control. Such clarification is needed because there are several points about controlling birth that are mistakenly thought to be highly disputed moral issues even though they are not. For instance, the issue is not whether children are the primary end of marriage in such a way that all other purposes of marriage are secondary. Earlier in the twentieth century the Church did speak of children as being the primary purpose of marriage, but as we saw earlier she carefully avoided this particular formulation in *Gaudium et Spes*. Thus, while we cannot eliminate openness to procreation as a major value in marriage, the birth control discussion is not at the present time focused on the notion of the primary and secondary ends of marriage. Our previous reflections on the nature of marriage should be recalled here to amplify this point.

Nor is the point at issue in the birth control dispute the question of world population. The Church in her official teaching has recognized that population is a moral issue,[51] though she and all of us might realize that in a world with a growing percentage of older people the population issue is quite complicated and not to be resolved simply through a reduction in the birth rate. It should also be noted that when a reduction of the birth rate is desirable (as sometimes it surely is), one of the most important ways to help reduce the birth rate is by raising people's standard of living through development programs. Those who spend their time arguing either for or against artificial contraceptives while ignoring the low standard of living that prevails in so many places are missing a critically important means of helping the world at large to control its population level.[52]

The birth control dispute is not centered upon the matter of whether couples can make decisions about the size of their families. The Church does recognize that for a variety of reasons (medical, psychological, economic, etc.) couples might very legitimately make decisions to limit the size of their families.[53] It should be acknowledged at the same time that couples do not always have good reasons for choosing to limit the size of their families. Selfishness, economic greed, and other unacceptable motives for birth control can exist, especially in a society such as ours wherein a contraceptive mentality is present in many quarters. Thus couples should be careful to see that their particular reasons for practicing birth control are good ones.

Once it is recognized that none of the above points is the major issue in the birth control discussion, we are in a position to see what the real birth control issue is in the Roman Catholic context. The issue is the question of the means that might be used to practice birth control. To say that the issue is an issue of permissible or moral birth control means in no way suggests that this is a trivial or unimportant issue. All we need to do is reflect that for many in our society, abortion is an acceptable birth control means in all sorts of circumstances whereas for many others, including Roman Catholics, abortion is always or almost always morally wrong. Thus the means question vis-à-vis birth control is hardly an indifferent matter. Our considerations on means of birth control will be divided into three parts: contraceptives and temporary sterilization procedures, permanently sterilizing measures, and abortions. After these issues are discussed, we will make some comments on artificial insemination.

Contraceptives and Temporary Sterilization Procedures

Moral reflections: Some birth control devices (condoms, diaphragms, foams) are aimed at preventing the union of sperm and egg during intercourse, whereas other birth control devices such as the pill may possibly work (we are not certain) by preventing ovulation. Technically, it might be more accurate to consider those devices that prevent the union of sperm and egg as contraceptives and those devices that prevent ovulation as temporarily sterilizing devices. Most would agree that the moral questions about contraception and temporary sterilization are essentially the same and we shall proceed on this basis herein.[54] The official teaching of the Church as affirmed in *Humanae Vitae* is that the use of contraceptives or temporarily sterilizing devices constitutes an objectively grave moral evil in all circumstances.[55] It is well known that *Humanae Vitae* drew a great deal of comment, qualification, and dissent throughout the Church. In general, the responses given to *Humanae Vitae* can be divided into two categories.

The first type of response to *Humanae Vitae* can be found in the words of those individuals and groups who did not directly dissent from anything in the encyclical but who pointed to a variety of elements in the Roman Catholic tradition in the light of which it could be argued that Catholics who, for serious reasons and in good faith, disagreed with the magisterium on birth control could remain members of the Church in good standing, receiving the sacraments, etc. Among the elements developed in this type of commentary on *Humanae Vitae* have been the theology of conscience, the theology of Catholics' responsibility to the non-infallible magisterium, and the theology of sin. All of these issues were treated above in chapter three. A great deal of this not directly dissent-ing commentary on *Humanae Vitae* fell into the objectively grave/subjectively not culpable category, i.e., this commentary agreed with the encyclical's point that artificial birth control is always an objective moral evil, but it held that there could be a variety of cases in which Catholic couples practicing birth control are not guilty of mortal sin. The American Catholic bishops, both in their November 1968 statement and in their recent pastoral letter on moral values, took positions that could be interpreted as belonging to the objectively grave/ possibly not subjectively culpable approach to birth control.[56]

As we noted earlier when dealing with the objectively grave/subjectively not culpable approach in the context of matters such as masturbation and homosexual acts, this ap-proach can be used with a great deal of pastoral sensitivity. But we also noted that, in some cases involving extremely complex circumstances, the objectively grave/subjectively not culpable approach does not seem to reflect the mainstream of today's moral theology which holds that the morality or immorality of any action is determined only when we see the action in union with all of its circumstances. Since many couples considering the possibility of birth control are faced with very weighty circumstances in view of which they cannot agree fully with the Church's position, it seems necessary to go beyond the objectively grave/subjectively not culpable approach to *Humanae Vitae*. Thus it is that a variety of authors have devel-oped a second sort of response to *Humanae Vitae*,[57] a response that respectfully disagrees with the encyclical's conclusion that there are no circumstances in which artificial birth control might ever be moral. The present author agrees with this second type of response to *Humanae Vitae*.

Those who have respectfully disagreed with *Humanae Vitae* have done so using various methods and nuances. The present author's approach follows closely our handling of some previous matters. In other words, contraceptive mea-sures, both because of their non-openness to procreation in individual acts and because of problems with the various birth control methods, are always ontically evil. They always lack the fullness of human possibility that might be associated with sexual intercourse. Paul VI was stating the most ideal human possibility for intercourse when he rejected artificial birth control and he should be given credit for this. In some ways, due to our increased knowledge of the limitations of the various birth control methods, Paul's position looks somewhat better than when he first formulated it.

At the same time, however, it does not seem arguable that the ontic evil of artificial birth control becomes a moral evil in all sets of circumstances. If a couple face serious medical, psychological, or economic problems, their need for the human values involved in sexual communion would seem to give moral justification to their use of birth control devices. Such a decision by a couple will be undertaken with some regret (due to the ontically evil elements in birth control), but with a good conscience and with the conviction that, all things being considered, their action is objectively moral.

Some significance might be attached to the fact that in light of all the objections to *Humanae Vitae* the Church has not prominently reasserted her official position on birth control in the last few years, even though she could have easily done so in documents such as the *Declaration on Sexual Ethics*. The notion of probabilism (i.e., that one may follow a probable theological opinion) is a long-standing notion in moral theology. The fact that the Church has not spoken prominently on the reasons against artificial contraception and temporary sterilization since *Humanae Vitae* would seem to increase the probability of the arguments of those theologians who have disagreed with the official Church on this matter.[58]

The Different Birth Control Methods: There are limitations to every specific method of contraception and temporary sterilization. The pill is extremely effective in preventing birth (nearly 100% effective when properly used) and it does not interfere with the spontaneity of intercourse itself. But many women experience disagreeable side effects (nausea, headaches, etc.) especially in their early use of the pill, and there are a significant number of women (perhaps twenty percent) who should not take the pill at all for one or another medical reason (circulatory problems, etc.). As this implies, no woman should take the pill without competent medical advice. Moreover, while there are no clearly known major medical dangers to most women from the use of the pill, the fact is that it takes about twenty years for all the possible effects of a drug (including its cancer-causing potential) to show up. Since the pill went into widespread use around 1960, we will not have a full assessment of its medical consequences until the early 1980's. Finally there is the fact that in some of the forms in which it is currently prescribed, the pill may well be an abortifacient that does allow sperm and egg to unite but prevents implantation in the uterus.[59] This point will be commented upon further in a later section.

The I.U.D. or intrauterine device, a loop or coil inserted in the uterus, is nearly as effective as the pill in preventing birth. In the first year its failure rate is one and one-half to three percent after which it becomes even more effective. While the I.U.D. must be installed by a doctor, it does have the advantage of not needing daily remembering like the pill, a fact of particular significance in those parts of the world where the education needed for effective use of the pill is difficult to achieve. Like the pill, the I.U.D. has disagreeable side effects for some women (uterine cramps, heavier menstrual flow) and there are other women, particularly those who have recently had pelvic infections, who should not use it at all. There have been a very few cases (about 1 in 10,000) in which the I.U.D. has perforated the uterus and these cases, a handful of which have been fatal, may have been related to the professional skill of the doctors who installed the I.U.D.'s. As with the pill, we do not yet have a complete medical picture of possible dangers connected with the I.U.D. There are actually a variety of I.U.D.'s that have been used and some seem to involve more complications than others. Most are made of plastics, which have also been used in prosthetic surgery in other parts of the body. So far there is no known proof of these plastics' causing cancer.

Thousands of years ago, the Arabs put small pebbles in the uteri of their female camels before long journeys in order to prevent pregnancies, so the use of the I.U.D. has been known for many centuries. But it is still not known exactly how the I.U.D. works. The most probable theory is that it permits fertilization of the ovum but prevents implantation of the fertilized ovum. Thus it is quite likely that the I.U.D. is an abortifacient.[60]

The most widely used contraceptive devices in the narrow sense of the term (i.e., devices that prevent fertilization/conception rather than preventing ovulation or implantation) are the diaphragm, a rubber cap covering the opening of the cervix, and the condom, which is a sheath for the penis. Both of these devices are often used in conjunction with vaginal foams that kill the sperm. These devices have increased in popularity in recent years as the possible problems connected with the pill and the I.U.D. have become more widely known. Diaphragms and condoms do avoid the medical problems associated with the pill and I.U.D., but they have some difficulties of their own. While rather effective when used carefully, they are never as effective as the pill or I.U.D. At best they would be ninety-five to ninety-seven percent effective and up to ten to fifteen percent less than this when used without great care. In addition, these devices interfere with the spontaneity and physical sensations involved in intercourse. The woman must plan ahead to install her diaphragm and foam or do it in the middle of sex play. The condom cannot be put in place until erection has been achieved.[61]

All of these reflections ought to substantiate the notion that the presently available methods of artificial birth control involve ontic evil.[62] Obviously, much more research is needed into birth control methods. Where this research might lead is uncertain. If ways can be found to predict more exactly when, in the female cycle, ovulation and pregnancy are likely to occur, it may well be that the one means of birth control the Church has approved, periodic abstinence, will emerge as the most desirable birth control method. As of now periodic abstinence is not effective enough for use in the complicated cases some couples face, but for other couples it is already an adequate method for controlling the size of their families. This is especially the case with the method of periodic abstinence known as Natural Family Planning. We surely should not dismiss periodic abstinence as if it were irrelevant. It is a method worthy of further study.[63]

Permanent or Irreversible Sterilization
The central argument proposed in the last section was that there can be cases in which the good to be gained through contraceptive devices or temporarily sterilizing measures is of such proportion that the ontic evil always contained in contraception or temporary sterilization is morally justifiable. Once this argument has been made there seems to be no reason why its basic structure (which is ultimately the structure of all moral decisions) cannot be applied to permanent sterilizations as well as to temporary sterilizations and contraceptives. The only difference would be that, because of their permanency, a greater proportionality of value to be gained would be necessary to justify irreversible sterilizations such as tubal ligations or vasectomies.

Indirect Sterilizations: For the sake of moral discussion, permanently sterilizing procedures can be divided into three categories. The first of these categories involves medical pathology in the human reproductive system, pathology that would be a threat to the person's life or health even apart from further intercourse or pregnancy. Fibroid tumors in the uterus or cancer of the cervix are two common examples of reproductive pathologies that fall in this first category. Even in traditional Roman Catholic moral theology, sterilizations in these cases are considered to be morally licit. The traditional argument allowing such sterilizations has held that it is the person's good health that is directly intended in these cases, with the sterilization being an indirect result of the efforts to restore the person to health. Since the sterilization is not directly intended and since there is a proportionate reason for letting it happen (good health or even life), the Church holds that such sterilizations are moral.[64] The most common type of surgery used in these indirectly intended sterilizations is the hysterectomy or removal of the uterus. Some studies indicate that one third of American women who reach the age of sixty-five have had hysterectomies.[65]

Direct Sterilizations for Medical Reasons: The second category where permanent sterilization is discussed concerns the cases of women who have significant medical pathologies other than in their reproductive systems, pathologies that would be aggravated, possibly even fatally, by further pregnancies. Examples of the types of pathology in question would include diabetes and heart disease. These kinds of cases of sterilization have caused a great deal of interest in recent years. We realize that sexual intercourse is very important for the communion and life of the married couple. We also realize that some of the temporary methods of birth control are medically unsafe for certain women and that no temporary methods are effective enough for a woman whose very life may be threatened by a further pregnancy. Thus many have proposed permanent sterilizations (through tubal ligations or vasectomies) as the solution to those cases wherein the woman's health or life would be threatened by another pregnancy.

The traditional position of the Church[66] holds that sterilization is never morally permissible in the cases we are now considering because the sterilization is directly intended as a means to secure the good health of the woman. One philosophical issue involved here is the double effect principle and its theory on relation of the direct and indirect intentions of a human act. The traditional analysis of the double effect principle held that when an act has two effects (sterilization and good health), the bad effect (sterilization) was immoral if it physically preceded and therefore directly caused the good effect. The other philosophical issue is the use of the principle of totality. The Church has understood this principle to mean that since the reproductive system has such an important value for each person, it cannot be directly sacrificed for the total good of the person and her/his relationships; in other words, while the principle of totality can be used to justify other direct medical interventions for the good of the person (surgery to remove a cancerous limb), it cannot be applied to justify direct sterilizations.[67]

Both the double effect principle and the principle of totality have undergone a great deal of theological analysis by contemporary moral theologians.[68] The current thinking on the double effect principle is that, while the physical relationship between two outcomes of the same act remains an important moral consideration, it is not absolutely decisive of the morality of the act. The more decisive aspect of the double effect principle is the proportionality between the good and bad effects of the act, and at times this proportionality can justify a situation in which the bad aspect of the act produces the good aspect. The idea is that the good and bad elements of an act are so intertwined in the psychology of the person intending the act that we ought not always let the physical relationship of the good and the bad in the act be the norm for determining the morality of the act. Some would assert that in this use of the double effect principle we are still not directly intending the evil outcome of an act, since it is the good outcome that is prior in our minds when we look at the act as a whole. Others would say that in this use of the double effect we are directly intending the (ontic but not moral) evil because this evil is necessary to attain a proportionally more valuable good end. The present author prefers the second of these approaches (that we may directly intend the ontic evil) and will use corresponding terminology, but he recognizes that the dispute is not resolved completely.[69]

As far as the principle of totality is concerned, some theologians today would hold that the value of the reproductive system for the person and for those around him or her is a value that is understood in concert with other values, other life-giving and sustaining ways in which the person relates to society.[70] Decisions about totality must be made in this broader context. While the reproductive system is a basic value for society, it is not a value to be judged independently of all other values.

In the light of these considerations about the double effect and totality principles, the real issue in cases of sterilization to avoid aggravating serious physical pathology through pregnancy seems to be the issue of proportionate reason. Is there a sufficient reason to cause the ontic evil of sterilization in cases where the physical dangers associated with sterilization are such that complete abstinence from intercourse may be the couple's only other real option? Qualified theologians, conscious of the values inherent in the couple's physical communion, and conscious of the limited choices they face, would say yes.[71] The values to be gained through these sterilizations appear to outweigh the values lost, especially when one realizes that such couples may be quite unlikely to bear more children anyway. The present author agrees with the morality of sterilization in such circumstances.

Further Questions on this Type of Case: There are three follow-up questions to this second category of sterilization cases. First, if it is accepted that sterilizations in such cases are permissible, does it make any difference which of the two marriage partners has the sterilizing surgery? Would it be just as acceptable for the husband to have a vasectomy (which is easier and cheaper) as for the wife to have a tubal ligation? Some authors, noting that the marriage is a total unit, would seem to assert that it is as equally acceptable for a couple to choose a vasectomy as a tubal ligation in the cases just described.[72] There are, however, some reasons weighing against such a position. The pathologies we have discussed are in the wife's system. She is the partner who is not suited to bear more children. Assuming the couple live out their lives together, it will make no difference which of them is sterilized. But if the wife should die at an untimely age (and granted her medical situation, this is possible) the husband, if unsterilized, would be perfectly able to be a father in another marriage. Indeed, his opportunities for a happy second marriage may be lessened if he is sterilized. Some women may be less interested in marrying him because of his sterility. As of now, the possibilities for reversing the effects of a vasectomy are limited.[73] If vasectomies become more reversible, the considerations we have just made would no longer apply.

Second, what about the couple who know they are very likely to beget genetically defective children? In this case, the value of procreation has to be weighed not against the physical health of the mother, but against the physical health of a potential child. May this case be considered to be substantially the same as the case where the issue is the mother's health so that the same moral judgment might be made? The present author would think so. A couple facing this type of problem may want to use a temporary means of sterilization in the hope that medical science may one day discover ways of dealing with the genetic difficulty. Such a couple (especially if the odds are in their favor) may also make a good decision to hope for a healthy child. But a decision for permanent sterilization can be argued to be proportionate in this case, i.e., to be an ontic but not a moral evil. This would seem to be especially so when the likelihood of seriously defective children is very high and when temporary approaches to birth control are clearly unacceptable for a given couple. In this version of medically indicated sterilization, it seems that the normal course would be to sterilize the partner who is likely to cause the genetic defect.

The third follow-up question to this sort of sterilization concerns whether or not the reasons for it are clear enough that it could be established as a matter of public policy in Catholic hospitals. The American Catholic Bishops' 1971 Directives for Catholic hospitals declared all direct sterilizations to be immoral and this position was reinforced by the Vatican.[74] Bishops and others setting hospital policies seem somewhat divided on this matter, with at least some of them being open to the possibility of direct sterilizations for medical reasons in Catholic hospitals.[75] The present author would support this openness. An important facet of this question concerns the methodology under which such sterilizations would be allowed in Catholic hospitals. Some would argue that Catholic hospitals could permit these sterilizations by considering the hospital's role to be material (not formal) cooperation for sufficient reasons (the good faith of Catholics and others who disagree, the hospital's need for public acceptance in a pluralistic society) in morally evil acts.[76] The notion of material cooperation in moral evil is a valid theological notion. Its use here does avoid conflict with our tradition holding that direct sterilization is a moral evil. In a way the material cooperation notion puts the hospital in an "objectively grave, but we are not culpable" posture.

The difficulty with the material cooperation approach to direct sterilization for medical reasons is that once the material cooperation notion is used for these sterilizations, many would want to use this same notion as a basis for permitting other sterilizations or even abortions in Catholic hospitals. It seems clear that Catholic hospitals should stay away from the vast majority of cases of abortion.[77] Thus if another route besides material cooperation can be found to deal with cases of direct sterilization for medical reasons, such a route should be seriously considered. Above we proposed the idea that direct sterilizations for medical reasons are always an ontic evil, but an evil that is morally justifiable because of the difficult circumstances people face. Due to the clear medical facts involved in these sterilizations most people ought to be able to see why Catholic hospitals would accept them as ontic but not moral evil. The Church's position on life and sexuality would not seem to be unduly compromised by her hospitals' using the ontic evil approach to the class of sterilizations herein considered. The present author does not want to see our hospitals adopt any criteria that might lead them into the wholesale acceptance of non-medically indicated sterilizations and abortions. Hence he would urge Catholic hospital policy makers to give careful reflection to using the ontic evil approach as opposed to the material cooperation approach when dealing with a public stance on medically indicated sterilizations.[78]

Direct Sterilizations for Non-medical Reasons: The third major class of cases in which sterilization is discussed today relates to the cases in which direct sterilization is proposed as a means of birth control when there are no medical reasons for the control of birth, but rather psychological or economic reasons, etc. A great deal of caution is called for concerning this sort of sterilization. We live in a society some of whose members have become quite cavalier and indifferent in their attitude toward birth and life, a society that is sometimes all too ready to forget that every step in the practice of birth control involves ontic evil, even when this evil is morally justifiable. In this society sterilizations abound for all sorts of selfish reasons. One hears of men who have vasectomy parties to celebrate their vasectomies. In one of our cities, a local television station recently auctioned off a vasectomy to the highest bidder as part of a fund-raising project. In other words, there are a lot of poor reasons for this third class of sterilization cases. Because of these poor reasons, the witness of the Church in not permitting such sterilizations in her hospitals seems a fairly reasonable position in most situations.

At the same time, however, it does not seem that we can completely rule out the fact that in some cases the psychological, economic, and other non-medical reasons for sterilization are so weighty that the ontic evil in this type of sterilization might not become a moral evil.[79] This conclusion should not be drawn too lightly, especially with younger couples whose circumstances might change so greatly over the years. The children they have may die, their economic and psychological conditions might markedly improve, making them wish for more children. With couples who are older such considerations are not too prominent, and sterilizations for non-medical reasons are somewhat easier to justify. If a married woman is near or past forty, the permanency factor in sterilization means less, because such a woman has only a few years of fertility left anyway, with these years being somewhat more medically dangerous for childbearing.[80]

When the sterilization is done for non-medical reasons, the question of which spouse is sterilized seems less significant than in the case in which the pathology indicating the sterilization is clearly in one of the partners. Even in this case, however, if the couple is older the wife being sterilized will only be giving up a few years of fertility, whereas the husband could be giving up two or three decades. It may be, of course, that the reasons advanced for a non-medically indicated sterilization are reasons primarily in the husband, e.g., psychological indications that he will probably never again be effective as a parent. In such circumstances, the argument for the vasectomy of the husband would seem to be the weightier argument.[81]

Abortion

The Enduring Consensus: Perhaps one of the most significant facts about current Roman Catholic moral theology is that it has consistently insisted on the moral evil of abortion, in spite of the pluralism that has entered into so many other aspects of moral theology. The tradition of the right to life has been sacred in Western thought for centuries.[82] Catholic moralists do not seem at all ready to abandon this tradition in the area of abortion. They are not ready, on any widespread basis, to concede that the evil in abortion is an ontic but not a moral evil.[83] Hence the Church's stand on abortion remains a basically unified one,[84] granting that there are disputes about which strategies might best serve the Church as she seeks to articulate her moral values on abortion. Should she support a constitutional amendment or not? It is not our purpose to debate these strategic questions here, though the present author would tend to oppose the idea that a constitutional amendment is the best means for American Catholicism to speak out its convictions on abortion at this time.[85]

Traditional Double Effect Cases: On the subject of the morality of abortion, there are three exception-making distinctions that some respected Roman Catholic moralists might suggest. These distinctions would relate to only a very few of the millions of cases of abortion taking place in our times, but we will take note of them, since the full strength of the Catholic position on abortion will ultimately be better served if we make these distinctions. The first distinction is that some abortions are indirect results of other medical actions that are undertaken for very serious reasons affecting the mother's health and life. Such abortions (of a fetus in a cancerous uterus, an ectopic pregnancy, etc.) have been considered to be morally licit even in traditional Roman Catholic moral theology.[86]

When Life Begins: The second distinction related to abortion cases has to do with determining if and when fetal life is individually human, or more accurately, with whether there is any time at which fetal life is quite clearly not individual, personal, human life. The question about when exactly the human soul is infused has been debated by scholars for centuries, and in all probability we will never determine the precise moment when the soul is infused into the body. Some scholars do feel, however, that in the light of some recent biological developments we can make the assumption that fetal life does not become individual, personal, human life until at least two weeks after the sperm and the egg unite. During these first two weeks there are numerous spontaneous terminations of fetal life implying that it would not be "economic" for God to infuse individual human souls in such life. In addition, the phenomenon of twinning (one fertilized ovum dividing into two) can happen any time during the first two weeks, and it is rather difficult philosophically to conceive of one distinct individual human person being divided into two. Finally, there is the less fully verified phenomenon of recombination or chimeras, i.e., of two fertilized ova fusing into one. Again it is hard to conceive of two truly human individuals fusing into one. All these reasons support the opinion of some scholars that during the first two weeks after fertilization we are clearly not discussing individual, personal, human life.[87] It may well be that individual, personal, human life does not begin for some time after the first two weeks, but this latter unproven possibility does not seem to be sufficient to act on when we are dealing with a value as sacred as human life.[88]

Concerning the two post-fertilization weeks when we are quite certain that we do not have individual, personal, human life, what moral conclusions might we draw? Right away it must be admitted that there is a much greater continuity with individual, personal, human life in this immediate post-fertilization period than there was before fertilization took place. Thus, greater proportionate reasons would be needed to justify interference with the life cycle at this point than would be needed to justify contraception. Only in cases with especially complicated circumstances could we act in a way that might possibly interfere with the greater continuity with individual human life found in the first two weeks after fertilization.

Two cases of this sort can be proposed. The first case suggests that we give the benefit of the doubt to temporarily sterilizing devices (the pill and the I.U.D.) that may possibly function as abortifacients during the first two weeks after fertilization. Such an approach would permit the use of these devices if there are very serious reasons present and if the devices are medically safe for the woman using them. In this case we have the uncertainty as to whether the devices in question are truly abortifacients plus the certainty in the minds of many that, even if the devices are abortifacients, we are not yet dealing with individual human persons. The ambiguities surrounding this case are sufficient, in the present author's judgment, to permit the use of the devices in question.

The second moral case related to the current perspective on when individual human life begins concerns the permissible time frame within which efforts to prevent or stop pregnancy might follow a rape. Traditional Roman Catholic theology allowed efforts to remove the semen to go on for quite a number of hours after rape, even though fertilization may take place within thirty minutes of intercourse.[89] Past theologians took this position because in the light of the great evil of rape they wanted to give raped women the benefit of the doubt as long as there was any reasonable probability that fertilization had not taken place. In other words, our theology always used a "benefit of reasonable doubt model" when dealing with the victims of rape. Based on today's position that we are not dealing with individual, personal, human, fetal life during the first two weeks after intercourse, it seems reasonable to some theologians that we should further extend the benefit of the doubt to rape victims by allowing efforts to prevent or stop pregnancy during the first two weeks after the rape occurs. There are various sources of doubt in rape cases. We are not sure whether or not there is a fertilized ovum in the first place. Nor are we fully sure how we should evaluate the morality of abortifacient procedures in the time before the life is individually and personally human. With these uncertainties and with the great evil that is involved in rape, the extending of the time to deal with rape to fourteen days seems acceptable.[90]

Conflict of Life vs. Life: The third distinction to be made concerning the morality of abortion is that, in view of the current analysis of the double effect principle (i.e., that when

dealing with an act with two inextricably intertwined outcomes, proportionate reason rather than the physical relationship of the two outcomes [which is physically more direct
than the other] is the decisive moral criterion), reputable
theologians would hold that an abortion is morally permissible
(while always ontically evil) whenever there is a case in which
the mother's life will be lost if the abortion does not take place.
In our modern medical technology such cases of abortion are
extremely rare, but some of these cases are accepted as moral
abortions, even by very conservative Catholic moralists such as
Germain Grisez.[91]

Once the structure of this third distinction—that we can
act directly to take fetal life by weighing this life proportionately against the mother's life—is accepted, the question
arises as to whether other human values besides life may ever
be weighed proportionately against life so as to justify an
abortion. In the history of Christian thought in the West,
there has consistently existed the notion that at times other
values—prevention of crime, protection of property, maintaining virginity, etc.—may be considered to be on a par with
life so that life may be attacked (war) or given up to secure
these other values. Some Roman Catholic moralists have
suggested that values other than life may on rare occasions
offer a sufficient proportionality to justify abortions.[92] The
present author recognizes that such argumentation is theoret-
ically sound, based on the contemporary position of Catholic
scholarship on the nature of moral decisions. Practically
speaking, however, he would be very cautious about supporting abortions based on such argumentation. Except for the
case of the life of the fetus vs. the life of the mother, it does not
seem that anyone has sufficiently thought through the kind of
proportionality that would be needed to justify taking the life
of the fetus (which is not the same as the life of a criminal
assailant, etc.). For the present, it may be best to consider the
immunity of fetal life from direct attack to be a virtually
exceptionless norm (other than in the life vs. life case and in
the context of the first fourteen days after fertilization).

It should again be emphasized that these careful distinctions on abortion open up only a very small number of cases

vis-à-vis the total problem of abortion in our society. There seems to be little likelihood that the main thrust of the Roman Catholic position on the sacredness of human fetal life will change.

A Pastoral Note: One further aspect of the abortion dilemma deserves mention. What about the case of someone whose abortion cannot be justified in Catholic thinking, but who has been put under a great deal of pressure to have the abortion (e.g., a teenaged girl being pressured by her parents)? Our first priority in relating to cases like this ought to be to try to eliminate the conditions that bring them about. But even with our best efforts, some of these cases will continue to exist. When such a case arises, it is important to be pastorally sensitive and understanding. In such a case the person getting the abortion may not be fully responsible for her actions. She may not be breaking her fundamental option for God, and she and others like her should certainly be treated with mercy and compassion.[93] Much the same thing should be said for those who are sterilized or practice birth control in similar circumstances.

Artificial Insemination

All of the techniques of birth regulation we have so far considered are pertinent to married couples who wish to limit the size of their families. But what about the couple who wishes to have their own children and cannot? The adoption of children is, of course, a very worthwhile goal for such a couple. It may be, however, that the couple has a deep desire for children who are biologically their own. If this is so, the issue that often comes up is artificial insemination.

The official teaching of the Catholic Church has opposed all forms of artificial insemination.[94] The Church's position on this matter is noteworthy, since in opposing artificial insemination the Church has been led to stress the great value of the sexual love of the couple, a matter the Church has not always emphasized as much as might be desired. It seems that the Church's reasons for opposing artificial insemination by a donor other than the husband (A.I.D.) are fundamentally

sound. Various traumas can enter a marriage through the use
of A.I.D. The husband can easily tend to be jealous, the wife
can sense the marital union as less important to her, etc.
Reputable moral theologians both Catholic and Protestant
have stated their opposition to A.I.D., though some would
accept it in certain circumstances.[95]

The matter of artificial insemination by the husband
(A.I.H.) is a more readily debatable issue. The fact that any
procreation through such insemination would not be
achieved through sexual union is clearly a disvalue or ontic
evil. If, however, the couple sincerely desire their own child
and have no other possible means to bring about a pregnancy,
it seems that in these special conditions the principle of proportionality implies that the ontic evil involved in A.I.H. is not
a moral evil.[96] In those cases where A.I.H. is considered to be
morally licit, masturbation to secure the needed sperm from
the husband would be moral. This whole artificial insemination topic points to the need for continuing research on the
human reproductive system. Finding better ways of helping
those couples who desire children to have them may also help
us find better ways to help those who in difficult circumstances
do not desire any more children.

Finally, we should note that all of these questions about
family size are extremely complex and difficult questions.
There are no simple answers. Couples facing these questions
need to do so with a real spirit of discernment, of listening to
the Lord. Above we have seen ways in which some couples
might make decisions about the size of their families differently than Catholic couples did in the past. But without doubt
God is calling many couples to be open to the wonder of new
life, i.e., to avoid sterilization, birth control, etc. Couples
should take care not to let the tone of today's society obscure
God's call to new life. Such a call, if truly discerned, should be
responded to with the generosity and sacrifice that are at the
heart of family life.

Divorce and Remarriage

As this chapter has sought to work its way through some
of the agonizing sexual ethics dilemmas faced by married

couples, the controlling perspective has been the belief that marriage has about it a goodness that calls for both fidelity and permanency. Thus it should be clear that marital indissolubility is the goal or norm under which the Catholic approach to marriage must operate. But it is also and unfortunately clear that in our society a great many marriages break up. In some places there seem to be nearly as many divorces as there are marriages.[97] We have already noted that when the Church faces the divorce crisis her greatest single priority must be to better prepare people for marriage in the first place, doing this through a deepened theology of marriage and through more thorough instruction on marriage for all people beginning with young children. But what about those cases in which divorce and remarriage do take place among Catholics? More particularly what about those cases in which Catholics are convinced before God that they should enter into second marriages or remain as partners in second marriages?[98] Even with our best efforts at marriage preparation, such cases will occur in our finite and sinful world.

Changes in Church Practice on Marital Annulments

One encouraging development related to such cases has been the increasing recognition in recent years by the official Church that many persons, through lack of maturity, etc., do not give a true enough consent to their first marriages. If such a lack of consent (e.g., in the case of a pressured teenage marriage) can be proven, first marriages can be declared null and void with the result that, in the Church's eyes, the partners are free to enter second marriages, since their first marriages were not really marriages. In addition to her deeper understanding of marital consent, the Church has also allowed American dioceses to simplify some of the procedures involved in attaining marital annulments, so that annulments are often more easily obtained now than they were in former times. This is especially the case in dioceses with larger tribunals, some of which can now process very substantial numbers of annulments in the course of a year. Some further deepening of the canonical criteria for annulments seems still to be desired, but the fact remains that a lot of progress has been made in this area.[99] If a person in or wishing to enter a second marriage can obtain a tribunal annulment of his or her first marriage, this is surely the most desirable course to be followed at this time.[100]

Granted the recent developments in the Church's policies and procedures on marital annulments, the question might still be asked whether the marital annulment process, with its attempt to safeguard marital indissolubility by establishing that some marriages never existed, is necessarily the best process for the Church to follow in dealing with the dilemma of divorce and remarriage. For one thing, the annulment process requires a fair number of capable tribunal personnel, a fact that can be especially burdensome for smaller dioceses. Additionally and perhaps more seriously, the annulment process can appear to be legalistic. Probably a lot of very happy and healthy marriages could be considered as null, as non-marriages, if the criteria for true marital consent were applied to the beginnings of these now-successful marriages.[101] But, of course, the criteria are only applied when the marriages have not worked out, meaning that in reality it is the current breakup of the marriage rather than the circumstances of its origin that inspires annulment procedures. These and other factors[102] suggests that the distinction between annulments (which the Church accepts) and divorces/remarriages (which she does not accept) is a distinction that may not be that helpful when it is applied in a wholesale fashion.

Developing Theories on Indissolubility and Second Marriages

In the light of these questions about the annulment approach to broken marriages, some biblical scholars, historians, and moral theologians have suggested another approach to broken marriages. As part of its background, this second approach to broken marriages holds that Jesus' words "What God has joined together let no man put asunder" (Matt. 19,6) and related biblical passages are to be understood as the basic norm for God's people, but that these words are not to be taken as a strict legal formula for every particular case in which a marriage breaks down.[103] This concept of Jesus' words as a norm, rather than a legal solution to particular cases, seems biblically sound since so many other statements of Jesus have always been understood by us in the sense of basic norms that do not solve all concrete cases. For example, while we respect the basic normative value of Jesus' words, "Those who live by the sword will die by the sword" (Matt. 26,52), we do not understand these words as ruling out all efforts at self-defense or all armament by political governments.

Another background facet of the second approach to the problem of divorce and remarriage has come from an historical examination of the practice of the Catholic Church and other churches across the centuries. This historical research has indicated that Christian history is not as clear and unambiguous a rejection of second marriages as we sometimes think. One leading modern Catholic historian, John Noonan, has argued that throughout her history the Church has become more and more conscious of her power to dissolve some marriages, with this power gradually being extended to different types of marriage cases.[104] As of now, the only marriage that the Church does not ever dissolve in favor of second marriages is the *ratum et consummatum* marriage (i.e., a sacramental marriage [two baptized Christians] legally witnessed to in which at least one act of sexual intercourse has taken place). The implicaton of Noonan's work and the work of others seems to be that with further historical development, even the *ratum et consummatum* matrimonial bond might be dissolved in some cases so as to permit second marriages.

Following on this exegesis of the pertinent scriptural passages and this reflection on the history of Church practice on marriage, various theologians would propose that whenever a marriage has irrevocably broken down,[105] a partner in that marriage who deeply and sincerely wishes to share in the life of the Church, and who at the same time does not feel that he or she is genuinely free to abstain from a second marriage, ought to be free to enter or remain in a second marriage and at the same time be a member of the Church in good standing, i.e., free to receive the sacraments. This solution would apply regardless of whether grounds for annuling the first marriage could be established, and regardless of whether the person entering or already in the second marriage is morally responsible for the failure of the first marriage.[106] If the person entering or in the second marriage were guilty in the breakup of the first marriage, it would be expected that he or she has sincerely repented of the wrong already done. Decisions to take full part in the life of the Church in such circumstances would be made by the persons involved in conjunction with their pastor. This would have the effect of bringing pastors more fully into these complex marital cases, whereas now such cases are too much the responsibility of tribunal officials who are somewhat removed from them.

Obviously this approach does not fully reflect the Church's ideal norm which is marital indissolubility. But the fact is that we all live in a very finite and imperfect world where complete fulfillment of our ideals is not always possible. It does not seem impossible that the Church could both proclaim her ideals on marriage and be merciful in difficult particular cases such as the case of the soldier who comes home from a long and heroic effort in a trying war (Vietnam) to find that his wife has left him for another man.[107] The approach of the Church in reluctantly but compassionately giving a qualified acceptance to some second marriages after what appeared to be valid first marriages would not be applied to any and every second marriage. As we noted, there would have to be no possibility of reviving the first marriage, and sincere good faith in God on the part of the person seeking the second marriage, i.e., second marriages only for show or for the status of being married in the Church would not be accepted.

The type of second marriage we are talking about can be looked at both from the point of view of the persons involved in it and from the point of view of the Church. Either way, such a marriage must always be understood as containing a significant level of ontic evil.[108] It never actualizes the fullness of the Christian meaning of marriage. However, the persons involved in the second marriage may be certain that in their complicated life circumstances truly proportionate reasons[109] exist so that the ontic evil is not a moral evil. In this light such persons may judge that in God's eyes they are free to enter or remain in their second marriage and morally fit to receive the sacraments. From the Church's perspective, the main question about second marriages (once we agree that the norms of revelation and tradition do not solve each and every concrete second marriage case) is whether the harm done to our ideal of indissolubility by the Church's allowing some second marriages outweighs the harm done to Christian individuals in second marriages with good faith when the Church bars such marriages. In past cultures, it does seem that the harm done by allowing any second marriages would have outweighed the harm done to some persons by not allowing such marriages. Thus in former times the Church seems to have been correct in her prohibition of second marriages.

Today, with our changed culture, it can be said that the weights of the relative harms involved in this whole matter have shifted so that the harm done by forbidding second marriages is proportionally greater than the harm done in permitting them. People in the developed countries live nearly three decades longer than they did at the beginning of the twentieth century. This implies that while in the past divorced persons usually had only a relatively short period of life left, today's divorced persons, as a whole, face many more years of life than in previous centuries. This fact makes divorce without remarriage much more burdensome than it used to be. Our longer life span also probably helps explain why the divorce rate has increased so much in the first place. In former times, death would have ended many marriages before they reached the point of divorce.

Another result of the industrial revolution is that people no longer live in large extended families as was so often the case in the past when families typically included grandparents, aunts, uncles, brothers, sisters, cousins, nieces, nephews, etc. Today the typical family is husband, wife, and children. And these frequently live thousands of miles from any of the other relatives just mentioned. Formerly, when people lived in extended families, a person who was divorced tended to have a variety of close relatives at hand who could offer love, support, and understanding after the divorce. In our era the divorced person may well be completely devoid of other human sources of support after the divorce. This obviously increases the pain of divorce without remarriage. Considering these changed conditions of our society,[110] it can be said that, provided that the Church finds other ways to give clear witness to marital indissolubility (deeper theology of and preparation for marriage, etc.), the good to be done by permitting second marriages under certain conditions outweighs the harm such marriages might do.

Current Pastoral Practices

The present author favors the nuanced allowance of some second marriages over the annulment process and thinks that such an approach will ultimately prove to be the best method for the Church to use in relating to broken marriages. But whichever of these methods one favors, there is a problem today insofar as the status of married people vis-à-vis the Church is a matter of public record so that neither marital annulments nor the acceptance of qualified persons in second marriages can be fully accomplished without the official approval of the Church. While the Church is more open to annulments than in the past, some annulments are still not able to be accomplished officially. The marriage may be null but the evidence to prove this is lacking. The local marital tribunal may not have adequate personnel. The good reasons for the annulment may not be sufficiently recognized in Church law. On the matter of simply accepting some second marriages, the official Church is not yet doing this at all. Thus there is a problem about what should be done pastorally in the here and now for those who, either under the annulment approach or under the permission of second marriage approach, sincerely feel that they have a call from God to both their present marriage and to sacramental communion with the Church.

A number of persons have proposed that we deal with such cases by a solution that is usually called the good faith solution or the internal forum solution.[111] Essentially this solution holds that a person or persons who are in their present marriage in sincere good faith may be allowed to receive the sacraments as a matter of conscience even though their status is not officially recognized by the Church. It is sometimes said that such persons may receive communion only where they are unknown and thus will not give scandal.[112] But it might also be argued that nowadays scandal in this area of life is not usually a serious problem, since our population is so mobile and since many persons now have officially granted annulments, meaning that for the public there could easily be the thought that persons receiving communion in second marriages have been granted annulments. There is some debate as to whether this good faith solution ought to be used only by those couples who are convinced that their previous marriages were not valid marriages or also by those couples who feel that God is calling them to a second marriage even if their previous marriages were at one time valid marriages.[113] The present author would favor applying the good faith solution for both types of couples when there is truly a proportionate reason. However, the debate about how far the good faith solution should be extended is unsettled.

In the context of the good faith solution, the proposal has surfaced in some quarters that pastors should not only allow couples in second marriages to receive the sacraments of penance, Eucharist and anointing, but that they should also perform marriage ceremonies for such couples, explaining, of course, that these ceremonies are not officially recognized by the Church. Generally speaking, this author opposes these somewhat private marriage ceremonies. As with secret marriages of previously unmarried couples, these ceremonies may involve legal complications, though such complications can be avoided by having the couple go through a civil marriage. Such non-official marriage ceremonies might also be a source of confusion to various people, including the couple themselves. There may, however, be some special cases in which such non-official ceremonies would be advisable, if the couple has a clear understanding of what is involved, etc.[114] If the Church should in future years come to permit certain second marriages on a public basis, then it seems that there ought to be a ceremony for these marriages, even though this ceremony should differ in some aspects from the ceremony used for a first marriage.

A few years ago, the official Church insisted rather clearly that her official laws should be applied in the cases of persons in second marriages.[115] At the time the Church did this, some dioceses in the United States were establishing the good faith solution as a matter of public policy. Thus it seems reasonable to conclude that the Church's opposition to good faith solutions was primarily directed against the public or official establishment of these solutions. Priests, other pastoral ministers, and couples would still seem free to employ good faith solutions on a private basis. The notion of the internal forum, i.e., that in life with all its ambiguities pastors and people have a right to privacy on difficult matters, is a very sacred and long-standing notion in Catholicism.[116] While the official Church can surely take stands on public policies, the internal forum of conscience before God will always remain a factor in moral matters. A special committee of the Canon Law Society of America has held that no Church action should be taken against priests who privately use internal forum solutions to marital dilemmas.[117] All things being considered, this seems to be a very sound position.

By way of summary, this chapter has sought to do two main things. First, it has sought to uphold the basic strength and correctness of the Catholic approach to marriage. Elements of the basic strength of the Catholic position include the conviction that marriage is a personal and social union that calls for permanency, that genital sexual activity is a great good that fundamentally belongs in marriage rather than elsewhere, that children are an inherently important aspect of marriage, and that marriage for Christians is a form of faith witness, i.e., a sacrament. Second, this chapter has tried to face realistically some of the painful moral dilemmas relating to sexuality in marriage: premarital and extramarital intercourse, the communion of the couple, birth control, and divorce and remarriage. In the final analysis, the key question about the chapter is how well its two focuses have been brought together.

VII
Sexuality and Celibacy

One of the most interesting facets of human sexuality to come to the fore in recent years has been the concern over the psychosexual growth and development of celibates. As we have become more conscious of the fact that human sexuality touches people on every level of their existence, it has become clear that sexuality pertains not only to married persons who engage in genital sexual acts, but to all humans, regardless of their state in life. It is in this context that a fair amount of literature has begun to emerge on sexuality and celibacy.[1]

Strictly speaking, there is a difference between the law of celibacy that obliges diocesan priests and the vow of chastity taken by religious.[2] Practically, however, both groups need to make the same sort of sexual adjustment. Thus we shall use the one set of terms celibacy and celibates to refer both to persons obligated by the law of celibacy and those with religious vows. It should also be noted that the kinds of sexual adjustments we shall discuss in this chapter are pertinent to Christians who have chosen to remain single as well as to priests and religious. The motivations of people who choose the single life may not be the same as those of priests and religious (though often the motivations may be closer than we realize), but the life-style questions as regards sexuality can be quite similar for the celibate and the single person who has chosen to remain so, i.e., the single person who is not looking for marriage. Single people are sometimes the most forgotten people in the Church, so it is important that we not lose sight of them.

From the beginning, it must be said that the focus of this chapter is not the question of optional celibacy. Granted that there is not an absolute connection between priesthood and celibacy, the author does feel that convincing arguments for optional celibacy can be proposed and he would support such arguments. At the same time, none of these arguments ought to be accepted in practice without an effort by the Church to find other ways to promote celibacy if it is no longer legally required. We have already mentioned the importance of non-married people in society, and the fact is that Roman Catholicism is the only large institution in the modern world that gives structured support to unmarried life-styles. In the future we may legitimately move toward optional celibacy but in so doing we should not lose sight of the value of celibacy.[3]

What this chapter does intend to focus on is the place of sexuality in the lives of celibates and the meaning celibacy has as a loving life-style. Our considerations will be divided into three sections: general reflections on sexuality and celibacy, the celibate and some specific areas of sexual conduct, and the interrelationship between celibacy and marriage.

General Reflections on Celibacy and Sexuality
The first point to be made is that for celibates as for everyone else, human sexuality is a great and good gift of God. Celibates are called to serve God and their fellow people as sexed persons, not as people whose sexuality has somehow been neutralized or taken away. The love celibates bring the world is profoundly qualified by sexuality. Celibates love others as men and women. Celibates may thus be proud of their sexuality and of all that goes with it. They need not feel that they have to make major efforts to hide their masculinity or femininity. Rather they should gratefully realize that their sexual gifts—masculine and feminine—are an intrinsic element in their being, a basic modality of the way in which they live and love as celibate persons. Everything we said in the first chapter about sexuality as a basic human good touching all levels of human existence applies to celibates as well as to everyone else.

To get a bit more specific, what exactly is the loving life-style of celibates as sexed persons? If human sexuality opens up to all people the possibility for loving and responsible relationships to God, self, and others, how are celibates called on to love as sexed persons? It is crucial for us to get a good answer to this question. In recent times far too many priests and religious have opted for the "necessary evil" approach to celibacy, i.e., these priests and religious have accepted celibacy only because it is a required part of the package for priesthood or religious life. They have seen no real value to the celibate loving style in and of itself. Seminaries and religious formation programs have sometimes contributed to this "necessary evil" approach to celibacy by doing too little to help future priests and religious achieve any positive and spiritual understanding of celibacy. The present author happens to believe that celibacy does have a spiritual and human meaning as a loving life-style. He also believes that for the sake of the whole Church and for the sake of a more adequate theology of human sexuality the loving life-style inherent in celibacy needs to be better articulated.

The opening point of this articulation of the celibate life-style is that it is entirely coherent for Christians (and for all persons for that matter) to choose approaches to life and sexuality other than the approach of marriage. In this book we have laid great emphasis on the value of marriage, but this does not mean that all the possibilities of human life and human sexuality are exhausted by marriage. An ultimate biblical theme used in this work is the theme of covenant, i.e., that we humans are called into a loving union with God, others, and self. The simple anthropological fact is that all of us have available so many ways of living out God's loving covenant that none of us, even in a lifetime, can ever actualize all the loving possibilities God opens up to us. Thus each of us must make some choice in life about how we are going to love and how we are not going to love. Our status as finite creatures who live in limited spaces and for limited times forces us to make choices about our lives with every choice being a renunciation of other very good choices. Sometimes the things we give up when we make a choice that is good for us are so obvious that we are more keenly aware of the good we are giving up than of the good we are choosing. This point about our having to choose some goods and give up others is the foundation for the whole theology of asceticism or renunciation.[4] It is also the foundation for the idea that there are various vocations or states in life. Married people, as well as unmarried people, have to give up certain possibilities in life. The positive choice to marry someone is a giving up both of the single life and of other potential marriage partners.

Even if we abstract ourselves totally from the question of religion and religious dedication, we can see that in human living some people are going to choose with full logic and coherency not to marry. Sometimes this choice will be made so that the person can pursue an altruistic career for the whole of humanity (in medicine, politics, entertainment, science, etc.). Sometimes the choice will be made because of needs in one's family. There can be other reasons as well. Valuable as marriage is, it cannot be said to be an absolutely necessary value for the growth and development of each individual human person. One of the great cornerstones of our society is the notion of radical monotheism, a tenet holding that, in human affairs, there is only one absolute—namely, God—and that everything else in life is relative to our one absolute God.[5] Were we to say that marriage is absolute and that all other life states are inherently dehumanizing, we would be absolutizing something other than God.

Granting that a choice not to marry can be meaningful and still be an expression of human sexuality, we can go on to describe celibate loving and living as follows. In every human life there function two major kinds of love, two loves that all people need to experience. One of these loves is the love of mutuality, the love that is given in anticipation of a return from the beloved. This is a very wonderful love. Married love obviously involves mutuality but so does celibate love since celibates very much need human caring and support. The other major human love is freeing love, love that loves the beloved without expecting a return. Married love needs to be freeing love. The spouses in a marriage cannot be completely dependent on one another, and they surely have to love their children with a freeing or letting go kind of love or the children will never develop as they should. Celibate love also needs to be freeing love. The various ministries celibates take on must embody this freeing love, and freeing love is an important element in celibate friendships as in all friend-ships.[6]

The focal point of the difference between married love and celibate love (both of which are sexual and relational) begins to emerge when we compare how the two basic loves (mutual and freeing) are related to one another in marriage and celibacy. In marriage, while both loves are emphasized, the love of mutuality is more highly stressed than it is in celibacy. In celibacy, on the other hand, freeing love is more emphasized than in marriage. It is this greater emphasis on freeing love that makes the celibate life-style distinctive.

Care is called for in explaining why it is that celibates choose a life-style that gives greater emphasis to freeing love than does marriage. The decision for celibacy contains within itself highly personal elements and a high degree of religious mystery so that this decision, like the marital decision, can never be fully explained.[7] The decision for celibacy also contains clear elements of suffering and renunciation, a fact that is also true of the marriage decision.[8] Thus any effort to give a rationale to celibacy is by definition a provisional effort. With a sense of this provisionality the present author would suggest that celibates choose their more freeing approach to love as a means of giving witness to their faith in the resurrection. Celibates, by forgoing the type of mutuality found in marriage, are saying to us all that no human efforts or human projects can ever achieve the full destiny possible for humanity. Celibates are also saying that our full destiny is achievable, not by our own power, but through the power of Christ's resurrection. It is out of this resurrection faith that celibates voluntarily renounce marriage.[9]

The celibate life-style is thus a style of prophetic witness, a style that travels lightly and tries to set people free in this world, so that all might see more clearly the Christian faith in the coming resurrection of Christ. Once this is said, it emerges that there is a great deal of connaturality between the priesthood as a faith statement and celibacy as a faith statement. We have already noted that there is no absolute link between celibacy and priesthood, but this does not mean that the relationship between priesthood and celibacy is a purely indifferent relationship. The freeing love aspect of celibacy is a very great value for priestly ministers, a fact some of our Protestant brethren in the ministry have acknowledged.[10]

Some clarifications are needed concerning our notion of celibacy as a freedom stressing love taken on in mystery as a witness to the resurrection. First, it must be noted that married persons and single persons as well as celibates give prophetic witness to Christ's resurrection. This witness is given in the Church in a whole variety of ways, and celibates in no way have a corner on the market as far as eschatological or resurrection witness is concerned. Celibates (and single people) do give their resurrection witness in the specific way of renouncing marriage, and married persons obviously do not give resurrection witness in this exact way. But there are many other ways of witnessing to the resurrection.

Second, our remarks about the nature of celibate loving are not intended to make any judgment about the relative values of marriage and celibacy for the persons living in these states. The Church, as the communion of saints (such a crucial theme), needs both the emphasis on the more mutual love found in marriage and the emphasis on the freeing love found in celibacy. This means that the vocation that is best or highest for each person is the vocation to which that person is called by God. In the past, there has been too much triumphalism and division in the Church, with a lot of this division being articulated in "my vocation is better than your vocation" terminology. Such rhetoric is out of place, especially in an era in Church history when all of us (as the Church gets smaller) need one another so much.[11] Vatican II made the point that the call to holiness is universal and this norm must guide our theology of the states of life.[12] From the viewpoint of society as a whole, some theologians would still want to describe the celibate life-style as more exigent or more demanding than marriage.[13] From such a general viewpoint, this notion may well be correct. Our concern, however, is with concrete persons all of whom can achieve the same status before God in whatever vocation they are called to.

An especially noteworthy element in the way we have approached celibacy is that we have given it a basically personal anthropological description as a way of loving. We have not, in other words, used the physical aspect of celibate living as the central definition point in our approach to celibacy. Earlier in our description of marriage we held that it was necessary to begin our understanding of marriage by looking at the personal conjugal love of the marriage partners for one another. Only after we had developed this basic focus on marriage as conjugal love did we move on to talk about the physical sexual conduct of the couple and about their openness to children. In this chapter on celibacy we are using precisely the same line of reasoning. We have described what celibates are like as persons, what kind of lovers and what kind of sexual persons they are. Only after these personal identity questions have been reflected on can we talk about the celibate's conduct in various areas of life including the physical.[14] If we had begun to describe celibacy from a physical viewpoint, we would have missed the wholistic and personal level that is the key to all issues related to life states and to sexuality, and we would have been talking chiefly about what celibates do not do, instead of about the freeing loving that they do do.

Working out of this personal and broadly human notion of celibacy, we can say that for the celibate, as for all people, the central moral question is the question of responsible relationship to God, others, and self. What kind of a loving person is the celibate? How is he or she doing in living out the freeing love that is distinctive of celibacy? Is the celibate avoiding possessiveness and manipulation in the way he or she relates to other people? Or is the celibate using other people for selfish ends? To the extent that such questions can be answered favorably, the celibate is fulfilling the central moral demand of the celibate life.

When the central moral demand of celibacy is described in this way, it becomes obvious that the physical aspects of celibacy are not the single most significant element in celibate moral responsibility. We have already seen in other contexts that today's moral theology is moving away from a narrow physicalism. But what about the physical aspects of celibacy? Can we ignore them or say that they are unimportant? Surely not. Human sexuality, as we earlier stated, is best understood on the basis of a close union between body and soul in the human person in such a way that the personal moral commitments of individuals have physical implications. For celibates, the physical implication of their commitment to a certain style of freeing love is that they will abstain from genital sexual activity which includes not only sexual intercourse but also activities that are highly proximate to sexual intercourse. Sometimes today one hears the opinion suggested that as long as a celibate has the celibate mentality or attitude, he or she can engage in any physical sexual activities without violating the norm of celibate loving. It is true that celibate love has priorities that transcend the physical aspect of human life. Nonetheless, there remain certain physical sexual standards for celibates, and it would be a serious mistake to use our broader personal and communal approach to celibacy as a means of dismissing the physical aspects of celibacy.

An example can be suggested to try to interconnect and give relative priority to the various levels of moral demand involved in celibacy.[15] The example, which is not totally fictitious, involves two religious women. One of them lived in a certain convent for many years and because of her consistently selfish and unloving ways had a major negative impact on the life of the convent and on the life of the parish in which the convent was located. The second sister became sexually involved with a priest to the point of intercourse on a few occasions, though she was really trying to move away from such behavior. In a traditional or more physically oriented approach to celibacy, the behavior of the second sister would have been considered the worst possible failure against celibate love, while the behavior of the first sister would most likely have been interpreted as a series of relatively minor acts of uncharity. Part of the reason why the behavior of the first sister would have been seen as minor would have been because her acts of selfishness would have been looked at as individual isolated acts instead of as part of a larger picture. In the current or more wholistic and personal way of looking at celibate morality, the actions of both sisters would be considered as significant moral difficulties. The actions of both would contain notable degrees of ontic evil and, in all probability, of objective moral evil. But in the personalistic approach to celibacy, the ongoing selfishness of the first sister would be a greater failure against celibacy than the acts of the second sister. Both the personal/communal love aspect of celibacy and its physical aspect are important, but of these two aspects, the personal/communal aspect has the higher priority. We shall keep this in mind as we turn to specific questions of celibate sexual morality.

Specific Issues Involving Celibacy and Sexual Morality

Heterosexual Friendships

The first point concerning the celibate and friendships is that all sorts of friendships are important for celibates. Celibates need good friends of their own sex. Their lives will certainly be lacking in a vitally necessary dimension without such deep friendships with persons of their own sex. Celibates also need to be capable of friendships with young people and with aging persons of both sexes. Thus as we consider celibate friendships we should not limit our awareness to the question of celibates' having close friendships with members of the other sex who are of about the same age as they themselves are. Friendship is a tremendous gift and it touches each of us in a great variety of different relationships.

It does seem proper, however, for us to offer some special comments on same-age-bracket heterosexual friendships in which at least one of the partners in the friendship is a celibate. This is a work on human sexuality, and heterosexual celibate friendships with persons in one's own age bracket rather clearly involve human sexuality, granting, of course, that human sexuality is in some way operative in all human relationships. Moreover, heterosexual friendships involving celibates have not been very thoroughly treated in past literature on friendships, whereas other types of celibate friendships have been given more development in earlier approaches to celibacy.[16] Fears of human sexuality may explain why there has been relatively little said about heterosexual friendships for celibates. Many great saints of former eras had close heterosexual friendships and there were times in Church history when some religious of both sexes lived together in community; so the topic of heterosexual friendship for celibates does have some notable past precedents.[17]

The basic thesis herein proposed about deep heterosexual celibate friendships involving persons in the same age bracket is that such friendships are, generally speaking, very good for the persons sharing such friendships. We have stated that the challenge for the celibate is to learn to love all people in a way that is not selfish or manipulative, in a way that forgoes the reciprocity available in marriage. While the challenge to love in this way is always present to the celibate, it is especially present in the close heterosexual friendship. In such a friendship the impetus toward a marital type of reciprocity is quite strong. If the celibate can learn to love maturely—and celibately—in a close heterosexual friendship, there would seem to be a good possibility that he or she can achieve mature celibate love in other relationships as well. As this implies, heterosexual relationships involving celibates can be a school for their whole life of relationships.[18] Celibates who have close heterosexual friendships will surely experience meaningful degrees of mutuality and support in such relationships. At the same time, however, heterosexual friendships involving celibates will not move toward that degree of reciprocity that is found in the marriage relationship.

In an earlier chapter, we spoke of the need of all persons to integrate the masculine and feminine elements of their personalities. Celibate men and women need to integrate the masculine and feminine in themselves and they can be helped to do this through the experience of good heterosexual relationships. Male celibates, in their fear of the feminine, often take on patterns of social activity (sometimes involving certain types of jokes, sporting events, drinking, etc.) that might be more fully humanized were the men involved less afraid of the feminine elements of their own personalities. Perhaps the same might be said of female celibates. This is another reason why heterosexual friendship can contribute to the personal growth of celibates.

Far more than the personal growth of individual celibate men and women is involved in the matter of heterosexual relationships involving celibates. Heterosexual celibate relationships can be of benefit to the whole Church. Persons who take on the life-style of celibacy are called on, in various ways, to witness the Gospel to the entire Church. This means that celibates witness the Gospel to persons of the opposite sex as well as to persons of their own sex. Too often in the past this witnessing to members of the opposite sex was not done as well as it should have been. Many priests tended to be afraid of women, and as a result the spiritual needs of women were sometimes unmet. Religious communities of women frequently had structures that kept religious women from having much of any contact with adult men. Surely an important form of Gospel witness was lost here. Important Gospel witness was also lost because of the fears many celibates had of the masculine and feminine aspects of their own being. Hence, the personal development advantages of heterosexual celibate relationships, great though these advantages are, should by no means be seen as the ultimate issue in the discussion of heterosexual celibate relationships. The ultimate issue is that these relationships are needed for the good of the whole Church.

The foregoing paragraphs have used words like mature and sound when talking about heterosexual celibate relationships. As these words suggest, the heterosexual celibate relationships we are encouraging are not easy to achieve. The tendency toward a marital type of mutuality or exclusivity is very strong in many close heterosexual relationships and it takes a real maturity to love a member of the opposite sex deeply and at the same time keep away from exclusivity. This cautionary note is not presented to discourage celibates from close heterosexual relationships but to help them face realistically the difficulties involved in such relationships. Celibates are not made of stone and they should admit this. A strong spirit of Christian asceticism or renunciation is, therefore, a clear necessity in the life of every celibate who would have close relationships with members of the opposite sex. Asceticism in this context means a willingness to accept voluntarily the suffering involved in the fact that the celibate's best heterosexual relationships are not going to lead to marriage.

These reflections on heterosexual celibate relationships, maturity, and asceticism should not be taken as meaning that such relationships are the only way in which celibates can achieve asceticism and maturity in their approach to God and neighbor. A few times since the present author has written on heterosexual relationships for celibates, he has talked with very good celibates who have avoided deep heterosexual relationships in the past (probably because of the values inculcated in them in their religious or seminary formation) and who now have a "life has passed me by" sort of attitude. While celibate heterosexual relationships are good, they are not the only way to loving maturity as a celibate and there is no need for a "life has passed me by" sort of attitude.

Similarly, it does not seem that younger celibates of either sex ought to engage deliberately in a course of seeking out close heterosexual friendships. The whole premise of the celibate life is that celibates ought to love all those whom they meet and serve. Friendships for celibates (and indeed for all people) are not something to be grasped at. If close heterosexual friendships are to come in a celibate's life, they will come in their own good time and in appropriate and spontaneous circumstances. Like all friendships, heterosexual celibate friendships are gifts. We cannot make them happen.

A few comments might be in order on some of the activities and occurrences that might take place in celibates' close heterosexual friendships. First, while all celibate friendships would exclude dating (understood as an activity exploring possible marital compatibility), it does not seem that all time alone together is excluded for the partners in a close friendship in which at least one partner is celibate. Such time alone with a heterosexual friend would certainly not be the exclusive or even the main focus of a celibate's social life. But celibates are called to be open to all people whether alone or in groups and this fact would surely seem to permit occasional time alone for heterosexual celibate friends. This time alone could have many legitimate purposes (spiritual reflection and prayer, intellectual discussion, talk about mutual friends and loved ones, athletic activities, just plain fun, etc.). There is in our society somewhat of a prejudice against any man and woman who are not married to each other spending time

alone together, and celibates must be sensitive to this prejudice. At the same time, this prejudice should be overcome
since it is based on the unfortunate notion that the only reason
for a man and a woman's being alone together would be to
engage in sexual intercourse and related activities.

A presupposition underlying our remarks about the
legitimacy of a celibate in a heterosexual friendship being
alone with his or her heterosexual friend is that the celibate by
virtue of his or her celibacy will have a variety of heterosexual
friends rather than simply one heterosexual "other." Our
remarks also presuppose that celibates will have close personal
friends of their own sex and that they will do a lot of their
living and socializing in groups. All of these presuppositions
point out that the personal emotional context of a close het-
crosexual friendship involving at least one celibate is quite
different from the context of marriage, even when the friendship does involve some time alone.

Another comment on the context of heterosexual celibate
friendships is that it seems quite reasonable to suppose that
many of these friendships will not be purely Platonic, i.e., to
suppose that many of these friendships will include some
degree of feeling, emotion, and sexual desire. We indicated in
an earlier chapter that sexual desires are very common in
human experience and that these desires are often not a
phenomenon calling for major moral concern. This would
certainly seem to be true for most of the sexual feelings celibates may experience in their close heterosexual friendships.
Such feelings are a natural part of life. Celibates, of course,
will not act out such feelings nor should they enter into heterosexual friendships principally because of the sexual feelings involved. But when sexual feelings are occasioned in
celibates by heterosexual friendships, these feelings should
not be a threat. They may be recognized as a perfectly normal
human reaction. Often it would be well for the members of a
celibate heterosexual friendship to admit honestly to one
another that sexual feelings are occasioned by the relationship. Hiding the fact that the sexual feelings exist can make it
more difficult for celibates to deal with these feelings in a
manner appropriate to the celibate life-style.

On the subject of the expression of personal affection by

celibates, there are moderate degrees of showing affection (e.g., kisses, embraces) that can be entirely appropriate in certain contexts in celibate friendships. In our last chapter, when the topic of petting was discussed, the point was made that there are two kinds of petting: light petting that is clearly not an activity leading to intercourse, and heavy petting that is strongly oriented toward sexual intercourse and relationships in which intercourse is appropriate. Our point was that light petting, while it may cause some sexual arousal, can be a sign of affection that is acceptable and valuable in a variety of human situations and that need not be primarily oriented toward sexual intercourse and marriage. Celibates, like all other persons, need human affection and support, and kisses and embraces of a moderate sort can surely be a good part of the support which celibates (of the same and different sexes) give one another.

A certain degree of caution is called for in the use of heterosexual kisses and embraces by celibates lest these activities move the celibate toward intercourse and marriage. Related to this point, there is the question of where one draws the line between light and moderate expressions of affection and expressions that are heavier and clearly oriented toward intercourse and marriage. Because individual persons differ, there is no answer to this question that is totally satisfactory to all. There are some types of petting (cf. the following section) that would always seem to be ruled out. For this topic of the expression of affection and, indeed, on the whole matter of heterosexual friendships involving celibates, the advice of a good spiritual director would seem to be a highly valuable aid.[19]

Sexual Intercourse and Related Activities

Obvious questions come to the surface in the light of the position just taken on celibates and heterosexual friendships. What about celibates having sexual intercourse? What about their engaging in those forms of petting that are manifestly heavy (nudity, nights in bed together, protracted fondling of the genitals, etc.) and not to be classified with the light forms of petting we approved above for celibates in certain contexts?

Some voices are heard today suggesting that as long as one has the celibate mentality, sexual intercourse might be acceptable for celibates. To respond to these kinds of questions and opinions two main lines of thought must be developed.

The first line of thought belongs to what we might call the realm of pastoral sensitivity. It will happen in life that some celibates become more or less unwittingly involved in sexual intercourse and/or heavy petting. Especially in a time such as our own when many elements in Church life are in transition, incidents of somewhat unplanned sexual intercourse and heavy petting may happen in the experience of some celibates. Celibates who become involved in such intercourse or petting ought to be treated with respect and pastoral understanding. The intercourse and petting they become involved in may be due to circumstances (education, formation, family background, job situation, lack of acceptance by their religious communities or fellow priests, etc.) that are at least partly beyond their control. In view of such circumstantial factors, celibates who engage in sexual intercourse or heavy petting may not be breaking their fundamental option for God. There can, of course, be situations going in the other direction, situations in which the celibates engaging in sexual intercourse or heavy petting are guilty of a high degree of selfishness, irresponsibilty, and exploitative use of other persons. In these situations, celibates may indeed be breaking their fundamental options for God, especially if the intercourse and heavy petting go on for a long time.

The ambiguity surrounding the exact pastoral interpretation of intercourse and petting involving celibates requires that quick judgments be avoided about the future of celibates who are engaging in intercourse and heavy petting. Especially to be avoided is the quick judgment that the celibates we are considering should leave their vocations to the priesthood or religious life. Some celibates having intercourse or sharing heavy petting probably are called to leave their vocations and move toward marriage, but there are others who would do better to learn to transcend the intercourse or heavy petting and to stay in their present vocations. Time and maturity are needed to discern which alternative will be best for a given celibate, and counselors should be willing to allow enough time for a celibate in these circumstances to make a good decision.

None of the pastoral reflections just made deal with the specific question of the morality of intercourse and heavy petting on the part of celibates. Our second line of thought on this matter does take up the specific morality of celibates' having intercourse. Is there any way that such intercourse and petting might be morally justified for celibates? To put the question in another way, might there be any circumstances in which the ontic evil of intercourse and heavy non-marital petting might not be a moral evil for celibates? As far as the present author can judge, there would seem to be no circumstances that would give objective moral justification to intercourse and heavy petting on the part of committed celibates. Throughout this book we have opted for a close linkage of soul and body in the human person. This close linkage seems to imply that the spiritual state of celibacy cannot be without physical consequences. The notion that one can be spiritually a celibate (with the celibate mentality) but do whatever he or she pleases in the physical sexual order simply does not make sense. We do need to be pastorally sensitive to and caring for those celibates who may have intercourse or do heavy petting, but this does not mean that we can treat intercourse and heavy petting as a normal and fully acceptable form of behavior for celibates.

The position we have taken holds that celibacy and intercourse/heavy petting are morally irreconcilable. This position does not imply that a married priesthood is a moral or theological impossibility, nor does it imply that there could never be religious communities that include marriage.[20] These questions are surely deserving of further study along the lines mentioned at the beginning of this chapter. Our position on celibates' intercourse and petting is also not meant to exclude the possibility that a decision to leave the celibate life for marriage can be a perfectly moral decision. Our only point, therefore, is that celibacy as such can never be so spiritualized that it can be considered to be morally reconcilable with intercourse and heavy petting.

The observations we have made in this section have been directed to both celibate intercourse and celibate heavy petting. Both categories have been included because some have asserted that while intercourse could never be acceptable for celibates, all forms of sexual arousal short of intercourse (oral and anal sex, mutual masturbation, sleeping together in the nude, etc.) might be moral for celibates in some circumstances. This notion is sometimes called technical virginity (i.e., one engaging in such activities remains a virgin, technically speaking), and an appeal to certain medieval religious women (*virgines subintroductae*) who slept with monks without having intercourse is sometimes used as a precedent favoring technical virginity.[21] We have already taken the position that, while the distinction between light petting and heavy petting is not perfectly clear, there are some forms of sexual arousal (e.g., the instances cited earlier in this paragraph) that so much participate in the sexual communion belonging in marriage that they could not be given any moral justification outside of marriage except in those cases in which the couple has a commitment practically tantamount to a marital commitment. Since celibates by definition would never have such an exclusive commitment to one another, the activities categorized as technical virginity would not seem to be morally acceptable for celibates. Again, we must be pastorally sensitive to celibates who become involved in such behaviors, helping them to make the best decisions for their futures and realizing that fundamental options may not always be at stake in cases involving "technical virginity." But there seems no way to morally justify technical virginity for those who have truly chosen celibacy.

Masturbation and Celibates

Our chapter on masturbation held that in adults masturbation is always a reasonably significant ontic evil, so that it can never be looked upon simply as an indifferent matter. Our chapter on masturbation also held that there can be a variety of circumstances involving adults in which the ontic evil inherent in masturbation does not become a moral evil. In our present context, the key question would seem to be whether the argument that adult masturbation is an ontic but not necessarily a moral evil might be applied to cases of celibate masturbation. The present author holds that this question ought to be answered affirmatively. There are many cases in which celibate masturbation is not a moral evil. Two factors underlie this opinion. First, a number of the cases in which adult masturbation seems not to be a moral evil are cases involving single people who do not take the more typical marital route toward sexual integration and maturity. In this context, celibates are much like single people. Second, in spite of the challenge to human and sexual maturity intrinsic in celibate living, it is a fact that a significant percentage of celibates (a larger percent of celibate men than celibate women) have some incidence of masturbation in their lives.[22] Many times the celibates who experience masturbation are very good persons living well adjusted and Gospel-oriented lives. We have already noted that physical integrity is not the sole or even the most important criterion to be used in assessing celibate maturity. Hence it seems reasonable to hold that when the celibate is doing well as a loving celibate person, his or her masturbation, which may well be an uncontrollable habit, is quite likely not a moral evil, though it remains an ontic evil.

Our position does not mean that celibate masturbation is to be dismissed as a totally inconsequential matter.[23] Nor does our position deny that some celibate masturbation may be connected with behavior patterns that are significantly problematic and that might call for psychological or moral adjustment. We should also note that even if one does not accept the notion of morality implied in the term ontic evil and similar terms, there is still the possibility of holding that a good deal of celibate masturbation does not involve the breaking of persons' fundamental options.

Homosexuality and Celibacy
Our evaluation of heterosexual intercourse and heavy petting in the context of celibacy should make clear our basic position on celibacy and homosexual acts. Homosexual acts cannot be said to be reconcilable with celibacy any more than

heterosexual acts can. Thus any person who is engaging in homosexual acts on a regular and consistent basis is not a suitable candidate for the celibate life-style. In saying this, we are not saying any more than we would say of a heterosexual person.

Besides this basic position, there are three pastoral comments to make about celibacy and homosexuality, comments particularly pertinent to those in formation work in seminaries or religious communities. First, it should be no surprise or cause for major alarm that some candidates for the priesthood or religious life experience homosexual tendencies. Such tendencies are quite common among young people especially when they live in one-sexed environments. Very often these tendencies will be grown out of as the person matures. Many priests and religious who had some slight homosexual tendencies when they were young experience no recurrence of these tendencies in later life. The counselor should have this in mind and should seek to assist seminarians and young religious in growing beyond youthful homosexual tendencies. Assuming such growth takes place, the persons involved are surely apt candidates for the priesthood and religious life. Some of these cases of homosexual tendencies may call for psychological help, but often this is not necessary.

Second, in addition to homosexual tendencies in some seminarians and young religious, there sometimes occurs the case in which the seminarian or young religious acts out his or her homosexual tendencies on a few occasions. A central note of today's religious anthropology is that individual actions do not necessarily indicate the whole life orientation of a person. Thus a few homosexual acts may not indicate that a person is a true homosexual or that he or she will be engaging in homosexual acts on a regular basis throughout life. Quick judgments are to be avoided on what these few homosexual acts mean. If it emerges—perhaps with psychiatric help—that these acts, and for that matter the homosexual orientation that promotes them, are not likely to go on through life, the person should be helped to transcend such acts. If this transcendence is accomplished, the person can be a good candidate for the priesthood or religious life. This conclusion is important because in the past it was too readily assumed that once homosexual acts had taken place, the person could never be a good candidate for a celibate vocation.

Our first two pastoral comments have dealt with cases in which the presupposition was that homosexual tendencies, even when acted out, may well be overcome as a person matures. Our third comment concerns the case of a person who is irrevocably homosexual, but who is convinced and gives evidence that he or she can live a truly celibate life. In this context truly celibate life means that the true homosexual person can avoid all explicit sexual acts and live in the mature harmony and non-exclusive type of loving pattern that are the characteristics of the celibate life-style. Can such a person be a suitable subject for the priesthood or the religious life? In answering, it must be admitted that the case we are considering is quite rare. Celibacy, to begin with, is a rare gift among all people of whatever sexual orientation. In addition, the homosexual who wants to be celibate needs a special type of maturity to deal with the pressures of a one-sexed living situation and with the social pressures he or she will face. Hence the conclusion that a given true homosexual can live a genuinely celibate life-style is not a conclusion to be jumped to easily. However, when it is clear that a true homosexual can live a genuine life of celibacy, such a person need not be excluded from the priesthood or religious life simply because of his or her homosexuality. If such a person has the general qualifications needed for priesthood or religious life (health, intelligence, etc.), he or she should be given the opportunity to live out either of these vocations.

The pastoral comments we have made on celibacy and homosexuality have been phrased in terms of persons in formation, since this is where questions concerning homosexuality and the religious life or priesthood usually come to the fore. There are times when the same questions surface later in the life of the priest or religious. When this happens the same principles mentioned above can be applied.

To close this whole section on some of the sexual adjustment questions faced by celibates, it should be noted that our perspective in facing these questions has been the perspective of a caring pastoral realism, i.e., we have admitted that things like masturbation, intercourse, and homosexual acts sometimes happen in the lives of celibates, and then we have looked for the very best ways to help such celibates. Some lay readers of this book may find the cases discussed above a bit shocking. These readers might remember that celibates are human and sometimes in need of open, unthreatened reflection on the issues we have considered. All of us, moreover, might remember that there is another side to celibate love besides the pastoral realism referred to above. This other side is the perspective of transcendence of one's human weaknesses through prayer, spiritual direction, asceticism, and similar means of spiritual growth. To balance off the complicated areas mentioned above, it ought to be said that many priests and religious do achieve reasonable levels of spiritual growth and transcendence, so that they are not dealing with these complicated areas to any major extent. This fact can help all of us look at celibacy and its possibilities in an encouraging light, to look at it as the actuation of the other-centered love we described at the beginning of this chapter. The present author, with all his counseling experiences in the more delicate questions of celibate morality, remains deeply convinced of the religious and human value of celibacy for those who freely and maturely choose it.

Marriage and Celibacy's Need for Each Other

These reflections on the complexities and the deeper possibilities of celibate loving bring to mind an aspect of the goodness of human sexuality that we have not yet developed clearly enough. Sexuality's goodness is a frail or fragile goodness, a goodness that can readily be lost through human sinfulness, a goodness that is often in need of God's redeeming grace.[24] From the perspective of sexuality's fragile goodness it can very much be said that marriage and celibacy have a reciprocal need for each other. Marriage and celibacy each highlight different elements of the goodness of human love and human sexuality. The two states stand as counterpoints to each other, and when both marriage and celibacy are appreciated the likelihood is increased that human sexuality's frail goodness will perdure. There has not been a great deal of historical research on the interrelationship of marriage and celibacy, but there are at least some indications that societies that have held marriage in high esteem have tended to hold celibacy in high esteem and vice versa.[25]

To explain a bit further how marriage and celibacy need one another, married love, with greater stress on mutuality, always runs the risk that the marriage partners may use one another for what they can get out of each other. Such an approach tends·to reduce the marriage partners to objects or things instead of seeing them as persons. Celibacy, as more of a freeing non-return-expecting love, helps transcend this problem by insisting on the inherent values persons have, even apart from the benefits they bring to other people. Celibacy, on the other hand, runs the risk of not taking personal relationships and the mutuality they bring (even in the Trinity) seriously enough. This failure to appreciate mutuality makes some celibates quite withdrawn and unfeeling persons. Thus celibacy always needs the witness given by marriage on the value of mutuality. As all of this suggests, a world in which both marriage and celibacy are rightly appreciated and lived is the world most likely to preserve and maintain the goodness and spiritual dimensions of human sexuality. It was chiefly for this reason that this book needed a chapter on celibate love after the chapter on marriage.

VIII
Some Other Issues
in Human Sexuality

The past four chapters have taken up the basic areas of human sexual life and adjustment: autosexuality, homosexuality, heterosexuality, and celibacy. There remain a few important questions in sexual morality that did not easily fit into any of the basic areas. These questions will include major sexual offenses, sexual dysfunctions and therapies, and sex-changing surgeries. After reflecting on these questions, this chapter will conclude with an effort to reformulate a Catholic position on venereal pleasure and sexual morality.

Major Sexual Offenses

Repeatedly throughout this work we have appealed to the distinction between ontic (or premoral or nonmoral) and moral evil and we have used this distinction to argue that in areas such as masturbation, homosexual acts, and premarital sex, moral evil may not always be present even if ontic evil is always present. Our consistent use of this distinction may have caused some readers to wonder whether all matters in sexual ethics are more or less relative. It should thus be pointed out that there are a number of actions in the sphere of sexual morality wherein the ontic evil is so predominant that it becomes virtually impossible to conceive of any circumstances that could morally justify these actions. With this in mind, it can be said that the official Church's teaching on sexual morality and the opinions of theologians are really quite the same when it comes to most major offenses against sexual morality. The list of sexual actions that would always seem to include moral evil includes rape, prostitution, incest, the sexual abuse of children, and any form of sexual activity involving cruelty.

Some of these major sexual offenses require a few comments.

On the subject of rape, the evil involved is obvious and there seems to be no reason whatsoever to justify rape. It is, of course, understood that some rapists may be mentally ill, etc., rather than being fully responsible for their actions. What must also be said is that our focus in dealing with the evil of rape needs to be a large focus concentrating not only on the rapist, but also on certain attitudes in our society that tend to foster a rape mentality. We treated some of society's inadequate views of women earlier. These views, especially the notion that women are sexual objects at the disposal of men, help create the climate in which rapes happen. The widespread rape of black slave women during the slavery period in the United States and the great frequency of rape by conquering armies in wartime are examples that highlight the notion that women's bodies may be used by any male who is strong enough to do so. The fact that rape laws have been enforced much more strictly against oppressed groups of males (e.g., blacks, other racial minorities) than against men in general is another indication that society may not be as serious about the crime of rape as it should be. Thus our condemnation of rape as moral evil must reach beyond individual rapists to the broader issue of the social attitudes that can occasion rape. A very necessary part of our social reform approach concerning rape must be the reform of laws and police practices (e.g., mistrust of women who are raped, lurid attitude about the details of the rape) so that prosecutions can be accomplished more readily.[1]

Some similar remarks are in order on the subject of prostitution. While there seems to be no way to interpret prostitution as anything other than an objective moral evil, it does seem to happen reasonably often that prostitutes themselves are victims of social injustice in such a way that some of them experience themselves as having no choice other than to turn to prostitution. In ministering to prostitutes, it is therefore important to help them find other viable economic means of survival. Another element of evil relative to prostitution that must be combatted is the societal notion that it is all right for males to traffic with prostitutes. We mentioned before that the double-standard morality (man can have sex before marriage, but a woman cannot) is frequently called the oldest morality in the world. Until this double-standard morality is fully changed, the structures of society will probably always tend to force some women toward prostitution. The point of these reflections is not to completely excuse prostitutes from the moral evil of prostitution, but to point out that, as in the case of rape, there is a larger context of social evil that must be addressed when prostitution is considered.[2]

With our sophisticated modern knowledge, we rather quickly think of the genetic arguments against incest, i.e., that incest will lead to diseases and abnormalities produced by a combination of recessive genes. Actually, there is a much deeper argument against incest, an argument that goes back long before the facts of modern genetics were understood. This deeper argument holds that incest must be prohibited in all circumstances because of its disruptive influence on family life. Today when some sources question the value of family life, it is perhaps worth recalling that from time immemorial the prohibition of incest has existed as a statement of the importance of family life.[3] Almost all cultures have taboos against incest and many societies extend the degrees of kindred in which incest is forbidden farther than we do in the Western world.[4] Fortunately, incest of any type happens quite rarely. Of the parent-child incest that does take place, much more happens between fathers and their daughters than between mothers and their sons. This fact may reflect the unfortunate notion that daughters are their fathers' property. It is very important that proper pastoral compassion be shown to families who are victims of incest. It is also important that the guilty party or parties in incest be given adequate counseling, perhaps of a psychiatric nature.

The use of children to obtain sexual gratification, sometimes called pedophilia, is one of the most difficult and trying of all the problems related to sexual morality. As with incest, almost all adults who are prosecuted for pedophilia are males. The classic stereotype of the pedophile is that he is an older man, a stranger, and probably someone a bit deranged mentally. This stereotype does not fit the statistical facts that have been assembled. While pedophiles are older than many sexual offenders (those involved in incest are even older), their average age at conviction is only thirty-five. A small percentage of pedophiles are senile or mentally retarded, but the great majority are not. Most importantly, about eighty-five percent of pedophiles are not strangers, but friends, neighbors, relatives, etc., known to the family and even to the child. Hence, the old advice that little girls and boys should be wary of strangers may not be of much help in preventing their sexual abuse. Fortunately, physical harm to children occurs in only a small percentage of incidents of sexual abuse.[5]

On the subject of the sexual abuse of children, we should remember that adults tend to have higher levels of trauma vis-à-vis sexual matters than do children. Thus a great deal of the child's ability to come through a sexual-abuse incident without permanent psychological difficulties will depend on the attitude of the child's parents and other adults (pastors, teachers, etc.) who may have contact with the child. If these adults keep calm when talking with the child about the sexual incident, there is a much greater likelihood that the child will be able to survive the incident without lasting psychological harm.[6]

A disturbing note about sexual offenders in both incest and pedophilia cases is that as a group they tend to be very conservative, moralistic, and religious persons.[7] Possibly this fact implies that they have imbibed a great level of the (sometimes religiously inspired) fear of sexuality that was described at the beginning of this book. Their fears of sexuality may lead them to restrict their participation in normal, healthy forms of sexual expression with the result that they turn to obviously wrong and juvenile forms of sexuality such as incest or the abuse of children. Should this line of reasoning be correct, a necessary part of our approach to problems such as incest and the sexual abuse of children might be the effort to develop healthier attitudes toward sexuality on the part of society in general.

When we speak of the moral evil inherent in all forms of sexual expression involving cruelty, themes such as explicit sadism and masochism quite readily come to mind as, of course, they should. But there are also a whole variety of subtler forms of sexual cruelty. These subtler forms of sexual cruelty may not involve any physical violence but in their own way they can be very dehumanizing.[8] Both physical and non-physical forms of sexual cruelty can exist in marriage (cf. the alarmingly high incidence of wife beatings) and outside of it. Some sexual cruelty is related to mental disorders and can be helped through psychological counseling, but a lot of other sexual cruelty comes from persons who are apparently normal mentally.

Sexual Dysfunctions and Therapies

Previously we alluded to an excess physicalism in many contemporary approaches to human sexuality, a physicalism that Paul Ramsey characterizes as calisthenic sexuality. Human sexuality does involve all sorts of dimensions besides the physical, and these larger dimensions often enter into difficulties people experience concerning their sexual functioning. Many of the physicalist programs for improving sexual functioning are run by persons who are not professionally competent, meaning that there are clear dangers associated with some sexual dysfunction clinics and meaning also that governmental controls in this whole area may be necessary in the future.[9]

In spite of these unfortunate circumstances pertaining to sexual dysfunctions and therapies, the fact remains that human sexuality does contain highly physical elements. The physical elements of human sexuality, sometimes in combination with psychological and other elements of sexuality, can on occasion fail to function properly, meaning that the person is deprived of normal sexual experience and enjoyment. Since our position is that human sexuality is a very good thing, physical breakdowns of sexual function (frigidity, impotence, premature ejaculation, etc.) are clearly misfortunes that deserve correction if a reasonable way to correct them can be found. Thus, research into the more exact nature of healthy physical sexual functioning and the development of therapies to overcome physical sexual dysfunctions would seem to be worthwhile and to be encouraged from the moral viewpoint,[10] especially when this research and development of therapies is integrated into a broader vision of sexuality.

At the same time, it should be remembered that, in any area of scientific study, not every type of research that is technically feasible is necessarily moral, since research must be done in a fashion that respects our human dignity. In the area of sexual functioning the study of the normal physical sexual responses of a willing married couple (heartbeat, circulation, rate of breathing, etc.) would certainly seem to be moral. The depersonalization of some of this couple's acts of intercourse through the use of the measuring devices would be a loss of value proportionately outweighed by the good of the knowledge gained for humanity as a whole. On the other hand, the use of concentration camp prisoners for bizarre sexual experiments (e.g., testing whether persons nearly frozen to death could be brought back to normal body temperatures more quickly through sexual arousal) such as those done in Nazi Germany[11] would be manifestly immoral. In between these two cases of moral and immoral physical sexual research there are no doubt a variety of other cases that are much more gray than either case we have presented. Probably the most important thing to be said about such gray cases is that they call for an honest and trusting dialogue between the scientists doing sexual research and ethicians.[12] In the past, scientists or doctors researching sexuality have tended to mistrust ethicians, due partly to the narrowness of traditional moral views of sexuality. If both groups can learn to listen to each other, we may be able to achieve consistently suitable approaches to research into human sexual functioning.

Concerning therapies to correct sexual dysfunctions, it must be noted that some of these therapies are still at the experimental stages. Dysfunction therapies that are experimental must be evaluated by the standards that apply to any medical experiments. Thus persons trying such experimental therapies should be fully willing to do so. They should have the risks explained to them, with the rate of risk being at an acceptable level, considering the difficulties the person has and the possible good to be gained should the experimental therapy be successful. Standard medical ethics treatises can be consulted for further reflection on the moral guidelines to be followed in experimental procedures.[13]

Even when sexual dysfunction therapies are so well established as not to be experimental, they still need to be evaluated on the subject of whether a true moral proportionality exists to permit the use of such therapies. Some sexual dysfunction therapies would seem clearly to be moral. Psychological instruction and counseling of those with dysfunctions would seem to be moral assuming it is competently given. The use of physical stimulation exercises by the couple (following instruction) is certainly acceptable and it has accomplished much good in some cases. In this category of physical techniques to be used by the couple, we can list the often successful methods of overcoming premature ejaculation. The use of films and other sexually explicit materials (carefully and professionally chosen) would also seem to be a morally acceptable type of dysfunction therapy in some cases. No doubt other morally acceptable approaches to sexual dysfunctions could be listed. It is always regrettable (perhaps we could say ontically evil) for a couple's sexual functions to be adjusted by means of artificial techniques, but sometimes there is a proportionality favoring such artificial adjustment.

On the other side of the question, it would also seem that there are some sexual dysfunction therapies where there may not be a sufficient proportionality of ontic good to ontic evil so as to permit the use of these therapies. An example might be the use of surrogate sexual partners. Human sexuality involves such deep dimensions of personal commitment that it is difficult to see how the good to be gained through intercourse, etc., with a more experienced partner could outweigh the loss of the personal-commitment element of sexuality in the use of a surrogate. Thus, for the present, the author's moral stance would tend to go against the use of surrogate partners. Such a judgment is, however, a provisional judgment insofar as persons from a variety of disciplines should be willing to study further all types of sexual dysfunction therapies to see what exactly such therapies can accomplish, whether there are alternate means to the same ends available, etc. As this study takes place, more precise moral judgments about sexual dysfunction therapies might become possible.[14]

Sex-Changing Surgeries and Related Processes

There are two major types of cases in which sex-changing surgery is an issue. The first type of case concerns persons born with both testicular and ovarian tissue (hermaphrodites), and persons who are of one sex but in whom hormonal imbalances have produced characteristics of the opposite sex (pseudohermaphrodites). Related to this category would be the situation of persons whose sexual organs are in some way defective (e.g., men whose semen is discharged at the base of the penis instead of at the tip). In all such cases, the best moral judgment has held for some time that if medical science can find means of correcting these problems (through surgery, hormone therapy, mechanical aids, etc.), all well and good.[15] The question, of course, is whether medical science has at its disposal techniques that are really suitable (from the medical viewpoint) to correct the kind of difficulties just described. Some of the problems, such as female pseudohermaphroditism, can be quite successfully treated through hormone therapy and surgery, whereas in other cases the prognosis is not as good.[16] Fortunately, true hermaphroditism is very rare. Ongoing medical research into hermaphroditism and other physical defects in the sexual organs certainly seems to be called for.

The second major type of case involving sex-changing surgery is the case of the person with physically normal sex organs who wishes to be or sincerely believes that he or she is a member of the opposite sex. As we mentioned earlier, persons who fit into this case are usually called transsexuals. Traditional moral theology used to categorize all sex-changing surgery for transsexuals as immoral. Today, using the principle of proportionate reason, it might be argued that, if all other means of dealing with transsexualism (counseling, etc.) have been exhausted, sex-changing surgery might be used as a last resort. Not a great deal has been said in print on this subject by Catholic moralists, but the number of Catholic moralists who would at least privately accept transsexual surgery in certain circumstances seems to be growing.[17]

A moral perspective that must enter into our assessment of sex-changing surgery for transsexuals is the perspective of how successfully such surgery can be accomplished. Obviously no perfect means of sex-changing surgery (e.g., enabling reproduction) is now available, but it does not seem that a totally perfect change of sex would be necessary to justify sex-changing surgery for transsexuals. What can be said is that, as of now, the sex-changing process from male to female is much more satisfactorily accomplished than the change from female to male. Hence, as of now, it seems best to apply the last resort justification of transsexual surgery to the case of males who wish to be or believe they are females. If more effective female-to-male surgeries become available through additional medical advances, these surgeries might also be used.

The notion that seems to underlie the argument for the morality of last-resort sex-change operations for transsexuals is the notion that the human mind is an even more complex and mysterious reality than the human body. The implication is that when there is a major dissonance between the human mind and the human body, it may be easier (and perhaps more moral) to change the human body than to change the human mind. Obviously there are limits as to how far we can go in our efforts to change either the human mind or the human body, but some changes (operations, psychotherapies) are clearly agreed to be moral and ours is a position of continuing reflection on what humans may morally do to themselves with modern science.[18]

Nothing in our comments on sexual dysfunctions and sex-changing surgeries has referred to problems in sexual fertility. The same sort of prinicples apply to this subject. Research into fertility and therapies to correct the lack of fertility would in general be acceptable from the moral viewpoint. But not every technique of fertility research and therapy would necessarily be morally acceptable, so that regular dialogue between fertility scientists and ethicians ought to take place. We have already taken positions on two key issues in fertility research and therapy: masturbation for purposes of sperm testing and artificial insemination.

Many of the issues we have taken up so far in this chapter are not as pleasant to reflect upon or as common as most of the other specific topics in human sexuality we have treated. But these issues are a part of the whole picture in a contemporary approach to human sexuality. Our considerations on these issues complete our work on specific questions in sexual ethics. We shall close the present chapter with an attempt to state with precision and exactness the principles that guided us as we formed moral judgments on particular sexual issues.

Reformulating the Traditional Teaching on Venereal Pleasure

When we began to talk about specific questions in sexual morality, we had occasion to mention the traditional teaching of the Church and her theologians on the subject of venereal (i.e., physically sexually arousing) pleasure that occurs outside of marriage.[19] This teaching holds that the matter involved in venereal pleasure outside of marriage is always grave matter so that no one can in any way intend non-marital venereal pleasure, either as an end in itself or as a means to another end, without this pleasure being an objectively grave moral evil. This teaching does not assert that there can never be venereal pleasure outside of marriage without there being objective moral evil. Some venereal pleasure outside marriage occurs purely spontaneously and is not an objective moral evil in the traditional view. Other venereal pleasure outside mar-riage happens as the indirect result of actions undertaken for sufficient reasons (e.g., a doctor examining a patient). This pleasure is permitted by the human will rather than intended and it is not an objectively grave moral evil in the traditional view. The point of the traditional teaching on venereal plea-sure outside marriage is, therefore, that this pleasure is always an objectively grave moral evil when it is intended in any way. This, of course, does not mean that the tradition holds that all intended venereal pleasure outside marriage is mortally sin-ful. The direct intention that makes non-marital venereal pleasure objectively morally evil may not be of such weight as to involve the person at the fundamental option or mortal sin level.[20]

On our first mention of the traditional teaching on venereal pleasure we indicated that this teaching has been subject to occasional debate over the course of history and that in the light of many of the approaches this book would take to specific sexual issues, a reformulation of the traditional teaching on venereal pleasure would be necessary. Now that we have concluded our discussion of specific issues in sexual morality, we shall offer a reformulation of the tradition on venereal pleasure. Our reformulation, which will serve as a summary of much that has preceded, can be stated as follows.

All instances of non-marital venereal pleasure, excepting those which are basically spontaneous[21] and do not involve the human person in any notable way, contain within themselves a significant degree of ontic (or premoral or nonmoral) evil, i.e., these instances of venereal pleasure lack in a morally significant degree the due fullness of being that is open to human persons through sexual acts. In addition, many venereal pleasure causing actions within a marriage contain significant degrees of ontic evil, because these acts too are not open to the fullness of being possible in the human sexual experience. In both non-marital and marital venereal pleasure causing actions containing significant ontic evil, the exact degree of ontic evil present can vary somewhat with circumstances of age, etc.

The fact that significant ontic evil is present in all directly done non-marital venereal pleasure causing actions as well as in many marital venereal pleasure causing actions does not automatically mean that these actions are to be judged to be objectively gravely morally evil. Rather, the judgment about the objective moral status of venereal pleasure causing actions is made by looking at these actions in the totality of the concrete circumstances and reality in which they occur. If, in this total concrete reality, there exists a proportionate reason to justify ontically evil venereal pleasure, this pleasure may be permitted to occur or even directly caused without being an objectively grave moral evil. If, on the other hand, there is not a proportionate reason to justify ontically evil venereal plea-

sure, the positing or the permitting of such venereal pleasure
is an objectively grave moral evil. Even in those cases where
venereal pleasure clearly is an objectively grave moral evil,
mortal sin may or may not be present, depending on the
quality of the person's consent to and understanding of the
objectively grave moral evil. In making judgments about venereal pleasure, objective moral evil, and mortal sin, discernment of spirits is critically necessary.

Our proposal on venereal pleasure, by its use of the words
morally significant ontic evil,[22] stays with the tradition's main
insight that directly acted-for venereal pleasure in a non-
marital context is an occasion for notable human reflection
and a challenge to human growth and integration. It is never a
minor or completely indifferent matter, as some would have
us believe. Our proposal also stays with the tradition in recognizing that there is a difference between objective moral evil
and mortal sin. Our approach might well act on this difference
in practice more often than traditional theologians would
have.

Four ways can be mentioned in which our proposal
develops the approach of the tradition. First, our proposal
points out that the significant evil involved in non-marital (and
some marital) venereal pleasure can have degrees.[23] In the
past, the impression was sometimes given that this evil was
always of the same degree. Second, our proposal highlights
the fact that ontic evil is often contained in marital venereal
pleasure as well as in non-marital venereal pleasure. Hopefully, this will help transcend the notion that sex in marriage is
all right, even when it is exploitative, manipulative, etc.[24]
Third, our proposal insists on the need for discernment in
sexual decisions. While discernment has always been a theme
in our tradition, it has not been given its due in recent centuries, not only concerning sexuality but concerning many
other matters as well.

Fourth, and most significantly, our proposal develops the
traditional teaching on venereal pleasure by distinguishing
ontic from moral evil in sexual acts and by appealing to the use
of proportionate reason (carefully to be discerned) to determine when and if ontically evil venereal pleasure is also mor-

ally evil. On the basis of this approach, non-marital venereal pleasure may be directly acted for, at least in the psychological sense,[25] as well as merely permitted, when the totality of the action contains a truly proportionate reason for causing or allowing the ontic evil. Ultimately, the ontic evil may be directly done because it is not intended as a moral evil but, rather, reluctantly accepted as part of a total human action whose overall goodness allows the positing of the ontic evil in a world that is finite and sinful so that the fullness of good is never obtainable. Previously in this book, we have seen a number of examples of circumstances in which significantly ontically evil venereal pleasure may be acted for, and many other examples where it may not be acted for because the totality of the action does not offer a proportionate reason for the action.

In summary, our approach to the subject of venereal pleasure tries to maintain a real continuity with the Church's traditional moral concern about venereal pleasure while at the same time recognizing that this bona fide traditional concern needs to be developed today through the application of philosophical notions about morality that were not well understood in the past. In the next chapter, we shall consider some of the reasons why it might be advisable for the teaching Church to develop her own approach to venereal pleasure and sexual morality along the lines we have suggested in this book.

IX
The Recent Vatican Document on Sexual Ethics

On December 29, 1975, the Sacred Congregation for the Doctrine of the Faith, with the approval of Pope Paul VI, issued a document entitled *Declaration on Certain Questions Concerning Sexual Ethics*.[1] Because this document is the most prominent statement to come from the Vatican on human sexuality in recent years, and because the ideas outlined in this book might profit from some further interfacing with the teachings of the Church on sexuality, our final chapter will be a critique of the Vatican document on sexual ethics in the light of the positions we have taken in previous chapters.[2] Our critique will have four sections: a note on the means of composition and publication of the Vatican document, basic strengths found in the document, themes the document inadequately develops, and the most central area of disagreement between the document and contemporary moral theology.

A Note on the Document's Composition and Publication

In the months after the *Declaration* was promulgated, various sources released to the public the names of the theologians purportedly responsible for writing it.[3] With all due respect to the individuals involved, it must be admitted that these authors are not representative of those Catholic moral theologians whose approaches are most highly regarded by the theological community.[4] In an area as important and delicate as human sexuality, it seems very strongly that the Church's magisterium needs to dialogue with the most respected minds Catholic universities and seminaries have to offer. The magisterium also needs to dialogue on sexual matters with solid Catholic families to see what their perspectives are in our complex world. Thus, regardless of how one feels about the specific contents of the Vatican document on sexual ethics, it is regrettable that more consultation was not a part of this document's formation. On any issue facing the modern world, the magisterium needs to dialogue and this is particularly true in the field of sexual ethics.

Related to the question of how this document was composed, some comments might be made on the manner in which it was publicized by officially controlled segments of the Catholic press. Just after the *Declaration* was published, the present author had the honor of sharing a podium with the president of one of the Church's great missionary communities. In the flood of all the questions we were being asked about sexual ethics, this woman mentioned on several occasions how pleased and delighted she was with the Pope's recent Apostolic Exhortation on evangelization.[5] Though plenty of time for publicity has passed, one wonders how many Catholics have ever heard of this excellent document on evangelization. On the other hand, the editorial practices of *L'Osservatore Romano* and some other Catholic newspapers (with an assist from the secular press) made certain that large numbers of Catholics did learn about the document on sexual ethics. It is to be hoped that in the future the official Catholic press will provide a more balanced coverage of the Church's teachings on moral and social matters.

Basic Strengths Found in the Document

The recent Vatican sexual ethics document has two major areas of strength. First, it operates in a context that strongly believes in marriage and family life, a context that clearly asserts that genital sexual activity finds its truest meaning in marriage.[6] This insight about the unity of genital activity, marriage, and family life has always been the focal point of the Roman Catholic teaching on sexual ethics and it is an insight that needs assertion in our times, however contemporary theologians might wish to qualify its application to particular cases. Thus, the Vatican document deserves praise for the basic moral value that governs its approach to sexuality. The present book has consistently sought to respect this basic moral orientation of the Catholic tradition on sexuality.

The other major strength of the document is what might be called its pastoral sensitivity, its recognition of some of the very complex factors that people face in their sexual lives. Perhaps more than any previous document of its type, the *Declaration on Sexual Ethics* takes note of complex pastoral factors that somehow qualify the standing before God of persons engaging in certain types of sexual activity. One of the important pastoral factors the document notes is that some homosexuals are definitively such.[7] Another pastoral factor cited by the document is the approach of psychology into the meaning of adolescent masturbation.[8] Later on we shall remark that there are some questions as to the system with which the document applies its pastoral insights on subjects such as homosexuality and masturbation. But the fact remains that sensitive pastoral insights about sexual issues are notably more present in the recent Vatican document than in much that preceded it. This is a positive step in a good direction.

Some Themes Inadequately Developed by the Document

There are a number of themes the document touches on but develops quite inadequately. Such inadequate development was almost inevitable due to the brevity of the document, but some of the inadequacy seems also to be due to the relatively narrow base of theological consultation the document reflects. Probably the most significant theme the document develops inadequately is the meaning of human sexuality. Near the beginning, the document asserts a wholistic or comprehensive understanding of sexuality by referring to the many levels on which sexuality touches the human person.[9] Toward the end the document returns to this wholistic notion of sexuality in its call for sexual education.[10] However, in the document's remarks on sexual finality, and in its sections on premarital intercourse, homosexuality, and masturbation, rather little of the wholistic perspective on sexuality is evident.[11] Instead, the document appears in these sections to understand human sexuality quite physically. Especially for someone with a limited theological background, the document might serve to reinforce fears and negativities about sexuality. Many Catholics do have such fears of sexuality and thus need a deeper development of the wholistic notion of sexuality. Admittedly, the sexual ethics document is short and focused on certain problem areas. But the fact remains that its overall teaching on human sexuality is quite inadequate. No matter how one judges particular questions in sexual morality, this document ought to be filled out by a larger picture of human sexuality somewhat along the lines of what was proposed above in chapter one.

In its treatment of sin, the document clearly asserts that in the last resort a person's fundamental option determines his or her moral disposition before God. In the same section the document well notes that it more easily happens in sexual matters that full consent does not take place so that the level of fundamental option is not involved.[12] But here again, the document's correct statements on fundamental option are quite inadequately articulated with the result that ordinary people who read the document may end up rather uncertain as to exactly what sin and fundamental option mean.

Part of the difficulty in the document's treatment of fundamental options is that the document is anxious to correct an exaggerated notion of fundamental option, an exaggerated notion holding that sin has no reference to a person's external actions whatever, i.e., that sin purely and simply resides on the level of the person's relationship to God. It is true that some popularizers of the theory of fundamental option have completely dismissed external actions from their understanding of sin. Responsible Catholic moral theologians have not done so, however. As we noted, moral theologians do say that, in the light of the fundamental option theory, sin is far more likely to be found in a series of actions or pattern of life rather than in isolated external actions taken out of context. But this position does not write off external actions as unimportant.[13]

In the final analysis, the document spends so much time correcting this false notion of fundamental option that it leaves the impression that sin and individual external acts are simply to be equated. Especially for an ordinary Catholic, who was educated in the era in which we emphasized external acts much more than sufficient reflection and full consent, the document can reinforce an overly act-oriented notion of sin. In sum, the document insufficiently develops the notion of fundamental option; what results is in large degree only a caricature of the fundamental option theory as taught by our best theologians.[14]

At a number of points, the document supports its arguments by appealing to Scripture. Some of the citations from Scripture are well chosen. Questions can be asked, however, about the method with which the document uses scriptural passages. At times the method seems to border on proof texting, i.e., taking single scriptural passages as completely decisive for all moral cases that might relate to the passage. Today we are aware of the great difficulties involved in using any single scriptural passage as decisive for all cases. There is the question of the original context in which the passage was used, the question of how the passage's context may have been shifted by later biblical authors, and the question of how a particular scriptural passage relates to other passages on the same topic. These questions, and others like them, we earlier called the hermeneutic problem. The sexual ethics document, while it does not deny the hermeneutic problem (which has been officially recognized in prominent Catholic documents),[15] does not seem to give sufficient attention to hermeneutic issues pertinent to the biblical passages it cites. Throughout this book, we have tried to be aware of major biblical orientations on the subject of sexuality but we have not sought in the Bible for exhaustive answers to all sexual questions. The document, on the other hand, can leave uninformed Catholics with the impression that Scripture offers complete concrete answers to sexual dilemmas. Here again, if the document were lengthy and more complete, it probably could have spelled out the approach to Scripture more carefully, and thus have avoided the misimpressions it will create for some.[16]

The Major Area of Disagreement

In the remarks just made on sexuality, fundamental option, sin, and scriptural use, the limitations of the recent

Vatican document were described as inadequacies. This term was used because in the document itself or in other recent magisterial sources, perspectives do exist, which, if they were coherently and consistently presented, would serve to overcome the limitations in question. On these matters, therefore, any conflict between the magisterium and the theologians seems to be fairly readily open to reconciliation. Our attention now turns to an area in which the differences between the recent Vatican document and contemporary Catholic moral theologians are notably greater than on the subjects treated in the last section. Hence, the matter we are about to treat cannot be seen simply as something the recent magisterium accepts but failed to develop adequately in the sexual ethics document. Rather, the matter to be considered will call for a thorough reassessment on the part of the magisterium. The issue to which we are referring is the vital question of objective moral knowledge, the question of how we ultimately judge what is right and wrong.

We previously asserted that the two great strengths of the Vatican sexual ethics document are its sense of the most fundamental moral values pertinent to sexuality and its awareness of various pastoral factors that touch the sexual lives of different persons. Our question now is how the document interrelates these two basic strengths. The document operates out of the stance that the moral objectivity vis-à-vis sexual matters is to be determined totally by the fundamental moral values germane to sexual matters. If these fundamental values are fully actualized, sexual actions are objectively moral. If not, sexual actions are always objectively gravely immoral, no matter what their inherent circumstances are. Once this approach is taken, the only thing the document's pastoral insights (the irreversibility of some homosexuality, the psychology of adolescent masturbation, etc.) can be used for is to argue that sometimes persons are not subjectively responsible for their wrong actions in the area of sexual morality. The pastoral insights in such a view can in no way be seen as constitutive of the moral meaning of certain sexual acts. To use language we have used before, the document uses an objectivity grave/subjectively not culpable approach to sexual morality.

Surely the Church needs to proclaim fundamental moral values in the sphere of sexuality. But as we have tried to show throughout this book, it does not seem that total moral objectivity in sexual matters can be based on fundamental moral values alone. Instead, moral objectivity in sexual matters—and in all matters—is based on the interaction of fundamental moral values and the real concrete circumstances that are inherently part of people's actions. These circumstances may be so significant that they change the nature of the moral objectivity in given cases. Thus major pastoral circumstances qualifying sexual acts need not always be seen merely as occasions for judging that a person is subjectively not culpable for the morally wrong act he or she does.

As this book has noted, a number of contemporary moral theologians have distinguished moral evil from another level of evil (ontic, premoral, nonmoral evil) and stated that we are not on the level of moral evil until we look at the basic act and its inherent circumstances.[17] Whether this distinction is the very best way to articulate our understanding of moral evil is not certain. What does seem certain is that the best (and most deeply traditional)[18] moral theology needs to move beyond the notion in sexual matters, moral truth or objectivity is fully contained in the abstracted objects of acts so that the objectively grave/subjectively not culpable route is the only option open when judging problematic sexual behavior in which mortal sin does not occur.

The recent Vatican document, in spite of the excellent work done by some of today's best theologians (systematicians and biblical scholars as well as moralists), fails to approve any approach to problematic but not mortally sinful sexual behavior other than the objectively grave/subjectively not culpable approach. By this failure, the document stays in a fixed world view and natural law theory that seems inconsistent with the Scriptures, with Thomas Aquinas (properly understood on natural law), and with Vatican II as well as with contemporary scholars.[19] Thus it seems essential that the Church do some rethinking in its philosophy of moral norms and moral objectivity. The thrust of the *Declaration on Sexual Ethics* and of much else the Church wishes to do in the world today could be tremendously enriched through such rethinking.

This entire book has been written with a great deal of respect for the basic strength of the Roman Catholic tradition's understanding of sexuality, and with a great desire that the Church's teaching on sexual matters and all matters be such that the Church is truly a light to the world, a city seated on a mountain. The book has also been written with a conviction that for the Church to be a light to the nations on sexual ethics, she needs to reach down to her roots and better articulate her grasp of sexuality, of sin, of moral objectivity, and of a variety of specific sexual issues. Sociologists who examine such matters tell us that the Church's credibility as a moral leader in the world is not nearly as great as it once was. There are a variety of reasons for this lack of credibility, but it does not seem unfair that to say that one major reason for it is that the Church has failed to make vital developments in her approach to sexual ethics, even though she has the resources for such developments in her traditions, in her scholars, and above all, in her people.[20] Ours are confusing times and we need the Church teaching with full credibility. Thus, the present author, as a beleiving Catholic Christian,[21] hopes that the Church will move to revitalize her approach to sexual ethics. Otherwise, the risk is that all sorts of extreme and unacceptable approaches to sexuality will keep coming to the fore, without any unified credible Catholic witness to deal with them. Perhaps the lines of reasoning developed in this book can be a small contribution toward the revitalization of sexual ethics needed in Catholic Christianity.[22]

NOTES

Chapter I

1. Works on a Christian overview of sexuality include: Peter A. Bertocci, *Sex, Love, and the Person* (cf. abbreviation *SLP*); Sidney C. Callahan, *Beyond Birth Control: The Christian Experience of Sex* (New York: Sheed and Ward, 1968); Andrew M. Greeley, *Sexual Intimacy* (Chicago: Thomas More Press, 1973); Johannes Gründel, "Sex," *SM* 6, pp. 73-86; Abel Jeanniere, *The Anthropology of Sex* (cf. abbreviation *TAS*); Eugene C. Kennedy, *The New Sexuality: Myths, Fables, and Hang-ups* (Garden City, New York: Doubleday, 1972); Marc Oraison, *The Human Mystery of Sexuality* (New York: Sheed and Ward, 1967); W. Norman Pittenger, *Making Sexuality Human* (Philadelphia: United Church Press, 1970); Andre Guindon, *The Sexual Language* (Ottawa: University of Ottawa Press, 1976); Anthony Kosnik, et al., *Human Sexuality: New Directions in American Catholic Thought* (cf. abbrev. *CTSA* Study). For comments on the last of these works see chapter nine, note 22.

2. This is one of the central affirmations of the first creation story in Gen. 1,1-2, 4.

3. For a fuller explanation of gnosticism's origins and history, see Robert Haardt, "Gnosis" and "Gnosticism," *SM* 2, pp. 374-380.

4. For an explanation of the impact of gnosticism on early Christian positions on birth control, see John T. Noonan, *Contraception: A History of Its Treatment by the Catholic Theologians and Canonists* (Cambridge, Mass.: Belknap Press of Harvard University Press, 1965), pp. 57-70.

5. Cf. H. Richard Niebuhr, *Christ and Culture* (New York: Harper and Row, 1956), pp. 206-217.

6. St. Augustine, *City of God*, Book 14, chapters 16-27.

7. On the meaning of the notions of immortality of the soul and resurrection of the body, see Wolfhart Pannenberg, *What is Man?* (Philadelphia: Fortress Press, 1970), pp. 45-53.

8. Merkelbach 2, pp. 985-986.

9. No doubt a general cause for the inadequacy of past Catholic approaches can be found in the fact that so much of our theology of sexuality was taught by celibates whose concrete sexual experience was quite limited.

10. A prime example from these textbooks was the practice of bungling, i.e., of blistering the skin in the genital area so as to discourage masturbation.

11. *Catechism of the Council of Trent for Parish Priests* (New York: Joseph Wagner, 1923), pp. 343-344.

12. *Code of Canon Law*, no. 1013.

13. In *Seven Great Encyclicals* (Glen Rock, N.J.: Paulist Press, 1963), pp. 82-85 (nos. 19-30). For examples of the reflection on the ends of marriage

inspired by *Casti Connubii* see Hubert Doms, *The Meaning of Marriage* (New York: Sheed and Ward, 1939); John C. Ford, "Marriage: Its Meaning and Purposes," *TS* 3 (1942), pp. 333-374.

14. For a strong position on the union of the spheres (not necessarily all the individual acts) of procreation and married love see Paul Ramsey, *Fabricated Man: The Ethics of Genetic Control* (New Haven: Yale University Press, 1970), pp. 32-39.

15. A broad survey of the covenant theme in the Old Testament can be found in John L. McKenzie, "Aspects of Old Testament Thought," *JBC*, pp. 746-762.

16. Examples include: "J," *The Sensuous Woman* (New York: Lyle Stuart, 1971); Alex Comfort, *The Joy of Sex* (New York: Crown Publishers, 1972).

17. Eugene Kennedy, *The New Sexuality*, pp. 61-83.

18. More detail on Hefner's thinking can be found in his *The Playboy Philosophy* (Chicago: HMH Publishing, 1962-1965).

19. A female-oriented approach to shallow sensualism can be found in Helen Gurley Brown, *Sex and the Single Girl* (New York: Random House, 1962).

20. One of the most obvious examples of this romanticism of sex and marriage is found in the movie star magazines so prominent on our newsstands.

21. For a discussion of the question of sublimation see Norman O. Brown, *Life Against Death: The Psychoanalytical Meaning of History* (Middletown, Conn.: Wesleyan University Press, 1959), pp. 137-176; see also Herbert Marcuse, *Eros and Civilization: A Philosophical Inquiry into Freud* (New York: Vintage Books, 1962).

22. The great surge of genealogical research in our country may well suggest a revival of interest in families and family stability. The great success of Alex Haley's *Roots: The Saga of an American Family* (New York: Doubleday, 1976) and of its televised version is but one symbol of the growth of interest in genealogies.

23. For a thorough history of the development of Christian marriage which reviews some of the difficulties the Church had to deal with in earlier ages see Edward Schillebeeckx, *MHR*, pp. 225-380.

24. Contributions on genetics and morality include John F. Dedek, *CME*, pp. 87-105; Karl Rahner, The Problem of Genetic Manipulation," *TI* 9, pp. 225-252; Paul Ramsey, *Fabricated Man*.

25. A pivotal article on the whole theme of mystery is Karl Rahner, "The Concept of Mystery in Catholic Theology," *TI* 4, pp. 36-73.

26. For a basic outline of the theology of asceticism, cf. Karl Rahner, "The Passion and Asceticism," *TI* 3, pp. 58-85.

27. Key works on this theme of responsibility include H. Richard Niebuhr, *The Responsible Self: An Essay in Christian Moral Philosophy* (New York: Harper and Row, 1963); Albert R. Jonsen, *Responsibility in Modern Religious Ethics* (Washington: Corpus Books, 1968).

28. On this issue see Rollo May, *Love and Will* (New York: W.W. Norton, 1969), pp. 36-63.

29. Assessments of the biblical data on this point include D. S. Bailey, *The Man-Woman Relationship in Christian Thought* (London: Longmans, Green and Co., 1959); Pierre Grelot, *Man and Wife in Scripture* (New York: Herder and Herder, 1964); Paul K. Jewett, *Man as Male and Female: A Study in Sexual Relationships From a Theological Point of View* (Grand Rapids: Eerdmans, 1975).

30. See especially Ephesians 5, 25-34, and Matthew 19, 4-7.

31. This statement is not based on any one text or set of texts in the Scriptures, but rather on the Scriptures' overall treatment of sexuality, marriage, and morality.

32. For a basic explanation of the difficulties of biblical hermeneutics see Raymond E. Brown, "Hermeneutics," *JBC*, pp. 605-623.

33. Cf. Karl Rahner, "Christian Humanism," *TI* 9, p. 190.

34. There will always be a tension between the three elements of Christian anthropology (our created goodness, our sinfulness, and our call to resurrection). In this book we shall basically determine what is moral by looking at the totality of humanity's here and now situation. But there is another way of looking at what is moral, i.e., from the viewpoint of our resurrection destiny. In our forthcoming accommodations to the present world, we should not collapse all tension between the present and our call to resurrection. Hopefully our use of the term ontic evil (to be explained in chapter three) will challenge us to consider our call to resurrection when we make moral choices. Cf. Karl Rahner, "Church and World," *SM* 1, pp. 346-57, esp. 347.

35. Cf. Vatican II, *Declaration on Christian Education,* no. 8 (*DV2,* p. 646); *DSexEth* no. 13, pp. 15-16.

36. Materials on sexual education for children themselves include Walter Imbiorski, ed., *Becoming a Person Program* (New York: Benziger Bros., 1970); Michael Shimek, *The Body Person* (Infinity Series, Milwaukee: Winston Press, 1972). Materials for adults working with children include Dr. and Mrs. J. C. Wilkie, *How to Teach Children the Wonder of Sex* (Cincinnati: Hiltz Publishing, 1964); *idem, Sex Education: The How To For Teachers* (Cincinnati: Hiltz, 1970); Marcia Guttentag and Helen Bray, *Undoing Sex Stereotypes: Research and Resources for Educators* (New York: McGraw-Hill, 1976).

37. Helpful sexual education sources for adults include: SIECUS, ed., *Sexuality and Man* (cf. abbreviation *S&M*); Richard F. Hettlinger, *Human Sexuality: A Psychosocial Perspective* (cf. abbreviation *HSP*); Herant A. Katchadourian and Donald T. Lunde, *Fundamentals of Human Sexuality* (cf. abbreviation *K&L*).

Chapter II

1. Major sources on the history of the question include: George H. Tavard, *Woman in Christian Tradition* (cf. abbreviation *WCT*); Rosemary R.

Ruether, *Religion and Sexism: Images of Woman in the Jewish and Christian Traditions* (New York: Simon and Schuster, 1974). For further bibliographical data see Anne E. Patrick, "Women and Religion: A Survey of Significant Literature, 1965-1974," *TS* 36 (1975), pp. 737-761.

2. Cf. Rosemary R. Ruether, "Is Christianity Misogynist? The Failure of Women's Liberation in the Church," *Liberation Theology: Human Hope Confronts Christian History and American Power* (New York: Paulist Press, 1972), pp. 95-114.

3. Cf. Bernard P. Prusak, "Woman: Seductive Siren and Source of Sin," *Religion and Sexism*, pp. 89-116.

4. Tertullian, *On the Apparel of Women*, Book 1, chapter 1, (In *The Ante Nicene Fathers* 4, New York: Charles Scribner's Sons, 1926, p. 14).

5. Saint Jerome, Letter 54, 7-13 (In *A Select Library of Nicene and Post-Nicene Fathers of the Christian Church* 6. Grand Rapids: Eerdmans, n.d., pp. 104-107).

6. St. Augustine, *Soliloquies*, Book 1, chapter 10 (In *The Fathers of the Church: A New Translation*. New York: Cima Publishing, 1948, p. 365). For more material of the type just cited see Rosemary R. Ruether, "Misogynism and Virginal Feminism in the Fathers of the Church," *Religion and Sexism*, pp. 150-183; Kari E. Børresen, *Subordination et Equivalence; Nature et rôle de la femme d'apres Augustin et Thomas d'Aquin* (Oslo: Universitets-forlaget, 1968).

7. The argument as to what degree of responsibility the Church must bear for the historical difficulties of women will probably never be fully resolved. Should the Church have been able to use her resurrection faith (cf. Gal. 3,28) to break out of inadequate views of women? Or was her rooting in culture so strong that in her mistreatment of women she was only a victim of the times? Some would argue that the better position of women in the Christian countries proves that historically the Church has helped women. The power of the Gospel has undoubtedly helped women, but has this Gospel power helped women through (or in spite of) the actions of the official Church? We have no final answer, but it seems that the institutional Church must acknowledge at least some guilt in this area. For a statement of the case against the Church on this issue, see Simone de Beauvoir, *The Second Sex* (New York: Alfred Knopf, 1953). As an argument for the Church, see L.F. Cervantes "Woman," *NCE* 14, p. 944.

8. Background explanation of the origins of the double standard can be found in Susan Brownmiller, *AOW*, pp. 16-30, 219, 319, 375-376.

9. Cited in Helmut Thielicke, *The Ethics of Sex* (Grand Rapids: Baker Book House, 1964), p. 146.

10. Thomas Aquinas, *ST* I, 92, 1, a.l.

11. On the 40/80 day theory, cf. Russell Shaw, *Abortion on Trial* (Dayton: Pflaum Press, 1968), pp. 169-171. David Granfield in *The Abortion Decision* (New York: Doubleday, 1969), p. 32 refers to a 40/90 day theory.

12. Cited in Rosemary R. Ruether and Eugene C. Bianchi, *From Machismo to Mutuality: Essays on Sexism and Woman-Man Liberation* (New York: Paulist Press, 1976), pp. 47-48.

13. For a summary of the problem of pedestalism, see Mary Daly, *The Church and the Second Sex. With a New Feminist Postchristian Introduction by the Author* (New York: Harper and Row, 1975), pp. 147-165.

14. Cf. Beverly Wildung Harrison, "Some Ethical Issues in the Woman's Movement," (Unpublished paper delivered to the American Society of Christian Ethics, January 18, 1974), p. 12.

15. An example of this type of thinking can be found in Marabel Morgan, *The Total Woman* (Old Tappan, N.J.: Revell Pub., 1973).

16. Vatican II. *Dogmatic Constitution on the Church,* chapter 8 (*DV2,* pp. 85-96). For a summary of postconciliar writing on Mary see Eamon R. Carroll, "Theology on the Virgin Mary, 1966-75," *TS* 37 (1976), pp. 253-289.

17. For an excellent history of women in America see Eleanor Flexner, *Century of Struggle: The Women's Rights Movement in the United States.* (Cambridge, Mass.: Belknap Press of Harvard University Press, 1959).

18. A helpful discussion of pornography can be found in Harry M. Clor and Richard F. Hettlinger, "Should There Be Censorship of Pornography?" in Hettlinger, *HSP,* pp. 14-27.

19. More will be said on these issues in chapter eight. Especially to be noted is Susan Brownmiller, *AOW.*

20. For a more thorough study of this question see Haye van der Meer, *Women Priests in the Catholic Church?* (Philadelphia: Temple University Press, 1973). See also A. M. Gardiner, ed., *Women and the Catholic Priesthood* (New York: Paulist Press, 1976). As preparation of this book was drawing to a close the Sacred Congregation for the Doctrine of the Faith issued its *Declaration on Women's Ordination to the Roman Catholic Priesthood,* a document that clearly rejects women's ordination. Full theological critiques of the document are not yet available, but in any case the document will have to be evaluated in the light of the criteria for non-infallible magisterial statements that we will study in the next chapter. Discussion on the issue will inevitably continue, with the present author still favoring the ordination of women for the reasons outlined in the text above. The beginnings of more articulate theological dissent from the Sacred Congregation's position on ordination can be seen in a letter sent to Archbishop Jean Jadot by twenty-three faculty members of the Jesuit School of Theology at Berkeley. The full text of their letter appears in the *Los Angeles Times,* March 18, 1977, pt. II, p. 7.

21. Cf. Norma Ramsey Jones "Women in the Ministry," *Women's Liberation and the Church: The New Demand for Freedom in the Life of the Church,* ed. by Sarah Bentley Doely (New York: Association Press, 1970), pp. 60-69.

22. Cf. Rachel C. Wahlberg, "Abortion: Decision to Live With," *Christian Century* 90 (1973), pp. 691-693.

23. Mary Daly, "Feminist Postchristian Introduction," *The Church and the Second Sex,* pp. 15-51; idem, *Beyond God the Father: Toward a Philosophy of Women's Liberation* (Boston: Beacon Press, 1973).

24. Cf. Rosemary R. Ruether, "Women's Liberation in Historical and Theological Perspective," *Women's Liberation and the Church,* p. 36.

25. A good example is Marie Robinson, *The Power of Sexual Surrender* (New York: New American Library, 1959).

26. Thomas Aquinas, *ST* II-II, 58. For an articulation of justice in the context of today's women's movement see Margaret A. Farley, "New Patterns of Relationship: Beginnings of a Moral Revolution," *TS* 36 (1975), pp. 643-646.

27. *K&L*, pp. 245-247.

28. A great deal of caution is needed lest the physical qualities argument be pushed too far and extended into areas where it should not apply. But still the physical qualities argument is sometimes valid. Persons hired to model women's clothes will be women. For certain jobs, most women (not all) will lack needed physical strength. Some men of course will also lack the needed strength.

29. Since all of human life is intersubjective or relational, the difference in relational consciousness described above may be said to enter into all aspects of human life (without this fact excluding anyone from jobs, etc.). Thus, our statements on relationality as the focal point for interpreting the differences between the sexes is a beginning rather than an end of reflection on this subject. The difference in relational consciousness not only stresses the importance of our responsibilities to the opposite sex; it also enriches the quality of our relationships to members of our own sex. In focusing on the notion of relational consciousness, I have been particularly influenced by Abel Jeanniere, *TAS*, pp. 105-139, esp. pp. 109, 126-132. Also quite helpful are Margaret A. Farley's notions of activity and receptivity in "New Patterns of Relationship . . . ," *TS* 36 (1975), pp. 627-646.

30. Rosemary R. Ruether, "Women's Liberation in Historical and Theological Perspective," *Women's Liberation and the Church* . . . , pp. 26-27.

31. Ann Belford Ulanov, *The Feminine in Jungian Psychology and in Christian Theology* (Evanston, Ill.: Northwestern University Press, 1971), esp. p. 146.

32. With a greater feminine presence, perhaps the drive to compete and to win could be replaced with more of a willingness to share our goods. Economic distribution is an enormously complex problem that will not be solved simply or naïvely. But a feminizing of economics might be of real help.

33. George H. Tavard, *WCT*, pp. 147-150, 163-167, 170.

34. Cf. Margaret Farley, "New Patterns of Relationship . . . ," *TS* 36 (1975), pp. 638-639.

35. For further development of the biblical aspects of this theme, see J. Edgar Bruns, *God as Woman, Woman as God* (New York: Paulist Press, 1973).

Chapter III

1. Cf. Thomas Aquinas, *ST* I-II, 6.

2. Some authors who reflect this viewpoint will be cited below in note 9.

3. See especially Stanislaus Lyonnet, "St. Paul: Liberty and Law,"

Readings in Biblical Morality, ed. by C. Luke Salm (Englewood Cliffs, N.J.: Prentice-Hall, 1967), pp. 62-83.

4. A most interesting development of this theme can be found in Karl Menninger, *Whatever Became of Sin?* (New York: Hawthorn Books, 1973).

5. Cf. Louis Monden, *Sin, Liberty and Law* (New York: Sheed and Ward, 1965), p. 38.

6. Cf. Bernard J. F. Lonergan, "Cognitional Structure," *Collection: Papers by Bernard Lonergan,* ed. by F. E. Crowe (New York: Herder and Herder, 1967), pp. 221-239; Karl Rahner, "Dogmatic Reflections on the Knowledge and Self-Consciousness of Christ," *TI* 5, pp. 199-201.

7. Karl Rahner, "On the Theology of the Incarnation, *TI* 4, pp. 107-109.

8. Ultimately this is the position of the Council of Trent in its *Decree on Justification* (*DS* 1540, 1565).

9. Authors who use the fundamental option approach to sin include: Charles E. Curran, "The Sacrament of Penance Today," *CP,* pp. 7-26; John W. Glaser, "Transition Between Grace and Sin: Fresh Perspectives," *TS* 29 (1968), pp. 260-274; Bernard Häring, *Sin in the Secular Age* (Garden City, N.Y.: Doubleday, 1974); Richard A. McCormick, "The Moral Theology of Vatican II," *The Future of Ethics and Theology* (Chicago: Argus Communications, 1968), pp. 7-18; Timothy E. O'Connell, "The Point of Moral Theology," *CS* 14 (1975), pp. 49-66.

10. St. Alphonsus Liguori, the great 18th century moralist, placed serious matter last in his listing of the three conditions needed for mortal sin. (*Theologia Moralis* 2. Rome: ex typographia Vaticana, 1907, p. 748). The shift of serious matter from last to first place on so many nineteenth and twentieth century lists of the conditions for sin is a symbol of the overemphasis on external acts in much that has been written and taught in the past 100 years or so.

11. The earlier Karl Rahner, who studied for a time under Martin Heidegger, was sometimes accused of being overly individualistic. Cf. Johannes B. Metz, "An Essay on Karl Rahner," in *Spirit in the World,* by Karl Rahner (New York: Herder and Herder, 1968), pp. xii-xviii.

12. For examples of theologians' precision on the meaning of external acts see Karl Rahner, *Opportunities For Faith* (London: SPCK, 1974), pp. 108-120; Richard A. McCormick, "Personal Conscience," *CS* 13 (1974), p. 251.

13. Cf. Karl Rahner, "Justified and Sinner at the Same Time," *TI* 6, pp. 218-230.

14. Cf. Martin Luther, "Secular Authority: To What Extent It Should Be Obeyed," *Martin Luther: Selections From His Writings,* ed. by John Dillenberger (Garden City, N.Y.: Doubleday, 1961), pp. 363-402.

15. Pope Paul VI, *Evangelica Testificatio* (*On the Renewal of the Religious Life*), no. 12. *TPS* 16 (1971), p. 113.

16. Bernard J. F. Lonergan, "The Transition From a Classicist Worldview to Historical-Mindedness," *A Second Collection,* ed. by Willian F. J.

Ryan and Bernard J. Tyrrell (Philadelphia: Westminster Press, 1974), pp. 1-9.

17. Vatican II. *Dogmatic Constitution on Revelation,* nos. 7-19 (*DV2,* pp. 114-125).

18. Cf. Josef Jungmann, *The Mass of the Roman Rite: Its Origins and Development* (New York: Benziger Bros., 1951); Bernhard Poschmann, *Penance and the Anointing of the Sick* (New York: Herder and Herder, 1964); Burkhard Neunhauser, *Baptism and Confirmation* (New York: Herder and Herder, 1964).

19. Cf. John T. Noonan, *The Scholastic Analysis of Usury* (Cambridge, Mass.: Belknap Press of Harvard University Press, 1957).

20. Lawrence Kohlberg, "Moral Development," *International Encyclopedia of Social Science* 10 (New York: Macmillan, 1968), pp. 483-494. For a summary of Kohlberg's thought as well as a bibliography, see Ronald Dushka and Mariellen Whelen, *Moral Development: A Guide to Piaget and Kohlberg* (New York: Paulist Press, 1975).

21. An example of a topic on which this notion of differing moral expectations might be pertinent is Sunday Mass attendance. Studies have indicated that a great many older teenagers and young adults pass through an independence seeking phase in which they (hopefully only for a time) stop going to Sunday Mass. Cf. Pierre Babin, *Crisis of Faith: The Religious Psychology of Adolescence* (New York: Herder and Herder, 1968). Should our moral expectations concerning Sunday Mass be the same for such young people as for mature adults?

22. Thomas Aquinas, *ST* I-II, 94.

23. Cf. John C. Bennett, *Christian Ethics and Social Policy* (New York: Charles Scribner's Sons, 1946), pp. 116-124.

24. The classic twentieth century work on natural law is Odon Lottin, *Le Droit Natural chez Thomas d'Aquin et ses prédécesseurs,* 2nd ed. (Bruges: Charles Beyart, 1931).

25. Ulpian's viewpoint on natural law is cited in the *Digest* or *Pandicts* of the Emperor Justinian (Book l, t. l, n. 1-4). Ulpian's writings constitute about one third of the *Code of Justinian.* (Cf. *Encyclopaedia Britannica:* Micropaedia 10, 15th ed., 1974, p. 245).

26. For a summary of Ulpian's influence on Aquinas, see Charles E. Curran, "Absolute Norms in Medical Ethics," *AMT?,* pp. 115-119, 274-275.

27. Authors commenting on this type of physicalism include: Bernard Häring, "A Theological Evaluation," *TMA,* pp. 136-137; Peter Knauer, "The Hermeneutic Function of the Principle of Double Effect," *Natural Law Forum* 12 (1967), pp. 149-150; Richard A. McCormick, *AMC,* pp. 73-74.

28. Recent contributions on the natural law include: Edward A. Malloy, "Natural Law Theory and Catholic Moral Theology," *AER* 169 (1975), pp. 456-469; Bernice Hamilton, "A Developing Concept of Natural Law," *Month* 236 (1975), pp. 196-200; Charles E. Curran, "The Stance of Moral Theology," *NP,* pp. 5-22.

29. Cf. Paul Ramsey, *The Patient as Person: Explorations in Medical Ethics*

(New Haven: Yale University Press, 1970), pp. 187-195.

30. An especially interesting way to approach this whole question of moral absolutes and moral evil would be by exploring the implications for morality of H. Richard Niebuhr's concept of radical monotheism. Cf. H. Richard Niebuhr, *Radical Monotheism and Western Culture: With Supplementary Essays* (New York: Harper and Row, 1960).

31. In certain circumstances these minor evils are not so minor. For a person who needs physical exercise to spend all his time listening to Beethoven could be a serious matter.

32. Peter Knauer, "The Hermeneutic Function . . . ," pp. 132-161.

33. Louis Janssens, "Ontic and Moral Evil," *Louvain Studies* 4 (1972), pp. 115-156. This article is especially helpful in its sensitive analysis of how ontic evil may be intended (not for itself, but as part of a single composite act, pp. 140-142). Such an understanding is crucial for much that we will say in subsequent chapters.

34. Josef Fuchs, "The Absoluteness of Moral Terms," *Gregorianum* 52 (1971), pp. 443-447.

35. Bruno Schüller, *"Direkte Tötung—indirekte Tötung,"* *Theologie und Philosophie* 47 (1972), pp. 341-357; Richard A. McCormick, *AMC*, pp. 53-69, 72-76.

36. My leaning toward the term ontic evil is based on the fact that this term seeks to give some philosophical description to the evil we are discussing, rather than merely saying that this evil is not moral (as the terms premoral and nonmoral do). It might be argued on the other hand that ontic evil is too general a term since all kinds of evils in no way related to our present concerns (floods, earthquakes, etc.) are ontic evils. It is true that premoral and nonmoral are less general terms. They do tell us we are in a context where we must make a moral decision. In the text of the book I will usually use the term ontic evil. I will seek to avoid the generality problem associated with ontic evil by speaking of morally significant ontic evils, or more briefly, of significant ontic evils. In our context the term significant ontic evil will mean that the evil is weighty and that the human person has some freedom relative to the evil so that he or she cannot ignore it in making a moral choice. Whatever terms are used, there remains the question of whether the distinction between ontic/premoral/nonmoral evil and moral evil sufficiently maintains the challenge to the Christian to strive toward perfection and resurrection. Or does this distinction collapse the resurrection tension so that actions that are only ontic/premoral/nonmoral evils are too easily accepted and lose their power to challenge us to growth? I would hold that if proper nuance is used, the resurrection tension can be maintained. In any case, more discussion and searching is needed on this whole subject.

37. Thomas Aquinas, *ST* I-II, 18, 2-4.

38. Josef Fuchs, "The Absoluteness of Moral Terms," *Gregorianum* 52 (1971), pp. 415-457. For a summary of reactions to this article see Richard A.

McCormick, "NMT," *TS* 36 (1975), pp. 85-101. Other important contributions on this whole area of moral norms include: Bruno Schüller, *"Neuere Beiträge zum Thema Begründung sittlicher Norman," Theologische Berichte* 4 (Einsiedeln: Benziger, 1974), pp. 109-181; Peter F. Chirico, *ICD*, pp. 185-192.

39. For more detail on this proportionality theme see Richard A. McCormick, *AMC*, pp. 82-106.

40. McCormick, *AMC*, pp. 58-65.

41. The reason why most Roman Catholics would take this position is that to act physically directly against life, in this set of circumstances, would be too likely to undermine what it means to be human. The physical structure of our acts can sometimes determine their human meaning. Cf. Charles E. Curran, "The Principle of Double Effect," *OR*, pp. 196-197. For a differing and well-articulated opinion on the situation of the dying, see Daniel C. Maguire, *Death By Choice* (New York: Shocken Books, 1975).

42. Josef Fuchs, "The Absoluteness . . . ," pp. 433, 440, 445, 452.

43. Fuchs, "The Absoluteness . . . ," pp. 450-451.

44. For an anthology of recent articles on conscience see C. Ellis Nelson, ed., *Conscience: Theological and Psychological Perspectives* (New York: Newman Press, 1973).

45. Cf. Thomas Aquinas, *ST* I-II, 19, 5.

46. John Henry Newman, *Letter to His Grace, the Duke of Norfolk,* in *Newman and Gladstone: The Vatican Decrees,* ed. by Alvan Ryan (Notre Dame, Indiana: University of Notre Dame Press, 1962), p. 138.

47. For pre- and post-Vatican II summaries and critiques of magisterial social teaching see John F. Cronin, *Social Principles and Economic Life* (Milwaukee: Bruce Publishing Co., 1959), and *The Gospel of Peace and Justice: Catholic Social Teaching Since Pope John,* presented by Joseph Gremillion (Maryknoll, N.Y.: Orbis Books, 1976). See also Charles E. Curran, "Dialogue with Social Ethics: Roman Catholic Social Ethics—Past, Present and Future," *CMD*, pp. 111-149.

48. For a summary of the manuals' approach to the magisterium, see Joseph A. Komonchak, "Ordinary Papal Magisterium and Religious Assent," *Contraception: Authority and Dissent,* ed. by Charles E. Curran (New York: Herder and Herder, 1969), pp. 105-118.

49. Specific reflections on the moral magisterium can be found in Karl Rahner, "The Church's Limits: Against Clerical Triumphalists and Lay Defeatists," *The Christian of the Future* (New York: Herder and Herder, 1967), pp. 49-76; Daniel C. Maguire, "Moral Absolutes and the Magisterium," *AMT?*, pp. 57-107; Peter F. Chirico, *ICD*, p. 161, 185-92. Recent works on the magisterium as a whole include Avery Dulles, "The Theologian and the Magisterium," *CTSA* 31 (1976), pp. 235-246; Yves Congar, *"Pour une histoire sémantique du terme 'magisterium'"* and *"Bref historique des formes du 'magistère' et de ses relations avec les docteurs": Revue des Sciences Philosophiques et Theologiques* 60 (1976), pp. 85-98, 99-112.

Congar's articles report that the magisterium as we now know it began in the nineteenth century. The articles are an especially significant contribution on this theme.

50. Daniel C. Maguire, "Moral Absolutes and the Magisterium," *AMT?*, pp. 102-106.

51. For a biblical and historical survey of the discernment theme, cf. Edward Malatesta *et al., Discernment of Spirits* (Collegeville, Minn.: The Liturgical Press, 1970). On the Ignatian approach to discernment see John Futrell, "Ignatian Discernment," *Studies in Spirituality of the Jesuits* 2 (1970), pp. 47-88. Cf. also Philip S. Keane, "Discernment of Spirits: A Theological Reflection," *AER* 168 (1974), pp. 43-61.

52. Cf. Karl Rahner, "On the Question of a Formal Existential Ethics," *TI* 2, pp. 217-234.

53. Undoubtedly the most important single aspect of the renewal of moral theology is this effort to unite moral and spiritual theology. Cf. Bernard Häring, *The Law of Christ* 1-3 (Cork: The Mercier Press, 1963-1966); Gérard Gilleman, *The Primacy of Charity in Moral Theology* (Westminster, Maryland: The Newman Press, 1959).

Chapter IV

1. The fact that dreams are not a moral concern does not mean that they are irrelevant to the larger question of human growth and development. Reflection on dreams can help many persons come to a higher degree of human integration. Cf. C. G. Jung, "General Aspects of Dream Analysis," *Structure and Dynamics of the Psyche* 8 (New York: Pantheon Books, 1960), pp. 237-281.

2. For a typical manualist approach to venereal pleasure, cf. Merkelbach 2, pp. 934-937.

3. Cf. *K&L,* pp. 259-262.

4. Other etymologies of the word are possible. Some suggest that the first part of the word comes from "mas," meaning male seed. The later part of the word is sometimes said to come from "turbatio," meaning excitement.

5. Cf. Merkelbach 2, pp. 949-952.

6. Fallopio thought that the Fallopian tubes were ventilators so that the child could get air.

7. Sources giving the history of our knowledge of human reproduction include Richard A. Leonardo, *A History of Gynecology* (New York: Forben Press, 1944); Harold Speert, *Obstetric and Gynecological Milestones* (New York: Macmillan, 1958); *K&L,* pp. 111-115.

8. Cf. *K&L,* pp. 71-72.

9. *K&L,* p. 113.

10. For summaries of such myths on masturbation see Havelock Ellis, *Studies in the Psychology of Sex* 1 (New York: Random House, 1942), part 1, pp. 101-283; Alfred Kinsey *et al., SBM,* p. 513; *K&L,* pp. 281-282.

11. Cf. SIECUS, *S&M,* pp. 67-69; *K&L,* pp. 281-285. Much of the past concern about masturbation and health can be traced to the eighteenth century Swiss physician Tissot whose views are no longer accepted.

12. Alfred Kinsey et al., *SBM*, p. 502; *SBF*, pp. 154-155. Kinsey's actual figures showed an incidence of masturbation in ninety-two percent of males and fifty-eight percent of females, though for devout Catholic women the figure was only forty percent. Morton Hunt, *SB70*, p. 78, has figures strikingly close to Kinsey's from samples taken 20-25 years later. Hunt's figures are ninety-two to ninety-three percent for males and fifty-one to seventy-five percent for females with the lower figure representing women who are regular churchgoers.

13. Cf. the sources in the previous citation. See also SIECUS, *S&M* pp. 28-30.

14. As examples of such psychology in a Roman Catholic context, cf. Frederick Von Gagern, *The Problem of Onanism* (Cork: Mercier Press, 1955); George Haigmaier and Robert Gleason, *Counselling the Catholic* (New York: Sheed and Ward, 1959), pp. 73-93, 215-227; March Oraison, *Illusion and Anxiety* (New York: Macmillan, 1963), pp. 103-130.

15. *DSexEth*, no. 9, p. 8.

16. For a survey recounting the traditional magisterial statements on venereal pleasure, cf. John F. Dedek, *CSM*, pp. 31-37; Charles E. Curran, "Sexuality and Sin: A Current Appraisal," *CP*, pp. 163-167.

17. *DS* 2148, 2166. The Latin words of the censure are *"ut minimum tamquam scandalosae et in praxi perniciosae."*

18. Thomas Sanchez, *Disputationum de Sancto Matrimonii Sacramento* 3 (Venice, 1606), lib. 9, dis. 46, no. 9. Opinions similar to that of Sanchez were voiced in 1929 by P. A. Laarakkers. His book was withdrawn from circulation by a decree of the Holy Office.

19. Arthur Vermeersch, *De Castitate et De Vitiis Contrariis* (Bruges: Charles Beyaert, 1919), p. 357.

20. One of the most careful studies opening the way to a reform of the Church's teaching on venereal pleasure is H. Kleber, *De parvitate materiae in sexto: Ein Beitrag zur Geschichte der Moraltheologie* (Regensburg: Pustet, 1971).

21. Thomas Aquinas, *ST* I-II, 94, a.4.

22. Aquinas, *ST* II-II, 154, a.3.

23. In addition to the theological data given in this chapter, special emphasis should be given to the fact that many priests and Catholic people now view masturbation differently than they did in the past. Cf. Norbert Brockman, "Contemporary Attitudes on the Morality of Masturbation," *AER* 166 (1972), pp. 597-614. This data from the experience of the Catholic people is in some respects as important as the theological approaches developed in our text.

24. This statement is intended to cut both ways. The pastoral minister, in a desire to keep things simple, can either treat all masturbation as thoroughly indifferent or treat all of it as a major moral problem for which persons are almost always responsible. Neither of these approaches is acceptable. Masturbation is complex enough psychologically that it will always take some reflection to discover exactly what it means in the life of a given person.

25. *DSexEth*, nos. 9-10, pp. 9-12.

26. Works which seem to go in this direction (though with differing formulations) include: Charles E. Curran, "Masturbation and Objectively Grave Matter," *A New Look at Christian Morality* (Notre Dame, Indiana: Fides Publishers, 1968), pp. 201-221; *idem*, "Sexuality and Sin ... ," *CP*, pp. 175-177; John F. Dedek, *CSM*, pp. 44-65; Robert P. O'Neill and Michael A. Donovan, *SMR*, pp. 99-119.

27. Though the interpretation may not be completely fair to his text, Donald Goergen has given many the impression that masturbation should be looked upon as completely indifferent or as healthy in every respect. Cf. Goergen, *TSC*, pp. 196-204. See also the critique of Goergen in Bernard Tyrrell, "The Sexual Celibate and Masturbation," *RR* 35 (1976), pp. 399-408.

28. In proposing the notion of masturbation as ontic but not always moral evil, I by no means wish to leave the impression that the objectively grave/subjectively not culpable approach to masturbation is of no use. Sometimes this approach, which stems from a good tradition of pastoral sensitivity in Roman Catholicism, is indeed the right way to relate to masturbation or to other moral cases. For more on the positive aspects of the objectively grave/subjectively not culpable approach cf. Bernard Häring, "A Theological Evaluation," *TMA*, pp. 139-142.

29. Cited in Charles E. Curran, "Masturbation and Objectively Grave Matter," *A New Look at Christian Morality*, p. 221; see also Bernard Häring, *ME*, p. 100.

Chapter V

1. Cf. Donald Goergen, *TSC*, pp. 77-78, 209.

2. Goergen, *TSC*, p. 78.

3. For a summary of the great variety of types and degrees of homosexuality, see Wardell B. Pomeroy, "Homosexuality," *The Same Sex*, ed. by Ralph W. Weltge (Philadelphia: United Church Press, 1969), pp. 3-15; Evelyn Hooker, "Homosexuality: Summary of Studies," *Sex Ways in Fact and Faith*, ed. by Evelyn and Sylvanus Duvall (New York: Association Press, 1961), pp. 166-183.

4. For a spelling out of this distinction, cf. John R. Cavanagh, *Counselling The Invert* (Milwaukee: Bruce Publishing Co., 1966), pp. 20-21. Because of the great variation in homosexual adjustments, it must be admitted that the distinction between "true" homosexuality and other types of homosexuality will never be a fully clear or adequate distinction.

5. For a clear rejection of such myths see Wardell B. Pomeroy, "Homosexuality," *The Same Sex*, pp. 10-11.

6. John McNeill, in *The Church and the Homosexual* (Kansas City: Sheed, Andrews and McMeel, 1976), pp. 111-113, takes serious exception to the statement of Charles E. Curran (in "Dialogue with the Homophile Movement: The Morality of Homosexuality," *CMD*, p. 203) that "most homosexual liaisons are of the 'one night stand' variety." If, as Evelyn Hooker observes, we have only seen the tip of the iceberg in our studies of homosex-

uality (cf. E. Hooker, "The Homosexual Community," *The Same Sex,* p. 35), it would seem that we simply have no definitive proof one way or the other as to the character of the majority of homosexual liaisons. My own leaning is to suspect that more honosexual unions are stable than we thought in the past.

7. Alfred Kinsey *et al., SBF,* p. 488.

8. *K&L,* pp. 332-333.

9. *K&L,* pp. 332-333.

10. For a summary of opinions on psychiatry and homosexuality, see *K&L,* pp. 336-339. More negative opinions on the psychology of homosexuality include Irving Bieber *et al., Homosexuality: A Psychoanalytic Study* (New York: Basic Books, 1962); Edmund Bergler, *Homosexuality: Disease or Way of Life?* (New York: Collier Books, 1962). More positive positions on this issue include Evelyn Hooker, "The Adjustment of the Overt Male Homosexual," *The Problem of Homosexuality in Modern Society,* ed. by Hendrik M. Ruitenbeek (New York: E. P. Dutton Co., 1963), pp. 141-161; Wardell Pomeroy, "Homosexuality," *The Same Sex,* pp. 3-13; Dennis Altman, *Homosexual Oppression and Liberation* (New York: E. P. Dutton Co., 1971); Martin Hoffman, *The Gay World* (New York: Bantom Books, 1969).

11. For a review of the possible causes of homosexuality, cf. *K&L,* pp. 336-339. A thorough history and analysis of differing interpretations of homosexuality can be found in Arlo Karlen, *Sexuality and Homosexuality* (New York: W. W. Norton, 1971).

12. *K&L,* p. 338-339; George Weinberg, "The Case Against Trying to Convert," *Society and the Healthy Homosexual* (New York: St. Martin's Press, 1972), pp. 41-48.

13. National Conference of Catholic Bishops, *Principles to Guide Confessors in Questions of Homosexuality* (Washington: USCC, 1973), p. 5; *DSexEth,* no. 9, pp. 8-9.

14. Derrick Sherwin Bailey, *Homosexuality and the Western Christian Tradition* (London: Longmans, Green and Co., 1955), pp. 1-28. John McNeill's *Church and Homosexual,* pp. 43-50, relies heavily on Bailey's interpretation and does not note that the major biblical translations and commentaries to appear in the two decades since Bailey's book have not made use of his interpretation. Cf. *The Jerusalem Bible,* ed. by Alexander Jones (Garden City, New York: Doubleday, 1966), p. 35; E. H. Maley, "Genesis," *JBC,* p. 21.

15. *The Jerusalem Bible,* p. 269, note p; John McNeill, *Church and Homosexual,* pp. 53-56.

16. McNeill, *Church and Homosexual,* pp. 65-66.

17. McNeill, *Church and Homosexual,* pp. 62-63.

18. I am deliberately avoiding philosophical terms such as ontic or moral in this statement, since such terms are not the Bible's frame of reference.

19. Cf. Thomas Aquinas, *ST* II-II, 154, 11-12. Thomas shows his Ulpianist leanings in this passage by arguing that homosexual acts are the worst of all sexual sins. For a typical treatment of homosexual acts by a modern manualist, cf. Merkelbach 2, pp. 947-949.

20. Cf. Gilbert M. Cantor, "The Need for Homosexual Law Reform," and Lewis I. Maddocks, "The Law and the Church vs. the Homosexual," both in *The Same Sex,* pp. 83-94, 95-110.

21. As of 1975, the only states in which neither oral nor anal sexual acts are against the law are Connecticut, Colorado, Delaware, Hawaii, Illinois, Ohio, and Oregon (plus the District of Columbia). Cf. *K&L,* p. 499.

22. Major concern with legal reform concerning homosexual acts can be traced back especially to the publication in Great Britain in 1957 of the *Report of the Committee on Homosexual Offences and Prostitution.* Popularly known as the Wolfenden Report (after the chairman of the group who reported to Parliament), this document called for the removal of laws against private homosexual acts between consenting adults. Available as *The Wolfenden Report* (New York: Stern and Day, 1963).

23. To get a sense of the overall tone of *Dignity,* see its pamphlet *Homosexual Catholics: A Primer For Discussion* (available from *Dignity,* 755 Boylston St., Room 514, Boston 02116). My own personal contacts with this organization have been very positive.

24. To say that such homosexual acts are objectively immoral (i.e., unacceptable based on reasonable social and religious standard), does not mean that each homosexual who engages in such acts is guilty of mortal sin. In some of these cases (granted pressures from society, etc.) it may well be pastorally wise to consider the person subjectively not responsible and therefore not guilty of mortal sin.

25. John McNeill, *Church and Homosexual,* p. 165, makes this same point.

26. *DSexEth* no. 8, pp. 8-9. For an excellent pastoral approach to homosexuals see Bishop Francis Mugavero, "Pastoral Letter: The Gift of Sexuality," *Origins* 5 (1976), pp. 581-586. In this context of pastoral sensitivity to homosexuals, we might also mention the writings of John F. Harvey, e.g., "Homosexuality," *NCE* 7, 116-119; "The Controversy Concerning the Psychology and Morality of Homosexuality," *AER* 167 (1973), pp. 602-629. Fr. Harvey has done a great deal to make the point that the true homosexual is not responsible for his or her condition as such. While his research clearly opens up the possibility of subjective nonculpability in some cases of homosexual activity, Fr. Harvey is hesitant to draw this conclusion but keeps searching for ways to enable homosexuals to avoid homosexual acts. Cf. John Harvey, "A Critique of John McNeill SJ and Gregory Baum OSA on the Subject of Homosexuality," *LQ* 43 (1976), p. 76.

27. Gregory Baum, "Catholic Homosexuals," *Commonweal* 99 (1974), pp. 479-482; John McNeill, *Church and Homosexual.* At the 1977 meeting of the American Society of Christian Ethics, Walter Muelder of Boston University chaired a discussion on McNeill's book. Muelder stated that while accommodations to individuals are surely in order, he could not see how the relationship of homosexual acts to heterosexual acts could be a matter of "valuational indifference." I would agree.

28. *Dignity* is actually more of a movement than an organization at the

present time. This is as it should be at a time when so many in the Church are rethinking their approach to homosexuality. As a movement, *Dignity* embraces a variety of moral positions on homosexuality. Nonetheless, I think the description I give above of *Dignity's* moral stance is reasonably accurate.

29. Catholic authors who have inclined toward a mediating position on homosexuality (i.e., similar to my own, but without using the ontic/moral terminology) include Charles E. Curran, "Dialogue with the Homophile Movement . . . ," *CMD*, pp. 184-219; John Dedek, *CME*, pp. 80-86; John Giles Milhaven, Review of *Church and Homosexual, NCR* (Oct. 8, 1976), p. 12. In their helpful contributions just cited, both Curran (pp. 216-218) and Dedek (pp. 85-86) approach the type of homosexual acts we are now discussing by using the theory of a moral ideal that may be compromised. Granted that homosexual acts, even the best of them, are not the most fully ideal expression of human sexuality, there still remains the difficult question of when we might morally accept them and when not. Hence, I prefer the category of proportionate reason justifying ontic evil to the category of compromised ideals as the basic thought structure to use in relating to the homosexual acts we are now considering. Dedek also suggests this sort of refinement of Curran's notion of compromise. For a modern Protestant treatment of homosexual acts, cf. Helmut Thielicke, *The Ethics of Sex* (Grand Rapids: Baker Book House, 1964), pp. 269-292.

30. Such a position is taken by Norman Pittenger, *Love and Control in Sexuality* (Philadelphia: United Church Press, 1974), p. 30. Pittenger makes it clear that while marriage as such is not possible for them, homosexual persons ought to be able to form personal unions that are respected and protected by society in the same way marriage is. Our text suggests this same point. For more of Pittenger's stance toward homosexuality, see his "Homosexuality and the Christian Tradition," *Christianity and Crisis* 34 (1974), pp. 178-186. For another source proposing a position on homosexual persons and marriage similar to my own, cf. *CTSA* Study, pp. 215-216.

31. In speaking against the adoption of children by homosexual couples, I am not speaking against the many single adults who generously adopt children or who keep their own children. While families are still the ideal context for raising children, family contexts are not always possible, so that the generosity of single adoptive parents is surely a good thing.

32. Cf. *K&L*, p. 333, for a brief treatment of bisexuality. For a strong opinion that bisexuality is only an aspect of homosexuality rather than an independent condition, cf. Hendrik M. Ruitenbeek, *The New Sexuality* (New York: Franklin Watts, 1974), pp. 75-81.

33. If a bisexual person is able to develop a stable sexual orientation only by moving toward homosexuality, this would seem to be preferable to remaining in the state of bisexuality.

Chapter VI
1. For a recent statement of this basic value system, cf. Richard A. McCormick, "Sexual Ethics: An Opinion," *NCR* (January 30, 1976), p. 9.

McCormick also developed this notion in "NMT," *TS* 34 (1973), pp. 90-91.

2. Carl Rogers, *Becoming Partners: Marriage and Its Alternatives* (New York: Delacorte Press, 1972).

3. Cf. Karl Rahner, *The Trinity* (New York: Herder and Herder, 1970); Wilhelm Breuning, "The Communion of Saints," *SM* 1, pp. 391-394.

4. The theme of the above sentence is contained in the title of Edward Schillebeeckx's *Marriage: Human Reality and Saving Mystery* (cf. abbreviation *MHR*).

5. For a fuller development of this notion, cf. Leonard F. Gerke, *Christian Marriage: A Permanent Sacrament* (Washington: The Catholic University of America Press, 1965: Doctoral Dissertation).

6. On Vatican II's omission of the terms primary and secondary, see the *Pastoral Constitution on the Church in the Modern World*, no. 48 (*DV2*, p. 250, note 155). Actually, if the word primary is not taken to mean most important or most fundamental, but rather as meaning "what is most concretely unique about the possibilities available in marriage as compared to other love relationships," children could still be called the primary end of marriage. The problem is that the word is too seldom understood in this very precise and specific sense.

7. The notion of conjugal commitment as the basic focal point of marriage was developed very significantly by Hubert Doms in *The Meaning of Marriage* (New York: Sheed and Ward, 1939). More recently this theme (with a healthy stress on the physical values present in conjugal love) has been taken up by John Giles Milhaven in "Conjugal Sexual Love," *TS* 35 (1974), pp. 692-710.

8. Cf. Francis Mugavero, "Pastoral Letter: The Gift of Sexuality," *Origins* 5 (1976), pp. 581-586.

9. For examples of the continuing work of the Canon Law Society of America see *The Jurist* 30 (1970), pp. 1-74; Lawrence G. Wrenn, ed., *Divorce and Remarriage in the Catholic Church* (New York: Newman Press, 1973). For the work of the Catholic Theological Society of America, see "Appendix B: The Problem of Second Marriages," *CTSA* 27 (1972), pp. 233-240.

10. An opposite sort of danger can also exist. Some of those who want to move away from the overly physical approaches become so spiritual in their approaches to marriage that the physical and emotional values of marriage are lost sight of. Cf. John Giles Milhaven, "Conjugal Sexual Love," *TS* 35 (1974), p. 700.

11. Material on marriage preparation is relatively limited. One program is Martin Olsen and George Kaenel, *Two as One: A Christian Marriage Preparation Program* (Includes Workbook and Manual, New York: Paulist Press, 1976). Also very helpful is J. Murray Elwood, *Growing Together in Marriage* (Notre Dame, Indiana: Ave Maria Press, 1977).

12. Besides Schillebeeckx, *MHR*, other works on the theology of marriage include Karl Rahner, "Marriage as a Sacrament," *TI* 10 pp. 199-221; Franz Bockle, ed. *Concilium* 5, no. 7 (1970), Issue title: *The Future of Marriage as an Institution;* Rosemary Haughton, *The Theology of Marriage* (Notre Dame, Indiana: Fides Publishers, 1970); William Bassett and Peter Huizing, eds.,

Concilium 7, no. 9 (1973), Issue title: *The Future of Christian Marriage;* Bernard Häring, *Marriage in the Modern World* (Westminster, Maryland: The Newman Press, 1965).

13. While questions might be raised about some of its specific approaches, the basic outlook of the bestseller *Open Marriage,* with its stress on the variety of relationships possible for a married couple, seems quite sound. Nena and George O'Neill, *Open Marriage: A New Lifestyle for Couples* (New York: M. Evans, 1972).

14. For an historical background, cf. Schillebeeckx, *MHR*, pp. 231-380. Thomas Aquinas held that the bethrothal could take place at the age of seven (*ST* III, 43, 2). My comments on the limitations and impersonalism of some aspects of the medieval view of marriage should not be construed as denying the social nature of marriage, as denying that society can place some legitimate social expectations on couples planning to marry.

15. Important recent works on commitment include John Haughey, *Should Anyone Say Forever? On Making, Keeping and Breaking Commitments* (Garden City, New York: Doubleday, 1975); Margaret A. Farley, *A Study in the Ethics of Commitment Within the Context of Theories of Human Love and Temporality* (New Haven: Yale University, 1974, Doctoral Dissertation).

16. The first of the figures given for women having premarital intercourse (14%) comes from Alfred Kinsey *et al., SBF*, p. 298. The more recent figures come from Morton Hunt, *SB70*, p. 150. For no group of American males born at any time during the twentieth century did Hunt find less than eighty-four percent who had had premarital intercourse.

17. *K&L*, p. 314.

18. *K&L*, p. 313.

19. Kinsey *et al., SBF*, p. 437.

20. Morton Hunt, *SB70*, pp. 258-261. For the oldest group Hunt surveyed, (55 or older in 1972), forty-three percent of men and fifteen percent of women had had extramarital intercourse. For the youngest group he surveyed (age 25 and under), the respective figures were thirty-two percent and twenty-four percent. Figures for this youngest group will probably increase as their years of marriage increase.

21. Hunt, *SB70*, pp. 215-278.

22. Hunt, *SB70*, pp. 271-274.

23. In rejecting the theory of premarital intercourse for fun only, there is no denial that intercourse, when it is morally appropriate, can and should be fun. The point is that there must be more to sexual communion than the fun aspect.

24. One of the most widely read statements of the traditional case against premarital intercourse is Evelyn Millis Duvall, *Why Wait Till Marriage?* (New York: Association Press, 1968). Other statements of the case against premarital intercourse include Peter A. Bertocci, *SLP;* Robert O'Neill and Michael Donovan, *SMR*, pp. 129-168.

25. The human being does impose meaning on the world, but he or she also lives in a world where there is a level of pregiven meaning. Keeping the balance between receiving meaning from the world and giving it back to the

world is the art we all must learn. Extreme situationalism which says that philosophy is utterly useless and that there is no continuity of meaning in our world must be rejected. Karl Rahner has aptly called such extreme situationalism "massive nominalism" (in "On the Question of a Formal Existential Ethics," *TI* 2, p. 219). To attach any meaning whatever to sexual intercourse would be such a massive nominalism. On this point of sexuality and meaning, cf. Peter Chirico, *ICD*, p. 275.

26. I say "virtually no circumstances in normal life" to hold open the possibility that in some unusually bizarre circumstances proportionate reasons for extramarital intercourse might exist. Scholars sometimes debate the case of Mrs. Bergmaier, the concentration camp inmate who wishes to rejoin her husband and children and who can only do so by becoming pregnant. Cf. Joseph Fletcher, *Situation Ethics: The New Morality* (Philadelphia: Westminster Press, 1966), pp. 164-165. Without solving Mrs. Bergmaier's case, it does seem wise to suggest that our prohibition of extramarital intercourse is a virtually exceptionless norm, i.e., that the exceptions to it would exist only in the rarest of cases, cases that hardly ever happen in normal life.

27. While marriage's social witness is a natural value, it is also very much a Christian faith value. Pastors and parents who wish to help young people see the arguments against premarital intercourse should concentrate on developing a lively sense of Christian faith in such young people. Such a faith will be at least as valuable, and probably more valuable, than the rational arguments against premarital intercourse.

28. For a summary of the flaws in some of the arguments proposed for this kind of premarital intercourse see Charles E. Curran, "Sexuality and Sin: A Current Appraisal," *CP*, pp. 177-179.

29. Historically this notion of a person's having a right to marry emerged especially in the Church's insistence that parents could not force a marriage on children. Cf. Thomas Aquinas *ST* III, 47, 6. In the twentieth century the right to marry was clearly asserted by Pius XI in *Casti Connubii* no. 68 (in *Seven Great Encyclicals*, Glen Rock: N.J.: Paulist Press, 1963, p. 96). To say that people have a right to marry does not mean that every person has achieved the necessary maturity to exercise this right. Hence society and the Church can impose restrictions on who can exercise the right to marry (restrictions based on age, etc.). Perhaps pastors should be more ready than they are at present to refuse to marry obviously unprepared couples. In the text we are, therefore, speaking only of cases where couples truly are prepared to marry and society unreasonably and unjustly restricts their right to marry.

30. Based on this whole issue of delayed maturity in our society, the Church in the future may have to give serious consideration to postponing the usual age for marriage (and also for ordination and religious profession) till about thirty. The pros and cons of such a postponement are not, however, resolved.

31. While I have not seen anyone use the exact language I propose

here, similar sensitive approaches to this type of premarital intercourse include Charles E. Curran, "Sexuality and Sin . . . ," *CP*, p. 179-180; John F. Dedek, *CSM*, p. 42; Richard A. McCormick, "NMT," *TS* 34 (1973), p. 89-92; Bernard Häring, *"Voreheliche geschlechtliche Vereinigung," Theologie der Gegenwart* 15 (1972), pp. 63-77. For a position that opposes the type of calculation I suggest, see John M. Finnis, "Natural Law and Unnatural Acts," *Heythrop Journal* 11 (1970), pp. 365-387.

32. This problem of the exception being taken as the norm happens with many moral issues today. Those teaching moral values must take care to avoid giving the impression that the exception is the norm. Cf. Paul Ramsey, "The Case of the Curious Exception," *Norm and Context in Christian Ethics*, Gene Outka and Paul Ramsey, eds., (New York: Charles Scribner's Sons, 1968), pp. 67-135.

33. *DSexEth*, no. 10, p. 11, would seem to allow this interpretation.

34. For the premarital/preceremonial distinction see Paul Ramsey, "A Christian Approach to the Question of Sexual Relations Outside of Marriage," *The Journal of Religion* 45 (1965), pp. 110-118. For a critique of the legalism involved in assuming that a hindered firm intention to marry or a secret marriage removes completely the evil of premarital intercourse see Richard A. McCormick, "NMT," *TS* 34 (1973), pp. 88-90. McCormick suggests here a point we have already made, that the real answer to the dilemma of premarital intercourse is to enhance our theology of and preparation for marriage so that people will freely want to choose to wait for marriage to have intercourse.

35. Cf. Alfred Kinsey *et al.*, *SBM*, pp. 344-346, 365-373.

36. As we have already noted (chapter four, especially notes 16-20), much of the historical dispute about parvity of matter in the sexual sphere concerned a possible moral difference between those forms of sexual arousal that involve orgasm and those that do not. The fact of this historical dispute may suggest that we need to be especially open to rethinking our moral stance on mild and moderately arousing forms of petting.

37. Many theological interpretations of petting (cf. Peter A. Bertocci, *SLP*, pp. 94-97) hold that there is a more or less inevitable progression from petting to intercourse. Kinsey's data, on the other hand, might imply that there is enough new about twentieth century petting that we cannot be sure how to evaluate it. Thus there is an uncertainty that makes our remarks in the text tentative. For contemporary theological treatments of premarital petting, cf. John F. Dedek, *CSM*, pp. 42-43; Robert O'Neill and Michael Donovan, *SMR*, pp. 137-144.

38. For too long Catholic theology has concentrated on wrong or evil types of sexual expression. If we believe that physical sexual expression and the emotional and personal overtones inherent in it are good, we ought to take the basic stance that the physical and emotional side of sexuality is something to be appreciated rather than feared. Setting such a tone is the main intention of this section of the chapter. A deeper appreciation of the spiritual side of sexual interaction is also very much needed.

39. For some reflections on the connections between sexual intercourse and the Eucharist, see James Plastaras, "Marriage and the Eucharist," *Worship* 39 (1965), p. 457.

40. Cf. *K&L*, pp. 357-358.

41. The traditional or "missionary" position (husband on top of the wife) was held by some theologians in former centuries to be the only moral position in which to have intercourse. The allowing of only this position was based on the (now known to be erroneous) notion that this position was more likely than any other to result in pregnancy.

42. Paul Ramsey, "Death's Pedagogy," *Commonweal* 100 (1974), p. 502. Some of the current literature on sex is not only one-sidedly physical but contains suggestions that are very dangerous (e.g., Dr. Reuben's recommendation of douching with a bottle of coke), cf. Richard Hettlinger, *HSP*, pp. 262-263.

43. Statistics on the frequency of intercourse do suggest that its rate of frequency in marriage has increased in recent decades. The average frequencies of intercourse given by Morton Hunt, *SB70* are 3.50 times weekly for 18-24 year olds, 3.0 times weekly for 25-34 year olds, 2.00 times weekly for 35-44 year olds, and once weekly for couples over 45. No married couple should feel in any way coerced or constrained by such statistics.

44. Cf. Thomas Aquinas, *ST* III, 69.

45. Merkelbach 2, p. 948.

46. To date, very little has been said in print on this subject by Roman Catholic theologians. The *CTSA* Study, p. 110, no. 3, does suggest, as I do, that oral sex may be moral in some cases.

47. For a listing of the states where such acts are legal, cf. chapter 5, note 21.

48. Especially noteworthy are the techniques described in William H. Masters and Virginia E. Johnson, *Human Sexual Inadequacy* (Boston: Little, Brown and Co., 1970), pp. 101-115.

49. Greenwich, Conn.: Fawcett Publishing, 1964.

50. It is true that in some cases senility results in unacceptable sexual behavior. This fact should not, however, lead to an unfair restraint on the sexual lives of healthy older persons. On this subject, cf. Isadore Rubin, "Sexual Life in the Later Years," *S&M*, pp. 99-120.

51. Pope Paul VI, *Populorum Progressio*, no. 37, in *TPS* (1967), p. 156.

52. On the connections between population and development, see Arthur McCormack, "The Population Explosion: A Theologian's Concern?" *TS* 35 (1974), pp. 3-19; Peter Henriot, "Global Population in Perspective: Implications for U.S. Policy Response," *TS* 35 (1974), pp. 48-70.

53. Vatican II, *Pastoral Constitution on the Church in the Modern World*, no. 51 (*DV2*, pp. 255-256).

54. In the early years after the development of the pill some theologians did argue that the use of the pill might be moral whereas the use of contraceptives (in the narrow sense of the word) would not be. Cf. Louis Janssens, "Morale conjugale et progèsterones," *Ephemerides theologicae*

Louvaniensis 39 (1963), pp. 787-826. Such a moral distinction between temporary sterilization and contraception has not been widely used in the past ten years or so.

55. The key sections of the Encyclical, as far as the controversy is concerned, are nos. 10-14, in *TPS* 13 (1969), pp. 334-337.

56. National Conference of Catholic Bishops, "Human Life in Our Day," *TPS* 13 (1969), pp. 383-385; *idem,* "Pastoral Letter on Moral Values," *Origins* 6 (Nov. 25, 1976), p. 363.

57. For summaries of the many theological critiques of (as well as some support for) *Humanae Vitae* right after its publication see Richard A. McCormick, "NMT," *TS* 29 (1968), pp. 707-741; Robert Springer, *"NMT,"* *TS* 30 (1969), pp. 258-284; Richard A. McCormick, *"NMT,"* *TS* 30 (1969), pp. 635-668; Robert Hoyt, ed. *The Birth Control Debate* (Kansas City: *NCR,* 1968). Since the months right after the Encyclical, the volume of literature on the subject has dropped off considerably, but proposed reformulations and critiques of *Humanae Vitae* continue to appear. Cf. Bernard Häring, *ME,* p. 88; John Dedek, *CME,* p. 68-72. Articles supporting *Humanae Vitae* have also kept appearing. Cf. John F. Kippley, "Catholic Sexual Ethics: The Continuing Debate on Birth Control," *LQ* 41 (1974), pp. 8-25.

58. Richard A. McCormick, in "The Silence Since *Humanae Vitae,*" *America* 129 (July 21, 1973), pp. 30-33, very effectively argues that further dialogue between the magisterium, theologians, and others is greatly needed.

59. For a summary of issues related to the pill, cf. *K&L,* pp. 151-156. For the developing concerns about how the pill really works, see Paul Vaughn, "The Pill Turns Twenty," *The New York Times Magazine* (June 13, 1976). p. 9.

60. For a review of questions concerning the I.U.D. cf. *K&L,* pp. 156-160.

61. For details on such devices, cf. *K&L,* pp. 160-164.

62. In this light consider the interesting words of Bernard Häring: "It is a great blessing that Pope Paul did not give doctrinal sanction to a specific medical method. Otherwise . . . he would have had to shoulder responsibility from all the damage likely to ensue from that one method," Häring, *ME,* p. 87.

63. Actually there are several different birth control methods based on periodic abstinence. The original or rhythm method was based on the timing of the woman's menstrual cycle (and was more or less effective, depending on how regular or irregular the woman was). Another method of periodic abstinence has based itself upon measuring the woman's basal body temperature (BBT). More recently, interest has focused on the method mentioned in the text, Natural Family Planning. This method bases its estimate of the woman's "safe" period on changes in her cervical mucus. Cf. John J. and Evelyn L. Billings, *Natural Family Planning: The Ovulation Method* (Collegeville, Minn.: The Liturgical Press, 1973). Recently Bernard Häring published an article about the possibility that problems such as spontaneous

abortions and births of defective children are related to the use of periodic abstinence. Cf. Bernard Häring, "New Dimensions of Responsible Parenthood," *TS* 37 (1976), pp. 120-132. Should Häring's speculations prove true, some serious rethinking of periodic abstinence might have to take place. There are, however, some real doubts about the arguments Häring offers. For a statement of the case against Häring's arguments cf. Thomas Hilgers "Human Reproduction: Three Issues for the Moral Theologian," *TS* 38 (1977), pp. 136-152.

64. For an outline of the cases of sterilization that have been accepted under the traditional understanding of the double effect principle, cf. Thomas O'Donnell, *MM*, pp. 131-144.

65. *K&L,* p. 166. Without much doubt there was a time in the United States a decade or so ago when this surgery was done for insufficient medical reasons in some cases. Cf. Thomas O'Donnell, *MM*, pp. 142-143.

66. Cf. Pope Pius XII, "Address to the Italian Catholic Society of Midwives," (Oct. 29, 1951), *AAS* 43, p. 843. Though it is not our main concern, it should be noted that one aspect of the papal condemnations of sterilization has been the opposition to all forms of state-controlled sterilization such as punitive and eugenic sterilization. For opposing these forms of sterilization, the magisterium deserves much praise. Cf. Pope Pius XI, *Casti Connubii,* nos. 69-70. In *Seven Great Encyclicals,* (Glen Rock, N.J.: Paulist Press, 1963), pp. 96-97.

67. For outlines of the double effect and totality principles as traditionally interpreted, see Thomas O'Donnell, *MM*, pp. 39-44, 76-78. Pope Pius XII's statement of the principle of totality can be found in his "Allocution to the First International Congress on the Hystopathology of the Nervous System," (Sept. 14, 1952), *AAS* 44, p. 782.

68. A key article in the early stages of the reformulation of the double effect principle was Peter Knauer, "The Hermeneutic Function of the Principle of Double Effect," *Natural Law Forum* 12 (1967), pp. 132-162. Perhaps the most thorough statement of a reformulated double effect methodology (with a summary of much that preceded it) is Richard A. McCormick, *Ambiguity in Moral Choice: The 1973 Pere Marquette Theology Lecture* (cf. abbreviation *AMC*). More recently see Charles E. Curran, "The Principle of Double Effect," *OR*, pp. 173-209.

69. I am persuaded in favor of the second of these approaches by Richard A. McCormick, *AMC*, pp. 56-65, 72-82. McCormick well notes that directly intending ontic evil is different from merely permitting it and requires a greater proportionate reason.

70. For such a broader interpretation of totality, cf. Martin Nolan, "The Principle of Totality in Moral Theology," *AMT?,* pp. 232-248.

71. Catholic authors who would be open to such sterilizations include Richard A. McCormick, "Medico-Moral Opinions: Vasectomy and Sterilization," *LQ* 38 (1971), pp. 9-10; Bernard Häring, *ME*, pp. 90-91; Charles E. Curran, "Sterilization: Exposition, Critique and Refutation of Past Teaching," *NP*, pp. 194-211; John F. Dedek, *CME*, pp. 72-76.

72. Cf. Charles E. Curran, "Sterilization: Exposition . . . ," *NP*, pp. 206-207. I am not trying to completely reject the possibility of vascetomies in such cases, but only noting that there are significant reasons for preferring a tubal ligation when the sterilization is based on medical pathology in the woman. The *CTSA* Study, p. 136, no. 3, uses an approach similar to mine in determining which spouse should be sterilized.

73. Cf. *K&L*, pp. 165-166.

74. National Conference of Catholic Bishops, *Ethical and Religious Directives for Catholic Health Facilities*, nos. 18-20, (St. Louis: Catholic Hospital Association, 1975), pp. 10-11. The letter to the American hierarchy from the Sacred Congregation for the Doctrine of the Faith (March 13, 1975) is printed in *Origins* 6 (June 10, 1976), pp. 33 and 35. For a critique of some aspects of the methodology underlying this letter see Richard A. McCormick, "Sterilization and Theological Method," *TS* 37 (1976), pp. 471-477.

75. Cf. *Policy Manual for Committees to Advise on Requests for Obstetrical/ Gynecological Sterilization Procedures*. Rev. ed. (London, Ontario: St. Joseph's Hospital, 1974). There are Catholic hospitals in the United States that perform such sterilizations. Because of the present uncertain situation, such hospitals usually do not publicize the fact that they do such sterilizations.

76. For an outline of the traditional notion of cooperation in medical ethics, see Thomas O'Donnell, *MM*, pp. 44-52. The Vatican letter of March 13, 1975, did leave open the possibility of cooperation in sterilizing surgeries (nos. 3b and 3c, p. 35), a fact that partly explains why some are interested in this approach. For an interpretation of the March 13, 1975, letter that supports its basic stance and opts for the possibility of cooperation see Kevin O'Rourke, "An Analysis of the Church's Teaching on Sterilization," *Hospital Progress* 57 (1976), pp. 68-75.

77. In the next section of this chapter we shall be noting a very few types of abortion cases that Catholic moralists and Catholic hospital policy makers might possibly consider allowing.

78. It does not automatically follow that material cooperation in sterilizations would lead to material cooperation in abortion, but it seems quite likely that many outside sources would push for such cooperation. Charles E. Curran, "Cooperation in a Pluralistic Society," *OR*, pp. 210-228, has written a sensitive article on cooperation that moves the notion away from cooperation in others' objectively grave moral evil and toward an idea of cooperation as respecting others' freedom of conscience. On this basis, Curran argues that Catholic hospitals could cooperate in sterilizations while staying away from abortions. But the danger of being pressured to extend cooperation remains, and I hold that it is better to work toward hospital policies that use the methodology of proportionate reason (or ontic but not moral evil) in permitting some sterilizations.

79. Moral arguments for the possibility of this type of sterilization can be found in the sources cited in note 71.

80. Cf. *K&L*, p. 115.

81. Cf. Bernard Häring, *ME*, pp. 90-91.

82. John T. Noonan, "An Almost Absolute Value in History," *TMA,* pp. 1-59.

83. Full-length Catholic works on abortion (with differing emphases and outlooks) include Daniel Callahan, *Abortion: Law, Choice and Morality* (New York: Macmillan Co., 1970); David Granfield, *The Abortion Decision* (Garden City, New York: Doubleday, 1969); and Germain Grisez, *Abortion: The Myths, The Realities, and the Arguments* (New York: Corpus Books, 1970).

84. The overall unity of the Catholic attitude toward abortion was well underlined by the generally negative response of Catholic scholars to the January 22, 1973, Supreme Court decision on abortion. For a summary see Richard A. McCormick, "NMT: The Abortion Dossier," *TS* 35 (1974), p. 312-332. On the popular level unity in the Catholic attitude toward abortion, see Andrew M. Greeley, *The Communal Catholic: A Personal Manifesto* (New York: Seabury Press, 1976), p. 12.

85. For an excellent statement of the background for a Roman Catholic stance opposing a constitutional ammendment on abortion see Charles E. Curran, "Civil Law and Christian Morality: Abortion and the Churches," *OR,* pp. 107-143.

86. For a summary of this approach, see Thomas O'Donnell, *MM,* pp. 155-226.

87. For the biological bases for this theory, cf. André E. Hellegers, "Fetel Development," *TS* 31 (1970), pp. 3-10; James J. Diamond, "Abortion, Animation, Hominization," *TS* 36 (1975), pp. 305-324. A philosophical approach to the question can be found in Joseph F. Donceel, "Immediate Animation and Delayed Hominization," *TS* 31 (1970), pp. 76-105.

88. Some scholars hold that, based on cortical or brain development, or on the concept of human relationality, we can prolong beyond the first two weeks after fertilization the period when individual personal human life is clearly not present. Cf. Bernard Häring, *ME,* pp. 81-85. Such an opinion has drawn quite a bit of criticism, even from progressive Roman Catholic moralists. Cf. Charles E. Curran, "Abortion: Its Legal and Moral Aspects," *NP,* pp. 181-184; Richard McCormick, "NMT," *TS* 35 (1974), pp. 335-338.

89. Charles J. McFadden, *Medical Ethics* (Philadelphia: F. A. Davis, 1951), pp. 153-154, held that efforts to remove the semen could go on for up to ten hours after a rape. Estimates of the time to be allowed varied from author to author.

90. Theologians who would hold that, based on the lack of individual personal human life in the first fourteen days after fertilization, some possibly abortifacient actions might be permissible include: Richard A. McCormick, "NMT," *TS* 35 (1974), pp. 338, 354-355; Charles E. Curran, "Abortion: Its Legal and . . . ," *NP,* pp. 188-189; Paul Ramsey, "The Morality of Abortion," *Life or Death: Ethics and Options,* ed. by Daniel H. Labby (Seattle: University of Washington Press, 1968), pp. 61-63.

91. Grisez, *Abortion: The Myths, the Realities, and the Arguments,* pp. 333-334, accepts such abortions, but on the basis that they are an indirectly intended part of an inseparable human act. He will not consider these abortions to be direct, nor will he extend his reasoning to the cases taken up

Notes 217

in the next paragraph of our text. For critiques of Grisez which hold that such abortions are direct, cf. Paul Ramsey, "Abortion: A Review Article," *The Thomist* 37 (1973), pp. 211-226; Richard A. McCormick, *AMC*, pp. 40-53.

92. Catholic authors cautiously considering such an approach include Robert Springer, "NMT," *TS* 31 (1970), pp. 492-493; John F. Dedek, *Human Life: Some Moral Issues* (New York: Sheed and Ward, 1972), pp. 81-90; *idem, CME*, pp. 127-135; Richard McCormick, "NMT," *TS* 35 (1974), pp. 354-355; Charles E. Curran, "Abortion: Its Legal and ... ," *NP*, pp. 190-193.

93. Cf. Bernard Häring, "A Theological Evaluation," *TMA*, pp. 139-142. It is interesting to compare Häring's reflections with the approach of James M. Gustafson to the very same case. Gustafson, "A Protestant Ethical Approach," *TMA*, pp. 101-122.

94. Pope Pius XII, "Address to the Fourth International Congress of Catholic Doctors," (Sept. 24, 1949), *AAS* 41, pp. 557ff.

95. Contemporary theologians taking stands generally against A.I.D. include Paul Ramsey, *Fabricated Man: The Ethics of Genetic Control* (New Haven: Yale University Press, 1970), pp. 39-52; Bernard Häring, *ME*, pp. 91-92; John F. Dedek, *CME*, pp. 100-101. In addition to the factors mentioned in our text, both Häring and Dedek cite abuses connected with sperm banks (big business, breeding of a super race) as part of their argument against A.I.D. Dedek in his phrasing leaves the door open for future developments that might tip the balance in favor of A.I.D. in some cases. Even more open to the possibility of A.I.D. is Charles E. Curran, *Politics, Medicine, and Christian Ethics: A Dialogue with Paul Ramsey* (Philadelphia: Fortress Press, 1973), p. 217. The *CTSA* Study, pp. 138-139, also seems rather open to the possibility of A.I.D. Based on the principles of contemporary moral theology (proportionality of ontic good over ontic evil), I do not think A.I.D. can be absolutely ruled out in all circumstances humanity might conceivably face. However, the circumstances that might justify it would be extremely rare.

96. For statements open to the possibility of A.I.H., see Richard A. McCormick, "NMT," *TS*, 32 (1971), pp. 96-97; Bernard Häring, *ME*, pp. 92-93; John F. Dedek, *CME*, pp. 100-102.

97. In California in 1975 there were 159,598 marriages and 129,144 divorces. In Florida, the comparable figures were 86,152 and 63,267. Cf. *The World Almanac and Book of Facts, 1977* (New York: Newspaper Enterprise Association, 1976), p. 952.

98. For an excellent summary of the voluminous literature to appear on this subject over the past decade, cf. Charles E. Curran, "Divorce: Catholic Theory and Practice in the United States," *NP*, pp. 212-276; see also Richard A. McCormick "NMT," *TS* 36 (1975), pp. 100-117.

99. For an outline of the pertinent canonical developments, cf. Charles E. Curran, "Divorce: Catholic Theory and ... ," *NP*, pp. 213-223. A more detailed survey of the grounds for marital annulments can be found in Lawrence G. Wrenn, *Annulments* (Hartford, Conn.: The Canon Law Society of America, rev. ed., 1972).

100. The Church is a social or public community (in addition to her

deeper, more mystical unity). Since annulment is the only recognized Church process permitting second marriages, it is better for persons to use this procedure (when possible), so as to be fully incorporated into the social structure of the Church.

101. In fact, many marriages are probably invalid from the viewpoint of true consent at the time they begin. This fact opens up an agonizing question: how can we better prepare people for Christian marriage and have higher standards for who should marry, without at the same time being overly idealistic about the level of maturity we should expect in young people wishing to marry?

102. For a presentation—based on personal experience—of some of the problems of the tribunal system, cf. Stephen J. Kelleher, *Divorce and Remarriage for Catholics?* (Garden City, New York: Doubleday, 1973). See also John T. Finnegan, "Marriage Law," *CS* 15 (1976), pp. 297-299.

103. Statements of this perspective on the biblical texts include: Bruce Vawter, "The Biblical Theology of Divorce," *CTSA* 22 (1967), pp. 223-243; Dominic Crossan, "Divorce and Remarriage in the New Testament," *The Bond of Marriage*, ed. by William W. Bassett (Notre Dame, Indiana: University of Notre Dame Press, 1968), pp. 1-33.

104. John T. Noonan, *Power to Dissolve: Lawyers and Marriages in the Courts of the Roman Curia* (Cambridge, Mass.: The Belknap Press of Harvard University Press, 1972).

105. The fact that second marriages should be permitted only after first marriages have irrevocably broken down underlines the importance of good marriage counseling and all other efforts to keep first marriages alive. Within the efforts to keep first marriages alive and growing we should include not only the effort taken when first marriages are in crisis, but also all efforts to enrich marriages and foster marital growth so that the crisis stage is not reached in the first place. In this context we can praise (without endorsing every single aspect of) the marriage encounter movement. Sources aiding growth in marital life include Howard and Charlotte Clinebell, *The Intimate Marriage* (New York: Harper and Row, 1970); J. Murray Elwood, *Growing Together in Marriage* (Notre Dame, Indiana: Ave Maria Press, 1977); Herbert A. Otto, ed., *Marriage and Family Enrichment: New Programs and Perspectives* (Nashville: Abingdon Press, 1976). What this chapter says about divorce and remarriage makes no sense at all except in the context of all possible efforts to promote stable marriages in the first place.

106. For reflections of this type, cf. Charles E. Curran, "Divorce: Catholic Theory and . . . ," *NP*, pp. 271-272; *idem*, "Divorce in the Light of a Revised Moral Theology," *OR*, pp. 105-106; Charles Whelen, "Divorced Catholics: A Proposal," *America* 131 (1974), pp. 363-365; Stephen Kelleher, *Divorce and Remarriage for Catholics?*, pp. 190-192.

107. For reflection on this specific problem cf. José Montserrat-Torrents, *The Abandoned Spouse* (Milwaukee: Bruce Publishing Co., 1969).

108. Earlier (chapter 5, note 29) I indicated that the notion of an ideal not fully realized is a helpful but less than completely satisfactory way to

relate to moral dilemmas. I stated at that point that the notion of ontic evil morally justified by proportionate reasons is ultimately a more precise and satisfactory way to relate to moral dilemmas. In the present context of divorce and remarriage, I have used the notion of indissolubility as an ideal not always completely realizable in concrete cases. Some type of acceptance of this notion—which is found in much of the literature—is necessary before we can talk about any new approaches to second marriages after valid first marriages. But in the case of second marriages after valid first marriages— as in all other cases we have treated in this book—we ultimately must calculate the proportionality of ontic good to ontic evil. Hence our text now turns to the crunch issue of calculating proportionality, both from the point of view of the persons involved and from the point of view of the Church. Cf. Richard A. McCormick, "NMT," *TS* 36 (1975), pp. 108, 117. I do not, however, agree with McCormick's very passive tone on how the Church should relate to couples in second marriages after valid first marriages (pp. 113-115). I would hold that the Church must give some positive support— admittedly a carefully qualified support—to the decisions couples make to enter second marriages. It must at least be officially clear that the Church will respect such couples' decisions by welcoming them to the sacraments. Later, I will suggest that the Church's welcome to such couples might be appropriately expressed in a carefully qualified marriage ceremony. It seems that the Churchs "overall educational purposes" which McCormick says argue against the Church's witnessing second marriages could be served in other ways.

109. The truly proportionate reasons for entering such second marriages have already been suggested: a sincere judgment that the first marriage has irrevocably broken down, a conviction that one cannot live except in a second marriage (i.e., celibacy is not a possible alternative), and sincere belief in the sacraments and in one's need to share in them.

110. For a description of the changed sociological factors related to broken marriages, see Abel Jeanniere, *TAS,* pp. 174-178.

111. The terminological waters are a bit muddy as regards the pastoral approach to invalid marriages. The term "internal forum solution" clearly refers to the case resolved privately by the couple and a pastoring person. Another term, "good conscience solution," is often used to describe a more official admittance of invalidly married couples to the sacraments, with this admittance being given by diocesan tribunals. Questions concerning this more official approach will be discussed in the text. Actually there is no reason why a term like "good conscience solution" could not be used to describe private pastoral approaches to the situations of invalidly married couples. To most people such a term might be more understandable than the term "internal forum solution." In the text, I use the term "good faith solution" to refer to private pastoral approaches. Once, in a case where the context is clear, I use this term to refer to the more public approach.

112. Cf. Anthony Kosnik, "The Pastoral Care of Those in Canonically Invalid Marriages," *The Jurist* 30 (1970), pp. 43-44.

113. A position limiting good faith only to those cases where the previ-

ous marriages are seen as null can be found in Anthony Kosnik, "The Pastoral Care . . . ," pp. 31-44. The broader position can be found in Leo Farley and Warren T. Reich, "Toward an Immediate Internal Forum Solution for Deserving Couples in Canonically Invalid Marriage Cases," *The Jurist* 30 (1970), pp. 45-74. John T. Finnegan, "Marriage Law," *CS* 15 (1976), pp. 300-303, is less explicit, but does not appear to exclude the good faith or internal forum solution for those in second marriages whose first marriages were surely valid.

114. I am not quite as open to these private ceremonies as is Charles E. Curran, "Divorce: Catholic Theory and . . . ," *NP,* p. 246. Only if I am very certain that the couple understands what the non-official ceremony means and shows a real desire for it would I incline to go in this direction. On the other hand, John Finnegan, "Marriage Law," *CS* 15 (1976), p. 302, seems too restrictive in his opinion on this subject.

115. The Sacred Congregation for the Doctrine of the Faith sent a letter on this matter to all bishops on April 11, 1973. For a commentary on the subsequent interpretation of this letter, cf. John Finnegan, "Marriage Law," *CS* 15 (1976), p. 303.

116. For a brief history of the concept of the internal forum see Klaus Morsdorf, "Forum," *SM* 2, pp. 344-346.

117. Cited in Ladislaus Örsy, "Intolerable Marriage Situations: Conflict Between External and Internal Forum," *The Jurist* 30 (1970), p. 13.

Chapter VII

1. Examples of such literature include Donald Goergen, *The Sexual Celibate* (cf. abbreviation *TSC*); Matthias Newman, "Friendships Between Men and Women in the Religious Life," *Sisters Today* 46 (1974), pp. 81-93; Maurits DeWachter, "Celibacy in Man-Woman Relationships: A Case Study," *Louvain Studies* 3 (1970), pp. 83-98; J. F. McNulty, "Sexuality and the Celibate Priest," *Emmanuel* 79 (1973), pp. 298-304; Gerald Fourez, *A Light Grasp on Life: An Essay on the Evangelical Life and Celibacy,* rev. ed. (Denville, N.J.: Dimension Books, 1975); Philip S. Keane, "The Meaning and Functioning of Sexuality in the Lives of Celibates and Virgins," *RR* 34 (1975), pp. 277-314. Readers are referred to the last-named article for a more thorough description of my approach to many of the issues described in the present chapter.

2. The respective canons for priestly celibacy and the vow of chastity are nos. 132 and 487 in the *Code of Canon Law.* Since canon 487 refers to all of the evangelical counsels, the vow of chastity may be said to be rooted in a whole life-style of asceticism and evangelical witness. Canon 132, 1, simply states that those in major orders cannot marry. Hence, the faith context is not as explicitly present in the law of celibacy, though, in the long run, for a meaningful life of celibacy the faith context must be present anyway.

3. For a strong statement in favor of optional celibacy, see National Federation of Priest's Councils, *The Moment of Truth* (Baltimore, 1971). Cited in John Haughey, "The NFPC Celibacy Statement," *America* 124 (1971), pp.

341-343. Serious literature on the whole value of celibacy (with some pros and cons on the optional celibacy question) includes: Alfons Auer, Richard Egenter, and Fergal O'Conner, *Celibacy and Virginity* (Dublin: Gill, 1968); William Bassett and Peter Huizing, eds., *Concilium* 8, no. 8 (1972), Issue title: *Celibacy of the Catholic Priest;* Edward Schillebeeckx, *Celibacy* (New York: Sheed and Ward, 1968); Karl Rahner, "The Celibacy of the Secular Priest Today: An Open Letter," *Servants of the Lord* (New York: Herder and Herder, 1968), pp. 149-172; Roger Balducelli, "The Decision for Celibacy," *TS* 36 (1975), pp. 219-242. Also to be mentioned in this context is Pope Paul VI, *Encyclical Letter on Priestly Celibacy,* June 24, 1967 (Washington: USCC, 1967).

4. Cf. chapter one, note 26.

5. Cf. H. Richard Niebuhr, *Radical Monotheism and Western Culture: With Supplementary Essays* (New York: Harper and Row, 1960). For a similar viewpoint on the limitations inherent in all human values, see Karl Rahner, "Christian Humanism," *TI* 9, pp. 187-204.

6. Various schemas on the division of human love have been proposed. C. S. Lewis treats four kinds of love (affection, friendship, eros, and charity) in *The Four Loves* (New York: Harcourt, Brace, 1960). Gerald Fourez, *A Light Grasp on Life . . .* , pp. 65-66, proposes a structure of three loves. In the text, I use what is perhaps the more classic structure; i.e., two loves, *eros* and *agape*, presupposing, of course, that both of these loves are good, and that they can interrelate so as to manifest a great variety of loves. Cf. Angers Nygren, *Agape and Eros* (New York: Harper and Row, 1969). (Originally published 1932-39.)

7. For an excellent statement on the transcendent and therefore inexplicable character of the decision for celibacy, cf. Roger Balducelli, "The Decision for Celibacy," *TS* 36 (1975), pp. 219-242.

8. Though the ascetic element in celibacy is very real and very worthwhile, care must be taken not to so focus on this element that the positive aspect of celibacy is lost sight of. Too many persons who were formed for celibacy in the past saw celibacy only as a necessary evil. Hopefully this chapter's stress on the positive character of celibate loving (freeing love) will help avoid this difficulty in the future.

9. This critique of all human accomplishments out of a resurrection faith underlies not only celibacy but all aspects of a vowed life. No one, including the priest without vows, can truly live the celibate life and at the same time be excessively attached to material goods or other partial values. The attitude underlying celibacy must touch a person's entire life.

10. Especially interesting in this vein are the reflections of Mrs. Martin Luther King, Jr., on the relation between marriage and ministry in her husband's life. Coretta Scott King, *My Life with Martin Luther King* (New York: Holt, Rinehart and Winston, 1969). Catholic reflections on the connaturality of priesthood and celibacy can be found in John F. Dedek, *CSM*, pp. 89-90, and Edward Schillebeeckx, *Celibacy*, pp. 111-116, 134-142.

11. For a provocative proposal to the effect that the shrinking of the

organized Church is part of God's plan and, therefore, not to be feared, cf. Karl Rahner, "The Present Situation of Christians: A Theological Interpretation of the Position of Christians in the Modern World," *The Christian Commitment: Essays in Pastoral Theology* (New York: Sheed and Ward, 1963), pp. 3-37.

12. Vatican II, *Dogmatic Constitution on the Church,* nos. 39-42. (*DV2,* pp. 65-72.)

13. For a careful statement of this whole issue see Karl Rahner, "On the Evangelical Counsels," *TI* 8, pp. 133-167.

14. More accurately, the physical questions about celibacy are inherently part of the questions about the celibate's personal identity. Celibates cannot be subject to a body-soul dualism. Thus, when we speak about the physical questions about celibacy coming after the personal questions, the point is that celibates must begin by focusing on the wholeness of their personalities, not with the one-sided look at the physical order that marked too many past views of celibacy.

15. I developed this example in a fuller context in "The Meaning and Function . . . ," *RR* 34 (1975), pp. 288-289.

16. One thinks for instance of the almost reverential treatment given to friendships between priests. Cf. Arthur B. O'Neill, *Sacerdotal Safeguards* (Notre Dame, Indiana: University Press, 1918), pp. 66-84. While priestly friendships are valuable, some of the older literature on them undoubtedly promoted the separation of priests and other people.

17. Names of celibate men and women saints who were close friends include St. Francis de Sales and St. Jane de Chantal, St. Margaret Mary and Blessed Claude de la Colombiere, and St. John of the Cross and St. Theresa of Avila. For a history of heterosexual religious communities in earlier eras, see George H. Tavard, *WCT,* pp. 91-93. For a report on a heterosexual religious type community today see Enzo Bianchi, "Bose: An Interconfessional Community in Italy," *Concilium* 9, no. 9 (1973), pp. 111-119.

18. Some would see this question differently, holding that good heterosexual relationships are a result of a person's having "graduated" from a variety of other life experiences rather than a "school" helping one achieve a variety of mature life experiences. Obviously the truth runs in both directions. I have seen a great many celibates grow through heterosexual relationships toward a more caring attitude toward all people. Thus I stress this aspect of the celibacy and growth question.

19. This point was stressed in Gerald Broccolo and Ernest Larkin, *et al., Spiritual Renewal of the American Priesthood* (Washington: USCC, 1973), pp. 33-34. A follow-up on this document's concern for spiritual direction can be found in Louis J. Cameli, *Spiritual Direction for Priests in the U.S.A.: The Recovery of a Resource* (Washington: USCC, 1977).

20. In this context one thinks of Protestant sects like the Mennonites whose traditional life-style, except for the presence of marriage, has been so much like that of Roman Catholic religious communities. The classic source explaining the character of these Protestant sects is Ernst Troeltsch, *The*

Social Teaching of the Christian Churches 2 (New York: Harper and Row, 1960), pp. 691-807. (Originally published in 1911).

21. For the notion of technical virginity see Herbert Richardson, *Nun, Witch, Playmate: The Americanization of Sex* (New York: Harper and Row, 1971), pp. 93-96. For an explanation of the term *"virgines subintroductae"* (without any endorsement of the modern applications of the term), see George H. Tavard, *WCT*, p. 92.

22. Obviously this statement is not based on any measured statistics. Nonetheless, the pastoral counseling experience of those who work with priests, seminarians and religious will surely bear it out.

23. On this matter cf. the observations about Donald Goergen, *TSC*, made above in chapter 4, note 27.

24. For this notion of sexuality as a frail or fragile good see Abel Jeanniere, *TAS*, pp. 174-185; Pierre Grelot, *Man and Wife in Scripture* (New York: Herder and Herder, 1967), pp. 46-55.

25. On this theme of marriage and celibacy as complementary and as having developed complementarily during the Christian era (in spite of a variety of recurring erroneous notions), cf. Edward Schillebeeckx, *Celibacy*, esp. pp. 75-87.

Chapter VIII

1. For further articulate reflections on the problem of rape, cf. Susan Brownmiller, *Against our Will: Men, Women and Rape* (cf. abbreviation *AOW*).

2. A great deal of ink has been expended on the problem of prostitution across the centuries. At least as far back as Augustine, *De Ordinis*, book 2, chapter 4 (Migne: *Patrologia Latina* 32, col. 1000), it has been noted that the real problem with prostitution rests with the males who seek out prostitutes. Augustine also indicated that perhaps prostitution should be legally tolerated, because without it male lust would only show up in worse forms such as rape. Cf. also Thomas Aquinas, *ST* II-II, 11. Regrettably our society seems no closer than Augustine's to facing up to the real cause of prostitution. For a current bibliography see Vern L. Bullough and Barret W. Elcano, *An Annotated Bibliography of Prostitution* (Reference Library in Social Science 25, New York: Garland Publishing, 1976).

3. Cf. *K&L*, p. 342.

4. *K&L*, p. 343.

5. *K&L*, pp. 340-342.

6. On this subject see William Simon, "Sexual Encounters Between Adults and Children," *S&M*, pp. 83-98.

7. *K&L*, pp. 341 and 343.

8. On sexual cruelty, cf. W. Norman Pittenger, *Making Sexuality Human* (Philadelphia: United Church Press, 1970), pp. 69-78. In addition to the more major sexual offenses mentioned in the text, note can also be made of more rarely occurring behaviors such as voyeurism, exhibitionism, sexual relations with animals and corpses, and extensive sexual fetishes. Because these behaviors are so disruptive of human relationships, they must basically

be said to be objectively immoral. At the same time, we must remember that such behaviors very often spring from psychological compulsions within the person rather than from a clear desire to disrupt human relationships. Hence pastoral compassion is in order, and professional psychological help is often indicated.

9. Cf. Donald Robinson, "Swindlers and the Sex 'Clinics'," *Readers Digest* 107 (December, 1975), pp. 82-86.

10. Especially to be noted as basically positive contributions along this line are William H. Masters and Virginia E. Johnson, *Human Sexual Response* (Boston: Little, Brown, 1966). *Idem, Human Sexual Inadequacy* (Boston: Little, Brown, 1970). Thorough critical evaluations on Shere Hite, *The Hite Report: A Nationwide Report on Female Sexuality* (New York: Macmillan, 1976) were not available to me as the present book was being completed.

11. The Nazi atrocities in the sexual area are chronicled in William Shirer, *The Rise and Fall of the Third Reich* (New York: Simon and Schuster, 1960), pp. 988-990.

12. One of the most encouraging developments in ethics in recent years in the United States has been the establishment of centers for bioethical research (e.g., The Joseph and Rose Kennedy Institute for the Study of Human Reproduction and Bioethics, Georgetown University, Washington, and the Institute of Society, Ethics and the Life Sciences [The Hastings Center], Hastings-on-Hudson, New York.) Perhaps such Institutes could be a very effective location for the kind of dialogue I call for in the text.

13. Cf. Bernard Häring, *ME*, pp. 208-217; Paul Ramsey, *The Patient as Person* (New Haven: Yale University Press, 1970), pp. 1-58. Additional reflections on the morality of sexual dysfunction therapies can be found in *CTSA* Study, pp. 231-232.

14. I have made no mention in the text of the various venereal diseases because, regardless of any irresponsibility that may lead to a person's contracting a venereal disease, there is nothing morally wrong with the fact of having a venereal disease or with taking the proper medical steps to treat such a disease. There is often a fear or guilt associated with venereal diseases, and this sometimes prevents proper care. Hopefully, we can learn not to let fears stop the proper care of venereal diseases. For a summary of these diseases and their care, cf. *K&L*, pp. 359-366.

15. Thomas O'Donnell, *MM*, pp. 259-261.

16. Cf. *K&L*, pp. 41-42, 106-109, 334.

17. One Roman Catholic moralist who has expressed an openness to such surgery is John F. Dedek, *CME*, pp. 77-80.

18. A subject somewhat related to (but still clearly different from) transsexual surgery is transvestism, the psychic need to wear clothing that will cause one to be perceived as a member of the opposite sex. Older moralists used to condemn transvestism as immoral (cf. Thomas O'Donnell, *MM*, p. 261). While research on this phenomenon (which may or may not mean that the person wishes to belong to the opposite sex) is very limited, it would seem at present that no one really knows why the disposition to

transvestism exists in some persons or how to cause this disposition to change. Hence the moral approach to transvestites would seem to parallel the moral approach to homosexuals. They should be treated with understanding and compassion. Possibly there could be some situations in which the evil of transvestism is an ontic but not a moral evil.

19. For the pertinent sources, see chapter 4, notes 16-20.

20. To use the traditional language, a person might act for the venereal pleasure (a serious matter), but without sufficient reflection or full consent.

21. It would seem that the venereal arousal that takes place in children and passing instances of sexual fantasy in adults are so little a subject of consent for the human will that they do not fulfill the meaning of the terms significant ontic evil or morally significant ontic evil as we have used these terms in this book. To be morally significant, an ontic evil must somehow challenge a person in his or her moral decision-making process. Basically spontaneous instances of non-marital venereal arousal do not do this.

22. Once we admit that morally significant ontic evil is present in all directly acted for venereal pleasure outside of marriage, we would have to admit that this ontic evil would always be an objective and personal moral evil and even a grave sin for any person who possesses perfect understanding and perfect freedom. (Recall in this context that the great saints thought they could sin seriously over very small matters.) Thus, when we say—as we have rather often in this book—that the significant ontic evil in non-marital venereal pleasure is not a moral evil in some circumstances, what we are actually doing is making a pragmatic judgment that the degree of freedom that a typical or average person is capable of in a given set of circumstances is limited to the point that this typical or average person will not be operating in a context where an ontic evil will also be morally evil for him. Such a pragmatic judgment obviously does not exclude the possibilities of human freedom to transcend the ontic evil in some (non-average) cases. I would argue that it is precisely the business of moral theology to offer pragmatic judgments as to where the average person is likely to stand vis-à-vis a given situation. Otherwise, we run the risk of leaving people with only two options: a naïve perfectionism in which all people are believed to be so free that they can immediately and totally transcend any human limitations, or a viewpoint that so limits human freedom that people conclude they may as well give in to every kind of human corruption. In the sphere of sexual ethics, the danger of leaving only these two options becomes evident when we consider how often in history rigorously ascetic groups have metamorphosized into libidinous groups allowing even the most distorted forms of sexual expression. Thus the pragmatism of average judgments as to whether ontic evil becomes moral evil seems to be a practical necessity for moral theology. Each individual person (perhaps with a spiritual director) will have to determine how our average ("objective" in this sense) judgments apply to him or her. Spiritual direction in this context opens up the whole question of discernment of spirits and of each person's responsibility to strive as far as possible for Christian perfection.

23. Recall in this context the degrees of ontic evil suggested in our chapter on masturbation.

23. Besides its application to questions of manipulation, etc. (where the likelihood is that the ontic evil does become a moral evil), the fact of ontic evil in marital intercourse also serves as the basis for our position on contraception, i.e., that contraception is always ontically evil, but not always morally evil.

25. For a related phrasing see Richard A. McCormick, *AMC*, p. 75. The force of the word psychological as used above in the text is that the evil is directly acted for, not because it in itself is desired, but because it is a regrettably necessary part of an action whose overall good outcomes outweigh the evil it contains.

Chapter IX

1. Cited herein as *DSexEth*. Page citations to the USCC edition (Washington, 1976). The Latin text is in *AAS* 68 (1976), pp. 77-96.

2. This critique will be relatively brief since a lengthier critique would take us back over much ground we have covered previously in this book. Other critiques of the *DSexEth* include Richard A. McCormick, "Sexual Ethics: An Opinion," *NCR* (January 30, 1976), p. 9; Daniel C. Maguire, "The Vatican on Sex," *Commonweal* 103 (1976), pp. 33-40; Bernard Häring, *"Reflexionen zur Erklärung der Glaubenskongregation über einige Fragen der Sexualethik,"* *Theologische-praktische Quartalschrift* 124 (1976), pp. 115-126; James McManus *et al.*, "Moral Theology Forum: The 'Declaration on Certain Questions Concerning Sexual Ethics': A Discussion," *The Clergy Review* 61 (1976), pp. 231-237; Charles E. Curran, "Sexual Ethics: Reaction and Critique," *LQ* 43 (1976), pp. 147-164; John F. Harvey, "A Critique of John McNeill SJ and Gregory Baum OSA on the Subject of Homosexuality," *LQ* 43 (1976), pp. 175-178. Archbishop Joseph Bernardin's positive praise of *DSexEth* can be found in *Origins* 5 (1976), p. 487.

3. In the forum from *The Clergy Review* cited in the last note (p. 232), Fr. Sean O'Riordan names the three authors to be Fr. E. Lio, Fr. Jan Visser, and Cardinal Pietro Palazzini. Fr. Visser's pastoral sense is discussed on p. 233.

4. It must be acknowledged that there are reputable authors who would support *DSexEth*'s approach completely or almost completely. In addition to Fr. Visser, who is so highly pastoral in his own interpretation of the document, the names of some others we have occasionally cited in the footnotes come quickly to mind: John Finnis, John Harvey, John Kippley, and Germain Grisez. Still, I think it is not unfair to assert that such men are not in the mainstream of Roman Catholic moral theology today.

5. Pope Paul VI, *Apostolic Exhortation on Evangelization*. *TPS* 21 (1976), pp. 4-51.

6. This concept was developed at the beginning of chapter six of this book.

7. *DSexEth*, no. 8, pp. 8-9.

8. *DSexEth*, no. 9, pp. 9-10.

9. *DSexEth*, no. 1, p. 3.

10. *DSexEth*, no. 13, pp. 15-16.

11. A phrase such as "the finality of the specific function of sexuality" (*DSexEth*, no. 5, p. 6) surely seems to echo the one-sided natural law physicalism discussed above in chapter three.

12. *DSexEth*, no. 10, pp. 10-11.

13. Cf. the sources cited on this issue in chapter, 3, note 12.

14. Cf. Charles E. Curran, "Sexual Ethics: Reaction and Critique," *LQ* 43 (1976), pp. 159-160. It is also interesting to compare *DSexEth*'s approach to fundamental option with the approach taken in Sacred Congregation for Christian Education, *A Guide to Formation in Priestly Celibacy*, April 11, 1974 (Washington: USCC, 1974), no. 36, p. 34. This magisterial source seems more open to the contemporary theology of fundamental option than does *DSexEth*.

15. A compendium of the pertinent magisterial statements can be found in Raymond E. Brown, *Biblical Reflections on Crises Facing the Church* (New York: Paulist Press, 1975), pp. 109-118.

16. Cf. Richard A. McCormick, "Sexual Ethics: An Opinion," *NCR* (January 30, 1976), p. 9.

17. The basic sources are cited in chapter 3, notes 32-35.

18. One of the major thrusts of twentieth century Roman Catholic metaphysics has been a recovery of the dynamism inherent in the thought of Thomas Aquinas and in Catholic doctrine. Cf. Joseph Maréchal, *A Maréchal Reader*, ed. by Joseph Donceel (New York: Herder, 1970); Karl Rahner, *Spirit in the World* (New York: Herder and Herder, 1968); Bernard Lonergan, *Insight: A Study of Human Understanding* (London: Longmans, Green and Co., 1957). Once this dynamism is understood it becomes evident that a moral theology that refuses to be static, and instead always applies its principles to new concrete cases, is indeed the best—and the most traditional—moral theology.

19. Volumes of literature could be adduced to support this statement. For a major recent contribution to the perspectives involved in the statement see Peter F. Chirico, *Infallibility: The Crossroads of Doctrine* (cf. abbreviation *ICD*).

20. Cf. Andrew M. Greeley, William C. McCready, Kathleen McCourt, *Catholic Schools in a Declining Church* (Kansas City: Sheed and Ward, 1976), especially the chapter entitled "Council or Encyclical," pp. 103-154. At the end of this chapter, Greeley *et al.* conclude that *Humanae Vitae* was a "failure and an organizational and religious disaster" (p. 153). While Greeley *et al.*'s emphasis on *Humanae Vitae* as the major cause of the Church's recent problems may not have fully considered all the variables, their basic contention that the Church's sexual teachings are a key source of her credibility problems seems to be a sound contention.

21. The use of these words prompts the author to say that he knows he does not have all the answers and that theology is best done in the context of a believing community. The author has spoken out his convictions in a spirit of service to and dialogue with the believing community.

22. Shortly after the present text was completed, the study on human

sexuality commissioned by the Catholic Theological Society of America appeared in print (cf. abbrev. *CTSA* Study). The scope and importance of the study are such that, had it appeared earlier, I would doubtless have entered into a significant degree of dialogue with it in this book. As it is, I have added in footnote references at several places where it seemed especially significant that the *CTSA* Study either supported or disagreed with specific positions I have taken on issues of sexual morality.

In general there is a great deal of continuity between the *CTSA* Study and the approach to sexuality I have presented in this book. The study's basic and very helpful position that "Wholesome human sexuality is that which fosters creative growth towards integration" (p. 86) is quite close to the anthropology of human sexuality found in chapter one of this book. The approaches opted for in the *CTSA* Study's lengthy "Pastoral Guidelines" chapter (pp. 99-239) very often concur with the stances I have taken on similar issues.

Much can be said in praise of the *CTSA* Study. Besides its sound sexual anthropology and usually perceptive pastoral judgments it contains a wealth of biblical, historical and scientific information (though this information could at times be better articulated so as to show what is continuous and what is peripheral in the Roman Catholic tradition on sexuality). The *CTSA* Study offers worthwhile treatments of several subjects not directly considered in this book, e.g., the virtue of chastity (p. 100-102), child-free marriage (pp. 140-143), and the single state (p.175-183). One specific issue the *CTSA* Study did not treat carefully and explicitly enough is the role of women.

From the present author's perspective, the biggest weakness in the *CTSA* Study is that it does not make more use of the major insights that prevail in Roman Catholic fundamental moral theology today (cf. chapter three above). The *CTSA* Study is aware of the current trends in fundamental moral theology (e.g., pp. 96-98) but it does not refer to these trends that frequently in its approach to specific questions in sexual ethics. Had it made more use of contemporary fundamental moral theology, the *CTSA* Study could have been a more philosophically coherent and methodologically integrated document.

The *CTSA* Study's lack of emphasis on fundamental moral theology shows up in its treatment of *DSexEth.* Repeatedly (pp. 81, 86-87, 100, etc) the *CTSA* Study praises the genuinely positive aspects of the *DSexEth* such as its openness to a deeper sexual anthropology and its pastoral sensitivity. But rather little is said about the great differences between *DSexEth* and the *CTSA* Study in the field of fundamental moral methodology. My own opinion is that, until the impasse in the area of fundamental moral methodology is resolved, the many valuable insights in the *CTSA* Study will not be able to bear their full fruit in Roman Catholic life.

ABBREVIATIONS

AAS	*Acta Apostolicae Sedis.*
AER	*The American Ecclesiastical Review.*
AMC	*Ambiguity in Moral Choice: The 1973 Pere Marquette Theology Lecture.* By Richard A. McCormick. Milwaukee: Marquette University.
AMT?	*Absolutes in Moral Theology?* Ed. by Charles E. Curran. Washington: Corpus Books, 1968.
AOW	*Against Our Will: Men, Women and Rape.* By Susan Brownmiller. New York: Simon and Schuster, 1975.
CMD	*Catholic Moral Theology in Dialogue.* By Charles E. Curran. Notre Dame, Indiana: Fides Publishers, 1972.
CME	*Contemporary Medical Ethics.* By John F. Dedek. New York: Sheed and Ward, 1975.
CP	*Contemporary Problems in Moral Theology.* By Charles E. Curran. Notre Dame, Indiana: Fides Publishers, 1970.
CS	*Chicago Studies.*
CSM	*Contemporary Sexual Morality.* By John F. Dedek. New York: Sheed and Ward, 1971.
CTSA	*Proceedings of the Catholic Theological Society of America.*
CTSA Study	Anthony Kosnik, *et al. Human Sexuality: New Directions in American Catholic Thought.* A Study Commissioned by the Catholic Theological Society of America. New York: Paulist Press, 1977.
DS	Henricus Denziger and Adolfus Schonmetzer. *Enchiridion Symbolorum Definitionum et Declarationum de Rebus Fidei et Morum.* 32nd ed. Freiburg: Herder, 1963.
DSexEth	*Declaration on Certain Questions Concerning Sexual Ethics.* By the Sacred Congregation for the Doctrine of the Faith. December 29, 1975. Page citations to the USCC edition. Washington, 1976.
DV2	*The Documents of Vatican II.* Ed. by Walter M. Abbott. New York: America Press, 1966.
HSP	*Human Sexuality: A Psychosocial Perspective.* By Richard F. Hettlinger. Belmont, Calif.: Wadsworth Publishing, 1975.
ICD	*Infallibility: The Crossroads of Doctrine.* By Peter F. Chirico. Kansas City: Sheed and Ward, 1977.
JBC	*The Jerome Biblical Commentary.* Ed. by Raymond E. Brown *et al.* Englewood Cliffs, N.J.: Prentice-Hall, 1968.
K&L	Herant A. Katchadourian and Donald T. Lunde. *Fundamentals of Human Sexuality.* 2nd ed. New York: Holt, Rinehart and Winston, 1975.
LQ	*The Linacre Quarterly.*

229

ME   *Medical Ethics.* By Bernard Häring. Notre Dame, Indiana: Fides Publishers, 1973.

Merkelbach   Benedict H. Merkelbach. *Summa Theologiae Moralis.* 11th ed. Bruges: Desclee de Brouwer, 1962.

MHR   *Marriage: Human Reality and Saving Mystery.* By Edward Schillebeeckx. New York: Sheed and Ward, 1965.

MM   *Morals in Medicine.* By Thomas O'Donnell. 2nd Ed. Westminster, Md.: The Newman Press, 1959.

NCE   New Catholic Encyclopedia. New York: McGraw-Hill, 1966.

NCR   *National Catholic Reporter.*

"NMT"   Notes on Moral Theology (in *TS*).

NP   *New Perspectives in Moral Theology.* By Charles E. Curran. Notre Dame, Indiana: Fides Publishers, 1974.

OR   *Ongoing Revision: Studies in Moral Theology.* By Charles E. Curran. Notre Dame, Indiana: Fides Publishers, 1976.

RR   *Review for Religious.*

SBF   *Sexual Behavior in the Human Female.* By Alfred C. Kinsey *et al.* Philadelphia: W. B. Saunders, 1953.

SBM   *Sexual Behavior in the Human Male.* By Alfred C. Kinsey *et al.* Philadelphia: W. B. Saunders, 1948.

SB70   *Sexual Behavior in the 1970's.* Morton Hunt. Chicago: Playboy Press, 1974.

SLP   *Sex, Love and the Person.* By Peter A. Bertocci. New York: Sheed and Ward, 1967.

SM   *Sacramentum Mundi: An Encyclopedia of Theology.* Ed. by Karl Rahner *et al.* New York: Herder and Herder, 1968-70.

S&M   *Sexuality and Man.* Ed. by SIECUS. New York: Charles Scribner's Sons, 1970.

SMR   *Sexuality and Moral Responsibility.* By Robert P. O'Neill and Michael A. Donovan. Washington: Corpus Books, 1968.

ST   *Summa Theologica.* By Saint Thomas Aquinas.

TAS   *The Anthropology of Sex.* By Abel Jeanniere. New York: Harper and Row, 1967.

TI   *Theological Investigations.* By Karl Rahner. London: Darton, Longman and Todd, 1961- .

TMA   *The Morality of Abortion: Legal and Historical Perspectives.* Ed. by John T. Noonan. Cambridge, Mass.: Harvard University Press, 1970.

TPS   *The Pope Speaks.*

TS   *Theological Studies.*

TSC   *The Sexual Celibate.* By Donald Goergen. New York: Seabury Press, 1975.

USCC   United States Catholic Conference.

WCT   *Woman in Christian Tradition.* By George H. Tavard. Notre Dame, Indiana: University of Notre Dame Press, 1973.

Index

231